Michael Taussig

what color is the sacred?

THE UNIVERSITY OF CHICAGO PRESS, *Chicago and London*

Michael Taussig is professor of anthropology at Columbia University. He is
the author of numerous books, including *My Cocaine Museum* and *Walter
Benjamin's Grave,* also published by the University of Chicago Press.

The University of Chicago Press, Chicago 60637
The University of Chicago Press, Ltd., London
© 2009 by The University of Chicago
All rights reserved. Published 2009
Printed in the United States of America

18 17 16 15 14 13 12 11 10 09   1 2 3 4 5

ISBN-13: 978-0-226-79005-3 (cloth)
ISBN-13: 978-0-226-79006-0 (paper)
ISBN-10: 0-226-79005-3 (cloth)
ISBN-10: 0-226-79006-1 (paper)

Library of Congress Cataloging-in-Publication Data
Taussig, Michael T.
What color is the sacred? / Michael Taussig.
p. cm.
Includes bibliographical references and index.
ISBN-13: 978-0-226-79005-3 (cloth : alk. paper)
ISBN-13: 978-0-226-79006-0 (pbk. : alk. paper)
ISBN-10: 0-226-79005-3 (cloth : alk. paper)
ISBN-10: 0-226-79006-1 (pbk. : alk. paper)
1. Color. 2. Color (Philosophy) I. Title.
QC495.3 .T398   2009
390—dc22   2008040243

For Santiago and Olivia

If one of the most "sacred" aims that man can set for himself is to acquire as exact and intense an understanding of himself as possible, it seems desirable that each one, scrutinizing his memories with the greatest possible honesty, examine whether he can discover there some sign permitting him to discern the color for him of the very notion of sacred.

MICHEL LEIRIS

From "The Sacred in Everyday Life," a lecture to the College of Sociology, Paris, January 8, 1938

contents

iLLustratiONS

Part One

INTO THE IMAGE

1

тне face of world history

So far, all that has given colour to existence still lacks a history.

NIETZSCHE, *The Gay Science*

"Men in a state of nature," wrote Goethe in his book on color, "uncivilized nations and children, have a great fondness for colours in their utmost brightness." The same applied to "uneducated people" and southern Europeans, especially the women with their bright-colored bodices and ribbons. He recalled a German mercenary returned from America who had painted his face with vivid colors in the manner of the Indians, the effect of which "was not disagreeable." On the other hand, in northern Europe at the time in which he wrote in the early nineteenth century, people of refinement had a disinclination to colors, women wearing white, the men, black. And not only in dress. When it came to what he called "pathological colours," Goethe wrote that people of refinement avoid vivid colors in the objects around them and seem inclined to banish vivid colors from their presence altogether.[1] It is as if there are two presences glowering at each other, shifting uncomfortably from one foot to the other. It is as much a body thing, a presence thing, as conscious intellection. One "presence" is people of refinement. The other is vivid color.

As for our German mercenary, I see him in my mind's eye, promenading through the streets fresh from God knows what violence out there in America, with wild Indians, half-breeds, and crazed Europeans trading furs for whisky along with rings and mirrors, brightly colored great coats trimmed with lace, and, of course, paints for face and body, as much for the corpse as for the living. How many beaver hats bobbing up and down the wintry main street and hanging on the hat stands in the coffee shops in Frankfurt are owing to his efforts? And here he is with his Indian face, perhaps one half yellow, the other vermillion, asymmetrically joined, the face of world history. The "rarest, most precious colors have always been imported from exotic places," write two experts on dyes and pigments, Francois Delamare and Bernard Guineau.[2]

Not only kids, primitives, and southern women love bright colors—war does too. Could there be a connection? And even if brightly colored uniforms have given way to today's camouflage, you have to wonder whether camouflage is not, in its own right, a play in vivid color as well as a fashion statement for the warring class. Look at them at headquarters far from the front dressed neatly in their uniforms, staring into computer screens and about as inconspicuous as one of their humvees. It's as if the designers responsible for army gear had not been able to let go of the swirling jungle motif, allowing the ghost of Vietnam to return, this time to the desert sands no less than to the slums and highways of Baghdad, once the center of the world's indigo trade. The generals look good in camouflage, too, even though they never get close to anything more dangerous than Fox news. But the medals come colored.

French soldiers hung on the longest. Beginning his "storm of steel" in 1915 near the village of Orainville in Champagne, the German soldier Ernst Junger saw them dead and red in the sugar-beet fields lit by moonlight.[3] They wore bright red pants well into the First World War, when it was suggested that their appalling losses might be reduced if they decolored, a fate that was, according to Goethe, Europe's lot for many a year, "women wearing white, the men, black." Yet Goethe's primitives are engraved in the European image of what warriors should be.

Wandering through the darkened streets of Paris one night in 1916, about the time the Frenchmen were losing their red trousers, the narrator in Marcel Proust's *In Search of Lost Time* happened across a gay friend, the Baron Charlus, surreptitiously eyeing the passing troops. The narrator thought the marvelous display of color must have been similar to the passing of the troops in Napoleon's time exactly one hundred years before in the same place: "the Africans in their red divided skirts, the Indians in their white turbans were enough to transform for me this Paris through which I was walking into a whole imaginary exotic city, an oriental scene."[4] By African, he meant the Berbers from Algeria known as *zouaves*, one of whom was painted in blue, orange, yellow, and black by Vincent van Gogh in Arles in 1888 using oils so as to heighten what he called "the savage combination of incongruous tones," the zouaves being French infantrymen famous, so it is said, for their brilliant uniform and quick-spirited drill.[5]

That they go together, these quick spirits and brilliant colors, should not be lost on us. Isidore of Seville, the savants' savant, said in the seventh century AD that color and heat were the same since colors came from fire or sunlight and because the words for them were fundamentally the same, *calor* and *color*. Etymology like this is hardly a science, but he was onto something important, same as the famous connection between *color* and the *quick-spirited drill* of the Berbers incorporated into the colonial army. And note that in his *Etymologiae* Isidore of Seville did not say light, but sunlight, light that comes from the biggest fire of all, the one that gives without receiving.

Talking to Primo Levi, famous for his memoir of Auschwitz, the American novelist Philip Roth suggested that his imprisonment was in some sense a gift. Levi replied: "A friend of mine, an excellent doctor, told me many years ago: 'Your remembrances of before and after are in black and white; those of Auschwitz and of your travel home are in Technicolor.' He was right. Family, home, factory, these are good things in themselves, but they deprived me of something I still miss: adventure."[6]

Being a chemical engineer, Levi survived because he worked as a slave in the Chemical Komando in the factory set up at Auschwitz by IG Farben, the largest chemical corporation in the world, making everything from toothbrushes to the poison gas used for the final solution. *Farben* means *colors*, and it was the search for dazzling, standardized colors that in the mid-nineteenth century led to the new science of organic chemistry from which emerged a world of commodities beyond even the dreams of Faust, just as it was these same dazzling, standardized colors that gave the final spit and polish to what Karl Marx saw as the spirit-like character of the commodity. The brave new world of artifice created by chemical magic was to Germany what empire was to Britain and France and eventually, as nature gave way to second nature, came to far surpass that old-fashioned, graspable sense of imperial destinies which Proust and van Gogh so admired with the zouaves. To ask, What color is the sacred? is to ask about these connections and whether we have lost the language that could do that connecting for us: the way the primeval forests and swamps went under to become coal and petroleum, the way that coal gas came to illuminate nineteenth-century cities and excrete a waste product from which first colors and then just about everything else could be made in one mighty imitation of nature. We cannot see that as sacred or enchanting because we have displaced that language of alchemy by that of the chemists. We do not mistake *color* for *calor*.

To equate *calor* with *color* as did Isidore of Seville detaches us from a purely visual approach to vision and makes color the cutting edge of such a shift. Color vision becomes less a retinal and more a total bodily activity to the fairytale extent that in looking at something, we may even pass into the image. Three of my favorite authors relish this power of color: Walter Benjamin, William Burroughs, and Marcel Proust. They see color as something alive, like an animal, and all three expend considerable verbal talent in getting this across: Benjamin concentrating on the child's view of color and colored illustrations in early children's books; Burroughs on drugs, sex, and games with language; Proust on the fullness of involuntary memory transporting one's body to the event by chance recalled. All of which is to say color comes across here as more a presence than a sign, more a force than a code, and more as *calor*, which is why, so I believe, John Ruskin declared in his book *Modern Painters* that "colour is the most sacred element of all visible things."[7]

This or something like it can be experienced acutely in many non-Western societies, as when an anthropologist casually spoke of indigenous Australians as "color mad" (a compliment), and Ticio Escobar writes of the Chamacoco Indians of Paraguay in the 1980s as obsessed with colors, dyeing , as he puts it, the deepest conceptions of their culture. What does he mean by this arresting statement? What could it mean?

Here colors illuminate the backdrop of myths and set the body alight during ceremonies. Colors "force the object to release hidden meanings, meanings that are neither complete nor lasting, to be sure, but that can gesture, ever so obliquely, to truths that remain otherwise concealed."[8]

Escobar has a story.

Chapter 1

Clemente's niece Elena is a lovely and vivacious fifteen-year-old. Her proud grandfather assures me that she has shamanic gifts and that she will one day be a great *konsaha*. For now she sings, maraca in hand, in accompaniment to her teacher. Since Emiliano, the director of the Spanish TV crew, arrived, Elena has not taken her eyes off him. Her gaze is so direct, so natural that the Spaniard, more curious than uncomfortable, asked her one day: "Why do you stare at me like that?" Elena's dark eyes did not look away from his blue ones. "What is the color of the world to you?" she asked him. "The same as it is for you, of course," he answered. And she then said something to which he had no reply: "And how do you know what the color of the world is to me?"

That night we spoke of the Chamacoco obsession with colors. Emiliano, who remained silent the rest of that day, only commented that Elena's answer had Kantian overtones.[9]

Or listen to Victor Turner who, on the basis of his time among Ndembu-speaking people in central Africa in the 1950s found that their three primary colors, white, black, and red, were "conceived as rivers of power flowing from a common source in God and permeating the whole world of sensory phenomena with their specific qualities." And he went on to say that these colors "are thought to tinge the moral and social life of mankind with their peculiar efficacies."[10]

But first he has to clear some ground.

The hypothesis I am putting forward here is that magico-religious ideas of a certain kind were responsible for the selection of the basic color triad and for the assiduity with which its constituent colors were sought or prepared. It is not the rarity of the pigments that makes them prized but the fact that they are prized for magic-religious reasons that makes men overcome all kinds of difficulties to obtain or manufacture them. I could cite much evidence to demonstrate the quite extraordinary lengths to which societies will go to get red or black or white pigments.[11]

These colors are alive. As *mysteries* they are invoked in the seclusion of cults concerned with death and with the passage from adolescence to adulthood. In the funerary cult, boys and girls witnessed the priest dig a trench in the form of a cross, evoking sexual intercourse. Along the cross he placed antelope horns containing medicine, and filled the trench with water tinged red from a beheaded fowl, singing, "This is no ordinary river. God made it long ago. It is the river of God." Posing riddles when all three rivers of power, white, black, and red, were finished, the priest sang songs with archaic and bizarre terms.

Shamanic songs the world over often use archaic and bizarre terms. Could we dare think of color the same way? As that which is at odds with the normal, as that which strikes a bizarre note and makes the normal come alive and have transformative power? (Just a thought.)

Certainly color in this description by Turner is sacred, theatrical, and mysterious. What is more, the idea of a color code is inappropriate, a brutal gesture towards containment. Far from being symbols, distinct from their referents, the colors *are* those referents in a deeply organic sense and that is why they are thought of in reference to God no less than to the copulating, procreating, growing, and dying human body. As Turner says after his survey of research by anthropologists on color in several other non-Western societies, including India, a human physiological component is rarely absent from the contexts in which color is used in ritual.

What he means is that color is fundamentally involved in the making of culture from the human body.[12]

This helps me understand why Burroughs is drawn to color as an organic entity, alive and intimately related to the human body. His writing oozes color that serves him as an agent of metamorphosis. In this regard he is similar, it seems to me, to a Ndembu ritualist, tapping into rivers of color, making and remaking culture from bodily fluids and processes except that Burroughs's idea of metamorphosis is sardonic and revolutionary.

Thanks to Victor Turner and his Ndembu friends in the 1950s, our imagination is given some breathing room. To advocate a Ndembu sense or a Benjamin, Burroughs, or Proustian sense of color-sense is not to say color is really this or really that. Instead it is to speculate on some of the implications of the way the West talks about color, what relationship such talk has to world history, and what wonder lies obscured within, such that if we think about color as heat or even as weather that propels you into the image, we might never think the same about thinking itself.

Such attention to the way we talk about color is precisely what Wittgenstein was getting at in his remarks on color and his statement that "Colors spur us to philosophize. Perhaps that explains Goethe's passion for the theory of colours."[13]

Yet Goethe did not go far enough. Not nearly as far as the German soldier who painted his face in the manner of the North American Indians. For while it may appear that people of refinement, unlike "man in a state of nature," are averse to vivid color, the situation both in Goethe's time and in our own seems to me even stranger; that this distaste for vivid color is actually an unstable mix of attraction *and* repulsion, which the face-painted soldier got right. When Walter Benjamin, Marcel Proust, and William Burroughs bring out the fact that even in the West color is a whole lot more than hue, that color is not secondary to form, that it is not an overlay draped like a skin over a shape—they are not saying that "man in a state of nature" has gotten this right and we in the West are nonsensuous creatures who are frightened of passions and the body. To the contrary, it is the combustible mix of attraction and repulsion towards color that brings out its sacred qualities which, as Goethe's face-painted mercenary suggests, owe more than a little to the Western experience of colonization as colored Otherness.

2

Licensed transgression

How do you begin to explain a reaction as visceral as the one Goethe pointed to regarding vivid colors?

First of all let us note to what sort of colored matter Goethe refers — not the glorious sunset or the moody sky, but clothing, household interiors, and at least some of the objects in one's immediate vicinity. The aversion is dramatic and forceful. "People of refinement," as Goethe called them, "seem inclined to banish them altogether from their presence."[1]

Some nerve is certainly being touched here. Surely aversion to this degree implies stamping down desire which, faced with repression, means fear, masked as an issue of taste. And just as surely it is on account of this see-sawing ambivalence that my New York City friends *wish* to disagree with Goethe's "darkness at noon" thesis and, what is more, *can* disagree, because vivid color is in fact let through the toll gates of the West—in stops and starts, in spurts and florescence of licensed transgression.

Clearly my friends are disconcerted. Especially if I am wearing my magenta silk shirt from Calcutta. They question how long this banishment of the vivid has existed and they question what I see as its uninterrupted existence over centuries. They find religious reasons such as the Reformation to explain it away. They find a scarlet cardinal's uniform in early modern Florence or a brightly colored plate for sale in the gift store of the Museum of Modern Art in New York. I look around the seminar room where the cardinal's gorgeous red is raised to disprove the "darkness in Europe" theme. Yet everyone—but everyone—around the seminar table is dressed exactly as Goethe said was the approved color for "people of refinement." I look around the hotel bar in Midtown Manhattan, where my friend brings up the colored glass for sale around the corner at the MOMA. All around us dark blue suits, grey pants, muted colors, men and women pretty much the same, and much the same as it is in upstate New York, or Sydney or London or Berlin or Bogota, Colombia—places I get to quite often—but not necessarily the same on the subway ride to Brooklyn, where an African American man sits unperturbed in the elegance of the vivid color he wears.

Or take the philosopher's wife, scandalized by color—as described for us by Virginia Woolf in her essay "Old Bloomsbury":

The Post-Impressionist movement had cast—not its shadow—but its bunch of variegated lights upon us. We bought poinsettias made of scarlet plush; we made dresses of printed cotton that is especially loved by negroes; we dressed ourselves up as Gauguin pictures and careered around Crosby Hall [at the Ball for the second post-Impressionist Exhibition of 1912]. Mrs. Whitehead was scandalized.[2]

Not its shadow but its variegated lights.

Virginia Woolf went further with this licensed transgression. She built it into her being and into her prose, as when she distinguished between the critical and the imaginative powers displayed by men like her father, and to a large extent all the men, straight and gay, of Oxbridge and Bloomsbury. They lacked imagination—indeed they were crippled emotionally. "That type is like a steel engraving," she wrote, especially as regards her father, "without colour, or warmth, or body; but with an infinity of precise clear lines."

As for color, it was like a magical substance alive and flowing and human-bodied even if merely expressed in words. It was the idea, of color. It was the

Licensed Transgression

presence, of color—as when she wrote her sister Vanessa in 1938 about the Isle of Skye in Scotland: "One should be a painter. As a writer I feel the beauty, which is almost entirely colour, very subtle, very changeable, running over my pen, as if you poured a large jug of champagne over a hair-pin."[3]

The aversion to which Goethe refers us concerns things intimate to the person, to the body and the immediate surroundings. Unlike the glorious sunset or the moody sky, these are manmade things that express our personhood and, as with the drapes and tablecloth and furnishings in our bedroom and living room, are precious manmade mini-environments in which our soul is put to rest and refreshed. Together with the body-as-draped this environment encircling us "people of refinement" is what we might call the "color danger zone," where exquisite care has to be exercised as regards what otherwise comes across as the polluting and transgressive quality of bright color. A vividly colored tie is okay when the man is wearing a grey or dark suit, but if it's the other way around, watch out! (Imagine a bright yellow suit with a black tie.) A brightly colored Gauguin on the dentist's off-white waiting room is what you expect. But dare the other way around!

Yet this tiptoeing around the perimeter of the color danger zone is achieved effortlessly, lost in the everydayness of the maneuver. Is it therefore unconscious? Is that how we should talk about it? Or is it something else quite different, with all the qualities of a reflex, a question of "taste," we say when we can't think of anything better, taste endlessly repeated, handed down from generation to generation regardless of other dramatic changes in fashion, that handmaiden of the market ever bound to novelty? Such chromophobia speaks to a deep-seated bodily response whose dictates we blindly follow as second nature.[4] To call it *habit* is fine so long as we appreciate, as did the French ethnologist, Marcel Mauss, that what he called *techniques of the body*, including ways of walking, handling a shovel, swimming, love-making, sleeping, defecating, sensitivity to hot and cold, and laughing, are as much body as mind, privileged yet everyday activities in which what we call culture—a largely unconscious force—both manifests and maintains itself. Habits come and go, maybe, but are pretty resistant to change. To confront a habit such as chromophobia, extending maybe over a millennium, despite fundamental social, political, technological, and economic changes over that time, is to confront a very special habit indeed.

3

where stones walk like men

But now there is another, unprecedented change, planetary in scope. Never before has the divine vision of man and cosmos as organically interconnected been more meaningful. What happened in the West after the Middle Ages was the dislocation of the person from the center of the universe and from the heavens. Physical as well as spiritual geography was sundered. But in the past decade this has been reversed. No longer just a pretty or a religious metaphor, cosmos and man are now welded together by global warming, by what used to be called the Apocalypse.

As our bodies as well as our outlook change in a dangerous world now subject to rising seas, hurricanes, and pestilence, heat detaches the senses from the complacent view of the body as a fortress with peepholes and antennae sensing externalities, and instead encourages us to take a world-centered and not a self-centered approach to viewing, such that the self becomes part of that which is seen, not a sovereign transcendent. To thus consciously see ourselves in the midst of the world is to enter into ourselves as image, to exchange standing above the fray, the God position, for some quite other position that is not really a position at all but something more like swimming, more like nomads adrift in the sea, mother of all metaphor, that sea I call *the bodily unconscious*.

Let us recall for the moment the sage who taught in the seventh century AD that the world was spherical, the savant's savant, Isidore of Seville, with his equation of *calor* and *color*. For the question arises as to whether a new body will be formed as that other body we call planet earth heats up? Certainly changes are already happening down to the genetic level with insects and plants. As regards us humans equipped with a body whose thermostat will be reset together with other basic adjustments, might we not come to possess a new body-mind relationship such that our body's understanding of itself shall change? Even more important in changing the old-fashioned mind-body setup will be the cultural changes—that foreboding sense of cliff-hanging insecurity in a world ever more engaged with security in a climate gone terrorist.

The mere possibility that this could happen should be sufficient for us to consider other forms of the body's knowing itself as a consequence of planetary crisis and meltdown. It is when the machine begins to break down that you begin to see how it works. Likewise it is when authority is challenged that you begin to see the otherwise concealed workings of the power structure. This we could call apocalyptic knowledge, or *preemptively apocalyptic knowledge*, a thought experiment we can now conduct on ourselves and which in my case, which is the book before you, involves interrogating *color* as an offshoot of *calor*—for example, when you heat a pocketknife, as did Goethe, and feel the colors emanating therefrom, "passing like a breath," he says, flowing and changing at red heat to a beautiful blue and beyond.[1]

And beyond? Where would that be? This is not the unconscious we have known since Freud, made dull with usage. What I have in mind with the bodily unconscious is "thought" more like poetry, which proceeds outside of language and consciousness, what a famous student of shock on the battlefields of World War I by the name of Cannon called the "wisdom of the body."[2] Perhaps this was all metaphor for Cannon, this "wisdom," but not for me nor for Nietzsche, who argued that what we in the West call consciousness is but a tiny part of thought; that we think all the time and without language but do not "know" it and as such we are connected, as thinking bodies, to the play of the world.[3] This is that "beyond" to which color takes us.

Leaving the blood-soaked field of Flanders, Cannon provided us with another precious insight with his article "Voodoo Death" in the 1942 edition of *The American Anthropologist*. Drawing on reports from Western doctors in Haiti and remote Australia on deaths due to sorcery, he found confirmation of this "wisdom of the body" as that into which the sorcerer taps so as to kill people. No doubt Cannon's essay could be interpreted as a scientific explanation of mystical phenomena, but to me it suggests something quite different as well, another form of sorcery, perhaps, wherein and whereby bodies relate to other bodies, human and nonhuman—animals, plants, the seasons, tides, and the movement of the stars and the winds—forms of sensateness, of bodily knowing, that exist below the radar of consciousness and are all the more powerful for so being.

Song is the great medium. As breath and rhythm it collates and connects the vibratory quality of being. Emanating from the chest and throat, connected to dream and to body painting with red ochre, it connects a wide arc of possibilities and impossibilities. The song of the sorcerer in remote Australia from where Cannon drew his data was described by indigenous people in the late 1920s as the deadliest of all magic. The worst songs come from the "people of the south," which turns out to be no definite place but is where stones walk like men. "These stones walk around and sing these songs," the anthropologist Lloyd Warner was told, "and men follow and listen and learn them and sing them and make the men in the north sick."[4]

One of the deadliest songs is that of the whitefish. The breath of the victim becomes rapid and strained. This means that the fish has eaten the insides of that person and that the illness proceeds in a waxing and waning rhythm according to the movement of the tides.

You may not care to believe this could happen, or you may care to wonder about the stories anthropologists retell, it being the aim of my retelling of Lloyd Warner's retelling to paint the big picture, so as to indicate and evoke the poetry the bodily unconscious requires and provides. This poetry extends into nature, as in the nature made manifest by organic chemistry, itself a direct result of the search for beautiful dyes.

At one stroke Freud swept the rug out from under the maneuver I now wish to make when he asserted that the world of myth, involving nature as an animate being, retreated into the psychic unconscious of modern man. Subject to the codes and procedures of psychoanalytic jargon and hardened into dogma, this shift from outer to inner worlds, same as the shift from the manifest to the latent content of dreams, was a shift which effectively killed off the "people of the south" where "stones walk around and sing these songs." No! The bodily unconscious is not the Freudian one. The bodily unconscious has more to do with the abundance of ancient figurines of stone from the people of the south that sat on Freud's desk, figurines from ancient Mesopotamia and Egypt, which he loved to caress while listening to his patients, as the poet H. D. tells in lavish detail in her tribute to Freud.[5]

To make such an obscure function as the bodily unconscious more subject to our awareness and even control involves for me the restudy of early anthropology so as to learn from these stones that walk like men, just as it involves a sympathetic yet skeptical perusal of the centuries of Western fantasies about non-Western people, fantasies that effectively divided the world into chromophobes and chromophiliacs and made of Goethe's soldier such a fascinating anomaly. Color for the West became attached to colored people or their equivalents, such as kids and the women of southern Italy with their brightly colored bodices and ribbons. This way the West could have its cake and eat it, could admire the zouaves, sexually as well as aesthetically, while standing in the darkness of war, the darkness of night, and the darkness of those dark overcoats, coats, trousers, socks, and shoes that men wore then in 1916, for centuries before, and to the present day.

My sense of the bodily unconscious is that it now holds the future of the world in the balance as much as the other way around; that we have reached a time in world history when we can choose to press forward with the exploration of this "last frontier," which would, like the study of work habits by scientific management from Taylorism to the present, exploit, disfigure, and even destroy it, or else we can figure out a way of mastering our drive for mastery. That would mean we need to catch up with the way that, in the West, history turned the senses against themselves so as to control them. The mystery of color lies in the fact that it evaded this fate because, while vital to human existence, it could never be understood.

4

COLOR as CRIme

His face painted in the manner of the Indians, Goethe's soldier strolls the high street, jostled left and right by black and white. He stands out, this crossover man, because civilized nations and civilized people have long felt strange about color—meaning bold colors—being drawn to them, yet at the same time uneasy, even repelled, wanting them less wild, less bold, and less free to wander away from the ghettoes of "men in a state of nature," where they can be regarded from afar and enjoyed—from afar. Truth, on the other hand, comes in black and white for our philosophers as much as for us. Shapes and forms, outlines and marks, that is truth. Color, to tell the truth, is another world, a splurging thing, an unmanageable thing, like a prancing horse or a run in a stocking, something, this thing, this formless thing that we need to fence in with lines and marks, the boundary-riders of thought. Or else we need to grant color second-class citizenship as a poor cousin to form, essential to interior decorating, for instance, but not to architecture, because it is a luxury, an excess, a filler, a decoration, an add-on that came long after black-and-white TVs and movies and Kodak cameras got started.

Indeed, it is worse than any and all of that. Color amounts to crime. Derived from the Latin *celare*, to conceal, *color* is another word for *deceit* says my *Webster's*, while in Hebrew it's pretty much the same; *zava* means *color*, but *zavua* means *deception*.[1] Walter Benjamin agrees. Sharply distinguishing the child's view of color from the adult's, he suggests that adults understand color as a layer superimposed on matter to such a degree that they regard color "as a deceptive cloak."[2] Case in point, that formidable, fun-loving theorist of the visual world, Roland Barthes, becomes suddenly serious, very serious indeed: "I am not fond of Color," he writes in his famous book on photography, *Camera Lucida*, for "color is a coating applied *later on* to the original truth of the black-and-white photograph. For me, color is an artifice, a cosmetic (like the kind used to paint corpses)."[3] The redoubtable color theorist of modern times, Josef Albers, offers sound advice: "in order to use color effectively it is necessary to recognize that color deceives continually."[4]

How strange, therefore, that my dictionary goes on to say that color also signifies authenticity, as in "He showed us his true colors." Yet does not the very phrase "he showed us his true colors," venerable with age and usage, also suggest the opposite, that color is both true and untrue precisely because of its claims to authenticity? How can you ever be sure with which variety you are dealing, his true colors or his false ones? Is this why we in the West are drawn to color, yet made uneasy, even repelled by it, as by Mafia types like me in Hawaiian shirts? Who of you reading this text would even dream of painting the living-room wall bright red or green, or any color other than off-white? Then, safe in your whiteness, you can hang a wildly colored picture on the wall, secure in its framed being.

Take that unflappable stylist, Claude Lévi-Strauss, who set anthropology on its head for several decades. In an unusual display of pique, he writes on the first page of his acclaimed *Tristes Tropiques*, published in 1955: "Nowadays being an explorer is a trade, which consists not, as one might think, in discovering hitherto unknown facts after years of study, but in covering a great many miles and assembling lantern-slides or motion pictures, preferably in colour, so as to fill a hall with an audience for several days in succession."[5] "Preferably in colour." His anger seems boundless when, referring to Amazon Indians, he writes: "I can resign myself to understanding the fate which is destroying them; but I refuse to be the dupe of a kind of magic which is still more feeble than their own, and which brandishes before an eager public albums of colored photographs, instead of the now vanished native masks."[6]

Or Tobias Wolff in his little masterpiece, *This Boy's Life* ("My first stepfather used to say that what I didn't know would fill a book. Well, here it is."), reciting good advice in the 1960s, vintage USA on trangressions you must not commit if you want to look upper class: "Painting the walls of your house in bright colors. Mixing ginger ale with whisky. Being too good a dancer."[7]

"Colours were rich and heavy with an astonishing depth and sensuality," Christoper Pinney tells us in his book of riveting color plates displaying chromolithographs produced in India after 1870. Frequently depicting gods from the Hindu pantheon, whether for selling items such as matches or cigarettes, or used for religious reasons, these "things were horrible," declared an English lithographer in the 1930s, echoing not only the artistic elite of both England and India but also Tobias Wolff's wry advice on how to be upper-class American.[8] One reason why these vividly colored images were designated as horrible may have to do with what Pinney emphasizes as their apparent *tactility*—the way the color dissolves the visual modality so as become more creaturely and close, so close in fact that the image—or what was the image—becomes something which can absorb the onlooker. Exaggerated, perhaps, but nevertheless the same sensation Nietzsche described for the Dionysian, meaning absorption into the very being of the Other, as with music and dance and ritual, as contrasted with the Apollonian, meaning controlled vision that holds the Other at arm's length. Wrought thus as Dionysian, vivid color manifests its allegiance with the deepest streams of Orientalism, an interesting and fraught affair in which the visual turns in on itself, so to speak, in a medley of fear and fascination at being absorbed.

But you don't have to go to the rejection of Indian chromolithographs to see how color photography fares in the West. Take the first major exhibit of color photography (by William Eggleston) at the New York Metropolitan Museum of Art in 1976. Janet Malcolm ground her finger in the wound when she noted that hitherto color photography was "associated with photography's most retrograde application—advertising, fashion, *National Geographic*-type travel pictures, nature pictures, old fashioned arty abstractions of peeling walls and European traffic signs."[9] Poor Eggleston, doubly jeopardized—and doubly dangerous. Refusing to photograph gorgeous sunsets or Ansell Adams–type shots of the sublime West, his colored targets were the ordinary, everyday Amerikan trash that even back then filled the shelves of the supermarkets down south with engorged strips of Technicolor advertising toothpaste and breakfast cereal. There were also plenty of suburban driveways and lawns, sad but colored, yet not even a stray Diane Arbus freak to enliven the show. In the temple of high art that had previously only allowed black-and-white photography, his pictures looked "insignificant, dull, even tacky." If that's not enough, try "inartistic, unmodern, and being out of place in an art museum" on account of their atmosphere of slouching dejection and tentativeness "which the reviews of the show cruelly confirmed."[10] "Snapshot chic," was how Hilton Kramer buried this colorful subject, as compared with the work of a black-and-white photographer showing at the same time uptown and whose photos Kramer lost little time celebrating as having achieved "an extraordinary visual poetry."[11] Yet to the curator, John Szarkowski, that was beside the point. For him Eggleston's photos are not of shapes, symbols, or events. They are not even of color , but of experiences— which I take to mean that color lends itself, here, at least, to presencing rather than seeing.[12]

Which reminds me of growing up in Sydney, Australia, in the 1950s, where this same scenario was being played out with the torrent of poor immigrants entering the city a decade or so after my refugee parents arrived from central Europe and settled in the leafy suburbs. But it was the southern Europeans, the Greeks and Italians—those who grabbed Goethe's color-conscious eye two centuries before—who changed the drab Victorian terraces of inner-city Sydney. To your regular Anglo-Australian it seemed almost unpatriotic, certainly shocking and low class, the way they painted the outsides of their houses vivid yellows and blues, greens and reds. (Far away in the interior, Australian aborigines, especially the stockmen, were doing the same thing—not to their houses but to their bodies, by means of brightly colored clothing, and, out of White sight, on their bare skin with natural pigments for ceremonies.) The slums of Sydney exploded in a riot of color. Considering how strange this was, it really didn't take all that long for the real-estate investors to come in and buy big time. The Greeks and Italians left, for the leafy suburbs, I guess, and now those same inner-city suburbs, such as Paddington, are among the wealthiest in the world, the vivid colors painted over by ochres, greys, and white, or else stripped back to the original brick. You can't get realer than real estate, or, to put it otherwise, gentrification could suddenly find beauty and investment opportunity in the cramped inner-city terrace housing, but it could never ever go the wild color route.

Around the same time as the southern Mediterranean migrants were coloring inner Sydney, the Oxford-trained anthropologist from Arizona, Laura Bohannan, carrying out research among the Tiv-speaking people of Nigeria, had to make herself a new dress because of the rough treatment her cotton dresses received at the hands of her washer-women. She found what she called "Manchester prints" available in the local market. "They were," she says, "a bit gaudy for the station," meaning the colonial district officer's residence, "but much admired in the bush."[13] When the time came for a big dance, she became aware of what she called "African vogue," which included, for Tiv women, the kind of long knee socks Englishmen wear with their shorts, "but for African consumption, in greens, reds, and yellows . . . and gaudy scarves for the head."[14]

Tiv men could be equally voguish. When she first met chief Kako in the humble settlement where she carried out her fieldwork, there came with him "a glorious procession of elders in bright red hats, long white, yellow and purple robes, and blood-red goatskin shoulder bags." Nevertheless she scarcely noticed the robes and the reason she gives is instructive. It was because Kako's dignity of bearing reduced all that red, purple, and yellow to what she calls "a gaudy backdrop." All he wore by way of color was a tattered indigo cloth slung togawise over the shoulder.[15] To the anthropologist, at least, the blue-blackness of indigo trumped color. It seems like nothing much has changed since Goethe and his face-painting crossover man recently returned from America. Even our value-neutral professional anthropologist from Oxford and Arizona in the 1950s repeats Goethe's scheme a century and a half after he announced it, and repeats it point for point.

As for the ambiguity tied to color as both deceitful and authentic, take the mural, *Drain*, painted by John Pugh and described in the *New York Times* in 2005 as (and I quote) "a big rusty drainpipe etched with the letters LADWP, for Los Angeles Department of Water and Power, sucking the color and, metaphorically, the water out of the vista."[16] Here draining color stands for the belief that for close to a century Los Angeles has been stealing western rivers and indulging in scurrilous lies, as depicted in the film *Chinatown*, while at the same time color in this mural also stands for authenticity, for the lost vitality of nature being sucked out of the blue and green mountains in the distance, foregrounded by that nasty, efficient-looking, big, rusty pipe decoloring ever more parched flatlands.

"For them color is fluid, the medium of all changes," wrote Walter Benjamin with reference to what he took to be the child's view of color.[17] Tying color to water as the muralist John Pugh has done is useful because, like a river, color is a moving force, and like the world's water supply under the present climatic regime of politically enhanced global warming, color, like heat, is now subject to unpredictable oscillations which, in the case of color, amount to oscillations between deceit and authenticity, something that does not seem to have been factored in by that savant's savant, Isidore of Seville, when he drew attention to the similarities between *color* and *color*.

It is this oscillation that accounts for color's magic, thereby attracting that energetic stage magician, conjuror, and trickster, that master of deceit, Georges Méliès. No sooner had he begun to make films in Paris circa 1900, pulling rabbits out of hats thanks to the film editor's scissors, than he found it hard to resist painting colors over the black and white of his films. To the reality-effect of film was added the magic-effect of color. To the truth-effect of film, was added the deceit-effect of color. And so it goes. I don't know how they looked then, but now, a century later, the color is filmy and faint, like the whisk of a horse's tail, flourish of the color-spirit, not painting-by-numbers but that true excess of the heart that can only come across through the untoward hint.

Could it be that in this scheme of fear and desire, truth and deceit, color is the excess which allows forms to come alive and that this is why my *Webster's* tells me color is both pretext *and* sign of the authentic? Invitation to the fantastic? Sure. But something else as well; the too muchness that makes a philosopher such as John Locke desperately award color second-class, illegal-immigrant status to the halls of thought and truth, but for Denis Diderot gives forms their form. "Drawing gives shape to all creatures," says Diderot, but "color gives them life. Such is the divine breath that animates them."[18]

Divine? Animated? Is that why color lends itself to hyperbole and fantasy? Take that heart-gripping comic book artist, Art Spiegelman, creator of *Maus: A Survivor's Tale*, in his recent history of comic books suggesting that it was comics that introduced color to mass-circulation printing. It began with William Randolph Hearst's 1896 *New York Journal* proudly announcing its comic supplement: "Eight Pages of Polychromatic Effulgence That Makes the Rainbow Look Like a Lead Pipe!"[19] Colorful language indeed, as if color printing on a mass scale not only opened the doors to the palace of excess, but also cozied up to the language of advertising, so deliciously over-the-top that nobody can believe in it but only enjoy it—what we call sheer hype and therefore perfectly at home in color. But then, mindful of Goethe's observation as to how "men in a state of nature," uncivilized nations, and children, have a great fondness for colors in their utmost brightness, what else might you expect from the vulgar, anti-intellectual, and often downright rebellious medium of the comic strip, destined initially for immigrants to the Lower East Side of New York City with a poor grasp of English?

Generations later, color moved on. Migrating from the Lower East Side of New York City to California in the mid-1960s "was like switching from black-and-white to color," writes Robert Stone in his memoir of Ken Kesey.[20] In the psychedelic posters coming out of the Haight-Ashbury district of San Francisco advertising concerts at that time, an outstanding feature was the way words became flowing color, resembling hair. So much so that in the posters of Victor Moscoso, Wes Wilson, and Lee Conklin, it is only with utmost difficulty that you can make out the names of the musicians or the time and place of the concert. Imagine colored letters like those in a medieval manuscript, but giddily stretched to bursting, as if reflected in a fun-house concave mirror.[21] Walter Benjamin would have loved these hybrids, neither words nor pictures but somewhere in between, kicking up their heels in a fairyland of color. It is as if these are not advertisements at all, but anti-advertisements. Color has been snatched back from commerce in one of the few genuinely countercultural movements of the twentieth century. What is more, this is done not by replacing forms with streams of color, but by giving you a sense of the metamorphosis whereby— thanks to color—*form undoes itself.*

Or take that bible of business, the *Wall Street Journal,* dedicated to making rich people richer, which, after decades of black and white, decided in 2002 that it would come colored but according to its art designer, Mario Garcia, would make only restrained use of subtle, elegant colors on the front page. This is not in the style of a traditional newspaper. This is not *USA Today.*[22] No sir! And the palette—yes, the newspaper has a palette—is mint green, sky blue, and soft champagne. The names seem no less important than the colors. We have moved a long way from the days of coarse, solid colors, when the dollar was a greenback.

This self-consciously restrained use of color is made manifest in delicately tinted swaths of soft champagne, as, for example, in graphs and charts tracing the organic life of money. To date there are very few colored news photographs in the *WSJ*, and their color is notably cringing like a nude with her arms crossed over her body. The few black-and-white photographs are just as diminutive. And if the colored photographs are wan, the black-and-white ones are tiny, not much bigger than a postage stamp, and markedly distant in focus.

Is this coyness regarding photography related to the claims of drawing? The *WSJ* is known for its small black-and-white stippled drawings of smiling faces thought newsworthy, such as the one on the front page of the October 26, 2005, paper, with its drawing of the face of a dog called Caspar. In the case of Ken Lay and other Enron executives, having suffered the misfortune, unlike other *WSJ* readers, of having been caught with their hands in the till, swindling their own employees and the state of California, they are depicted sans smile, as is Hugo Chávez, long-term president of Venezuela, another superrich guy who has let the team down. The sixty-four-dollar question, of course, is what is the connection between (1) the business of America, (2) color-phobia, and (3) photo-phobia? I mean, if in 1896 the comics, which are drawings, too, encouraged "Eight Pages of Polychromatic Effulgence That Makes the Rainbow Look Like a Lead Pipe," what is it that works in quite the opposite direction in the *WSJ*, dedicated not to entertaining the immigrant workforce but making money out of them?

After all, restraint is not what strikes the eye when we turn the inner pages to find ourselves swept away by a maelstrom of color photography—not of the purported news, but advertising in full-page spreads of incandescent purples and blues displaying the wonders of photocopiers, German cars, and even double-page spreads in dark blues and pinks which, as you may have guessed, reveal the virtues of the barometer of business known as Dow Jones. And they have the nerve to call prostitutes painted ladies. And so it goes. As my *Webster's* informs, "He showed us his true colors." Like the devil, color is irresistible.

Is color divine? Maybe. Animated? Maybe. That is, if you ascribe to the notion that the divine is the flipside of evil and hence requires continual infusions of transgression—as with Walter Benjamin's observation that what he called "the language of color" was characteristic of the posters that flourished in the shopping arcades of Paris in the early nineteenth century, posters that were in his opinion the cousins of "obscene graphics." He recalled an advertising poster that reminded him of opera with Siegfried bathing in dragon's blood: the cape was crimson; the sylvan, solitude green; the flesh, naked. He noted that what he called "falser colors" are possible in the arcades, "such that nobody was surprised that combs were red and green. After all, Snow White's stepmother had such things, and when the comb did not do its work, the beautiful apple was there to help out—half red, half poison-green, like cheap combs."[23]

Such a beautiful example, this apple-become-comb thanks to color, illustrating thereby the new nature of the new-commodity world whereby industry was gearing itself up to fabricate cheaply what had previously been artifacts made by hand from natural products. (Snow White's vicious stepmother, the Queen, disguised herself as an old peddler woman by painting her face, and knocked at Snow White's door, crying out, "Pretty things to sell, very cheap, very cheap.")[24]

Thanks to their ability to mimic nature, the new industries of the famed *Industrial Revolution*, and most especially of the *chemical* industry, promised us utopias and fairylands beyond our wildest dreams, not merely colored, but magical, not merely colored, but poisonous. As the spirit of the gift, color is what sold and continues to sell modernity. As the gift that gives the commodity aura, color is magical and poisonous and this is perfectly in keeping with that view which sees color as both authentic and deceitful.

5

coLor waLks

Color lies at the chemical heart of the cosmos. Take alchemy. That mixture of magic and chemistry is said to have started with ancient Egyptians dyeing their grey cottons blue, like the blue thread in linen mummy cloth dyed as early as the Fifth Dynasty (2400 BC). From the dyeing of drab cloth there arose the idea of dyeing metals—so to speak—converting, by alchemy, drab metals into gold and silver.

Some say both alchemy and chemistry get their names from the name of Egypt itself, Kamt or Qemt, meaning the color black, in reference to the mud of the River Nile. This name was applied to the black powder resulting from the quicksilver process in Egyptian metallurgy, powder that was identified with the body of Osiris, god of the dead.[1]

Dying and dyeing. Nothing could be more magically tremendous than that other world, that world of the dead over which Osiris presides—nothing, that is, other than the world of color that emerges from the world of blackness.

As for that black mud, protoplasmic Osiris, we might say, drifting and compacting at the bottom of the meandering Nile, equivalent to the refuse remaining at the bottom of the alchemist's pot following combustion—hearken to the most mightily alchemical transformation conceivable, not of base metal into gold, but of black into living color, as when that cantankerous old writer of *Naked Lunch* fame, William Seward Burroughs, tells us of the mysterious jet-black cat, Smoker, that one day came in from the snow to the writer's boxcar by the junkyard by the river to lessen the despair of the writer-who-could-no-longer-write: "Smoker, a creature of the lightless depths, where life as we on the surface know it cannot exist, brought light and color with him as colors pour from tar."[2] That was in 1987.

As colors pour from tar. We've all been there. Pure magick. Sucks you in as though it were something more than visual, so you pour with them, adding to the effulgence of color flowing in black sands granulated with the body of the god of the dead.

As for this writer-who-can-no longer-write, Smoker allows him to get at least one thing straight: those colors that pour from tar are nothing less than words, words used to liberate words—in keeping with Burroughs's lifelong obsession. "Cut ups? But of course. I have been a cut-up for years . . . I think of words as being alive like animals. They don't like to be kept in pages. Cut the pages and let the words out."[3]

That was in 1964. Brion Gysin was his painter pal in those days, and when you look over Gysin's work, playing with color in relation to written words, let alone Burroughs's own color work, as in his 1960s scrapbooks and his 1980s paintings, it suddenly hits you that there is a tight connection between the mad desire to cut up, on the one hand, and this fascination with color, on the other.

As when, in his homage to Gysin, Burroughs invokes the idea of going on "color walks"—which are a good deal more than color-coded walkways through Tangier or New York or Paris; red on Wednesdays, blue on Fridays, or whatever. A delightful idea, to be sure. But that is only the beginning, because the idea here is that the very notion of a code be "cut up," meaning that color is invoked so as to loosen the restraint of coding and that there is something about color that facilitates this, as if colors love to betray themselves, like yellow meaning

FIGURE 1. Brion Gysin in Algiers, 1956.

gold, awesome, and holy, but also treason and cowardice, as well as having a long history in the Christian West to mark adulterous women, Jews, Muslims, prostitutes, heretics, witches, and executioners.

Could we not say, therefore, that with the color walk we are alerted to the singular and beautiful fact that color itself walks?

This would make color even more of a flaneur than Burroughs, who liked to call himself *el hombre invisible* in his walks through the market in Tangier in the late 1950s. What was invisible in Tangier became color in Paris, thanks to Gysin's paintings painted in Tangier. Maybe a person has to lose themselves first and become invisible as a long-term resident in a third-world country before being

FIGURE 2. William Burroughs and Brion Gysin together.

readied for the color walk? But then Burroughs was continuously marginal in utterly realistic as well as in utterly romantic ways. He was queer. He was a heroin addict. He loathed Amerika yet was quintessentially American. And he had weird ideas about most everything, especially writing. Being marginal can mean you switch on and you switch off because you are either too conspicuous or invisible. Too invisible, that's the point at which you emerge as color—walking color, at that.

And remember, the original insight for the color walk lay in Gysin's playing with letters, letters that form words. Here color and the decomposition of written language-signs go hand in hand. What also happens when Smoker comes in from the cold is that the old writer in the boxcar by the junkyard is once again able to write. As colors pour from tar, he unblocks. He pours. The cat purrs. And guess what? All his stories are animal stories. ("Of course," adds Burroughs.) The old writer finds them in an illustrated book. There is the Flying Fox with its long black fingers and sad black face, just like Smoker. There is a Fishing Bat peering from under its shell. There is the Black Lemur with round red eyes and its little red tongue, the beautiful Ring-Tailed Lemur hopping through the forest like on a pogo stick . . . "So many creatures, and he loves them all."[4]

The old writer caresses these pictures.

After all, "I have been a cut-up for years," the writer told us. "I think of words as being alive like animals. They don't like to be kept in pages. Cut the pages and let the words out."[5]

Now the words and the animals become united in the stories the old writer finds welling up inside himself as colors pour from tar.

6

tHe DIVeR

January 8, 1938, Paris. When that young blade Michel Leiris asked of his surrealist friends gathered in Paris on the brink of war in their new club, The College of Sociology, that each one ask themselves what color is the sacred, he must have known he was onto a good thing, like the diver facing empty space as her toes leave the security of the high board, arms outstretched into the blue sky revolving above and beneath.

It was an exquisite talk for an exquisite occasion, fitting right into the college's burning curiosity about religious and magical forces felt to be active in politics no less than in art. Such forces might seem irrelevant to modern intellectuals, but not to the college, with its fascination with what it called "sacred sociology," a fecund mix of Marx, Freud, and Nietzsche, to which was added the astonishing novelty of ethnography—the anthropological study of so-called primitive societies. It was just this anthropological study that provided the alchemical ingredient necessary to jolt a new sensibility into existence, clustered around the notion of the sacred in everyday life, the subject of Leiris's short talk.

The less presentable side to this interest was manifest in *Acéphale, The Headless Man*, a would-be secret society within the college whose aim was to create not so much a new religion as to relaunch the *sacred* in a world transformed by the death of god, "recasting man by changing his reality in accomplishing his own nothingness."[1] Indeed, members of *Acéphale* had gotten close, *so it is said*, to actually killing a fellow society member as an act of sacrifice on the outskirts of Paris in some utterly mythic locale, the forest of Saint-Nom-la-Bretéche, not too far from a convenient railway station and a quick hop back to the Left Bank. "I can tell you," Pierre Klossowski said later, "that it was very beautiful . . . There was a Greek fire at the foot of a tree struck by lightning. A whole stage set."[2]

But for the more intellectually oriented college, Leiris had turned in a charming performance under the title "The Sacred in Everyday Life." Based on his recollections of an apparently serene childhood—unlike the deeply disturbing memories of the one female member of the group, Colette Peignot, one of whose writings on the sacred begins, "What color does the notion of the sacred have for me?"—Leiris came at religion and magic from a totally unexpected direction.[3] He quickened one's interest in what he thought of as sacred with his snapshots of the dining-room stove, *La Radieuse*, with the warmth of its glowing coals; his father's nickel-plated Smith and Wesson revolver; the bathroom antics with his brother; the mysteries of his parents' bedroom; the coining of names; the sudden recognition that one has been mishearing and mispronouncing words; and so forth—in short, charged spaces, dangerous objects, and prohibited events, lifting you off from the world of ordinary reality.

"It was," writes Jean Wahl about this talk, "the first meeting in which one had the feeling of some intensity from beginning to the end of the lecture."[4] Yet there must have been a feeling that for all its charm and ingenuity, something was lacking in this way of proceeding, because right there, at the very end, as if everything that had come before had nothing whatsoever to offer, there, like an epitaph stuck upright in the soft turf of the text, was his exploding trick, as I paraphrase, *What color is the sacred?*

It was, as they say, a "rhetorical question," tweaking its own presuppositions, leaving nothing much more than whistling in the dark. It put the very notion of the sacred in question, bracing it, not erasing it, thanks to the peculiar swerve Leiris had inflected upon things holy.

Nothing much more than whistling in the dark. About which you have to first realize that Leiris had made the sacred an outcome of the adult's imagination of the child's imagination. He secularized the sacred, we might say, but preserved its magic in this way, allowing remembrance of the child's perceptions to enchant the things of the world. Please note the dialectic, no less common than strange, it being surely obvious that the adult's imagination of the child's imagination includes the child's imagination of the adult's . . . including the child's view of color. It seems so different from that of adults. More lively. More lovely. What happened, you ask, on the way to adulthood?

One thing that happened was what that these sacred sociologists inherited "the sacred" across generations of intellectuals, beginning with the founding father of sociology, Émile Durkheim, together with the latter's close reading of the ethnography of Australian aborigines and the Native Americans of North America. In fact Leiris himself wrote a doctoral thesis on the secret language of the Dogon people of East Africa and became a museum mole, keeper of secrets in the Museum of Man in Paris as well as an exponent of writing as an art form that self-effacingly thinks about itself as it moves across the page, inlaying its stream of jewels.

What made the ethnographic interest in "the sacred" strangely pertinent at this time was that Leiris and his friends wondered aloud whether that ethnographic sacred to which Durkheim had introduced them might not be hard at work as a living force in the modern world about them. This was the basis of their College of Sociology, dedicated as it was to sacred sociology. But this had little to do with religion as a church. Instead "the sacred" pointed to a replay of a spirit world thought to be long since obliterated by what had come to be called the "disenchantment of the world." The spirit-force sacred is what I wish to reclaim, too, what Burroughs called the "magical universe," as opposed to the OGU or One God Universe. It is my belief that color, or rather the child's view of color, will help me, yet I am aware that reenchantment is not the same as enchantment.

The *sacred* was a variant on the surrealists' *marvelous* with higher voltage and more horsepower because attraction and repulsion kept changing places so fast that most of the time you couldn't tell one from the other. If the marvelous still held something of the distanced contemplation so dear to the aesthete, then the sacred was what short-circuited that remove, took you into the eye of the hurricane and out again with some pretty putrid colors when occasion demanded, like the yellow of Burroughs's bunker in the Bowery, downtown Manhattan, earlier a YMCA locker room whose mustard tones owed much to decades of young men's sweating bodies. With a dash of sulfur, the sun that radiated out from van Gogh's sunflowers could revert to that other yellow, the yellow of hell and self-mutilation. The sacred likes to bite the hand that feeds it. It was scary, yet drew you in, not least because it was always just one step ahead of the game. "I kept myself going on coffee and alcohol," van Gogh wrote his brother and benefactor, Theo, in 1899, the year in which he mutilated himself then took his life. "I admit all that, but all the same it is true that to attain the high yellow note that I attained last summer, I really had to be pretty well keyed up."[5]

To propose that something like pagan magic was alive and well in the secular world around us and that this was not despite modernity but because of it—this was no less appropriately inappropriate than Leiris's question as to the color of the sacred. As a question that tore at its own moorings, as a question that begged the question, it was no less bewildering than it was mocking, light hearted, and unsettling—like the diver facing empty space as her toes leave the security of the high board, arms outstretched into the blue sky revolving above and beneath.

7

COULD a cat BE a WHaLe?

Colours spur us to philosophize.

LUDWIG WITTGENSTEIN, *Remarks on Colour*

Could it be that the question as to the color of the sacred is itself sacred, a *spiritual exercise* of the sort Herman Melville undertook in *Moby Dick* when he tells us that it was above all the whiteness of the great whale that appalled him? "But how can I hope to explain myself here," he continues, "and yet, in some dim, random, way, explain myself here I must, else all these chapters might be naught."[1] Melville confuses us with his appalling whiteness here. He confuses his having to explain the fear whiteness can assume, with having to explain himself.

Yet is this not Leiris's question in a nutshell, understanding yourself by searching within for some sign allowing you to discern the color of the sacred?

Then there is Burroughs's white cat, Margaras. "He can hide in snow and sunlight on white walls and clouds and rocks, he moves down windy streets with blown newspapers and shreds of music and silver paper in the wind."[2] Sometimes he is called *The Tracker*, a scary creature as capable of blending into nature as threading his way through computer files. Having no color, so William Burroughs tells us, Margaras takes on all colors.

Color walks. And as it walks, so it changes. It is not something daubed onto a preexisting shape, filling a form, because colors have their own "form," giving life and light to the world.

Is color an animal?

Sounds unlikely. But what then is an animal? And why does thinking of color as an animal throw us off, maybe down those same windy streets where we run the risk of getting mixed up with blown newspapers and shreds of music and silver paper in the wind?

Not only Margaras. There is Smoker, too. Smoker, the all-black cat who came in from the snow, Smoker from whom colors pour as from tar. One cat is white, the other black, and together they emerge from the one book in a flurry of color and music and wind. Are these cats colors that happen to come across as cats?

Could a cat be a whale, a white whale at that? Take the whale whose whiteness caused Ahab such commotion. Drove Melville crazy, too. The whiteness more than anything else. Here's what Melville has to say:

> Is it that by its indefiniteness it shadows forth the heartless voids and immensities of the universe, and thus stabs us from behind with the thoughts of annihilation, when beholding the white depths of the milky way? Or is it, that as in essence whiteness is not so much a color as the visible absence of color, and at the same time the concrete of all colors; is it for these reasons that there is such a dumb blankness, full of meaning, in a wide landscape of snows—a colorless, all-color of atheism from which we shrink?[3]

I stare out my window onto the snow-covered river below, trying to put myself in Melville's snowshoes. As far as the eye can see the ground is mantled with soft, even whiteness. It is spectacular. It is soothing. It is something you can never get tired of. But the seasons move along.

The road workers hired by the town ripped out a tree stump from the frozen ground the other day when I was not here, damaging the low stone wall around the front of the house. They did it to make things easier for the snowplow. When I talked with the man driving the town's truck looking for potholes to fill, he said apropos of nothing much that we should wait until spring to fix up the wall, when the stones half buried in frost would be free.

The seasons move, but I was locked in the frost and had forgotten time, which is to say the movement of the earth in relation to the sun. I had forgotten how a totally different temperature and thickness to the air will bring with it a palette of colors along with the thawing of the frost. There will come bold greens and delicate blues, the reds of the poppies in late May, the scattering of white roses along the edges of the forest in June. In August the colors will be purple and yellow; that is the driest month, when the river banks and swamps turn purple with what people around here think of as an "invasive weed," name of loose-strife. Along the edges of the road by my house in August will be blue cornflowers accompanied by tendrils of yellow goldenrod and clusters of intensely bright yellow flowers, black-eyed Susans, also wild, growing some six feet high. Lying down with Bina at that time, I saw a bright yellow bird balancing itself on the stem of these yellow flowers. I had never seen such a color on a bird around here. Then I saw another bird, exactly the same, perched just above it. So I assume the color of birds owes something to the color of other wild things as we tilt this way and that in our orbit around the sun. But night is another story. Every night in June and July there will be fireflies lighting up the dark in a disappearing trail of sparks. God knows how, but sometimes they get into the bedroom. The night before I left for a long trip in July there were two fireflies inside well after midnight, looping the loop together.

Fireflies light up the night in trails of sparks that could never be confused with the light of the sun. Why is it then that for most of my life I had confused the sun with the artificial light produced by that late nineteenth-century invention of Thomas Edison, the lightbulb? But now I'm wiser. The dawn is a great teacher. You see the light gradually creeping among the shadows in the forest left by the night. It is a warm, soft, blurry, creaturely substance, liquid light we might say, with a golden touch and depths to it as well. No. The sun is not a light switch.

But right now in February it's an all-white world except that the river flows black, with light glinting here and there. Large rocks in the river are covered with snow and ice to form ecstatic shapes never before drawn or seen in their stately unevenness.

At times the earth seems to glow and be lifting upwards. Bare of leaves, the ash trees and maples are spidery spikes staking down the earth, suspended in a nothingness. This is no longer a forest but a forest of silhouettes, two-dimensional cutouts of unnerving beauty, all form, so purely form that form collapses into the effervescence you feel late afternoon walking down the mountain with the sun setting like fire on the ridge to your left. The snow has a lot of ice that crunches loudly under your snowshoes. The sun becomes more orange as it sets. But what gets you really going, walking down the mountain with Kostas that late autumn afternoon, what caught your eye and very being in the first place, was the unnamable color—a type of light purple, some subtle mist of green and blue with some red and yellow in there too that was, you realize, more than color as in coloring but some other medium altogether. It was, you want to say, a curious light lightness, some quite other medium is what you want to say—floating, passing, radiating across the valley through the air, twisting through the branches of the forest as if it were the breath of the dying sun, glowing itself ever stronger as it passes behind the ridge of the Catskills to the north, darkening blue with every added ray of fire from the sun.

8

in the time of Lapis Lazuli

Some quite other medium, you now want to say, when all along you had thought it was color, just color, good old color, useful for wrapping up reality as a gift. *Some quite other medium?* But what could it be, this curious light lightness that floats, that passes, that radiates across the valley like the breath of dying sun? What could it be? I choose to call it *polymorphous magical substance.* It affects all the senses, not just sight. It moves. It has depth and motion just as a stream has depth and motion, and it connects such that it changes whatever it comes into contact with. Or is it the other way around? That in changing, it connects? My immediate point of reference here, my strong image, is with something that leapt into my imagination several years ago, that inchoate light lightness likened to the feathers of newborn birds said to fill the bodies of Selk'nam Indian shamans on Isla Grande in the Beagle Channel of Tierra del Fuego at the tip of South America.[1]

Hard to imagine, this human body composed of feathers of newborn birds. Even harder to imagine is that this same stuff is profoundly implicated in the act of vision of the shamans and that such vision can cure as well as kill and is linked to communication with spirits active in dreams and song. We find this ethereal substance or something like it in many Indian societies in lowland South America and it has been likened by Claude Lévi Strauss to *mana*, an auratic, sacred power emanating from persons and things and thought by the famous anthropologist Marcel Mauss to be the basis of all magic. One way of understanding this light lightness would be liken it to human stem cells, with their potential to become any one of the highly specialized cells of the body— heart, brain, spine, liver, kidney, etc.—only here it is not the human body, but the body of the world.

Drawn from the mouth, this white, feathery substance lends itself to all manner of conjuring. It may condense into a small, spinning disc revolving at great speed as if alive in the palm of the hand, then be stretched to arm's length to be abruptly swallowed, despite its immense size.[2] It is like no substance we have ever seen or can imagine, more like a substance which is no substance, suspending laws of time and space where substance gives way to movement, manifesting itself in a myriad of changing forms. This, then, is what I call polymorphous magical substance, and it is how I prefer to think of color, something more than a spot of red or blue on a page.

Perhaps the story of ultramarine is helpful here. Before it was produced in factories in 1830, ultramarine was gotten from the semiprecious stone lapis lazuli in Afghanistan. Under the microscope you can see why the natural and the synthetic varieties of ultramarine look different to the naked eye. While the synthetic pigment has homogeneous, round crystals that produce a consistent, all-the-same blue surface, the ultramarine derived from lapis lazuli has large, irregular crystals of varying transparency and, what is more, these crystals are clustered together with particles of mica, quartz, calcite, and pyrite, yielding what Anita Albus calls a color like the glittering firmament. The calcite crystals, she says, "sparkle like stars within the deep blue."[3]

Like fast food's effect on food, nineteenth-century color technology killed off the body of color and, as regards the fine arts as practiced by the likes of Jan Van Eyck and Vermeer, choked off centuries of craft, notably the tremendous work preparing pigments, fresh, each day; the underpainting or foundation of the painting; and, following that, the application of alternate layers of opaque colors and transparent varnishes, what Cezanne called the "secret soul of grounds" and others call "glazing." In enlargements of cross sections of paint samples from paintings made this way, what we see, says Albus, "would look like a landscape of geological layers of different shapes and colors."[4] Multilayering was the key and a crystalline, transparent density, the result. You not only see it in Vermeer but also in the iridescent cloth woven by the Flemish and the Italians in the fifteenth century, no less than in the iridescence of a butterfly's wing. As Albus puts it, color is the *interplay* between *body* and *tone* (meaning hue). Each pigment a painter used had a different body, she writes, "which refracts, reflects, and absorbs light in a different way."[5]

But is not Anita Albus a shade too conservative with her language of the glittering firmament versus the all-the same-sameness of synthetic paint? Is there not value in flat sameness, only we don't see it as romance so much as the heroic mysteries of the void? Take Yves Klein's *artificial* ultramarine, IKB, a.k.a. "International Klein Blue," the resort to acronym telling you just how daringly industrial, how daringly camp and modern this color is going to be, allowing its progenitor to shock the 1950s art world with his ultramarine that "literally takes on a life of its own," such that color "would become the springboard for the space without limit."[6] If Albus's *natural* ultramarine plays with space like the flitting wings of the butterfly, the spatial play of IKB is "vaporous, floating, time-less." But at the end of the day, the butterfly seems a lot more fun, I would say. After all, IKB is romantic too, for nothing is as romantic as being anti-romantic.

When we see a color, we are actually seeing a play with light in, through, and on a body, the body of color itself. Being a matter of texture, it is no wonder that color can seem to be what I call a polymorphous magical substance, twisting itself as if alive through the branches along with the dying sun. At least it would be of no wonder were it not for changes in the production of paints since the nineteenth century. "The very abundance of colors in the modern world," write Francois Delamare and Bernard Guineau quite recently, "seems to dilute our re-lationship with them. We are losing our intimate connection with the materiality of color, the attributes of color that excite all the senses, not just sight."[7]

It is not by chance, Anita Albus says, that now "the language of color nuances is always connected with *bodies*: *sky* blue, *lavender* blue, *turquoise* blue, *gentian* blue, *violet* blue, *cornflower* blue, *reed* green, *apple* green, *olive* green, *almond* green, *sea* green, *emerald* green . . ." What does she mean, "not by chance"? She points out that each name associates a color with a texture: "transparent or opaque, smooth, rough, dense, or friable bodies that shine, sparkle, reflect, or shimmer softly or harshly in the light."

Then there are the name choices for what are generally thought of as the first synthetic, meaning aniline, dyes discovered in the mid-nineteenth century, the best known of which is *mauve*, the French name of the common mallow plant; the crimson red named *fuchsin* after the fuchsia; and then that cross between mauve and fuchsin known as *dahlia*, soon followed by *Britannia violets*.

Such names are fake, allusions to what paints used to be before the industrial production of paints with which light has an easier time than before—easier in the sense that light is not whacked around as it might be with its passage through a series of differently shaped crystals, as in the case of lapis lazuli or, for that matter, in the case of the colors of the sky in storms or at dawn and sunset, when we suddenly sit up and see the color as if for the first time.

The fakeness of these bodies conjured by market hype is a fakeness brought about because the body was killed off by mid-nineteenth century. What took its place were these names as substitutes for what had gone, and the names were marvelous. Of course, the broad strokes of the colors of nature remain accessible to human experience in the seas, the skies, the plowed fields and forests, in the human face and body, no less than in the flash of fur and wing of animals and birds, not to mention the rusted edges of shop awnings and the mould in the bathroom.

Yet the very same chemical revolution of the nineteenth century that emerged from the search for color and drugs from coal tar, this very same chemical revolution polluted those broad strokes of remaining nature with new texture. The sunsets never looked so stunning as they did through the haze of factory smoke and soot. Surrealism arrived long before the surrealists caught on. The moon radiated chemical purple, streams ran with phosphorescent blue or thick green sludge. A stench and pall clung to the air. Small wonder the upper classes of England and Germany sought the beauty of the natural colors of Italy and the south of France, and raved about the "quality of the light" that hung like wings of gossamer over silky sunsets. And of course these purple moons and phosphorescent streams back home in the industrial north appeared all the more vivid on account of the dull, bleak carapace that coated everything else, including the human lung. Iron and coal dominated this period. "Their colour spread everywhere," writes Lewis Mumford, "from grey to black: the black boots, the black stove-pipe hat, the black coach or carriage, the black iron frame of the hearth, the black cooking pots and pans and stove. Was it protective coloration? Was it mere depression of the senses?"[8]

Thanks to the chemical revolution wrought from coal, we now live in an artificial world without much awareness as to its artificiality. Most everything around us derives from coal chemistry, and this applies especially to the way we have recast the color of the world such that we have confused the factory-made color world around us in our rooms and magazines, our clothing and automobiles, with the colors in nature, parallel to the way we have confused a photograph with reality.

The fake names of synthetic colors do more than what Anita Albus points to. These names take all that color had been with reference to the world of plants, bugs, and minerals, and adds the magic of artifice, frequently the colonial exotic—as when Roland Barthes notes in his quirky autobiography first published in 1975 that when he buys colors he does so according to "the mere sight of their name."[9] What he says is: "The name of the color (*Indian yellow, Persian red, celadon green*) outlines a kind of generic region within which the exact, special effect of the color is unforeseeable; the name is then the promise of a pleasure, the program of an operation."[10]

Barthes recruits the special but unforeseeable effect of these largely colonial color names to destabilize the very idea of a code, in the same way that Conrad in *Heart of Darkness* flits between the solid colors of the map of Africa and the evanescent colors of the flames racing across the water of the Thames in the rays of the setting sun when his narrator, a simple sailor by the name of Marlow, gives voice to his soul-cracking experience in the Congo with the curious statement, *the fascination of the abomination*. Barthes uses the solidity of the colonial category—for example, *Indian yellow*—to shake things up back home by the Seine, a task made easy by the mystery of India, let us say, making for an elegant play of the fixed and the elusive. A great student of reading and writing, film and photography, Barthes himself loved to paint and is credited with over seven hundred drawings and paintings, the few I have seen being spidery meanderings of dots and lines hell bent on evading the code, not unlike the work of Cy Twombly. Being unforeseeable introduces into color the element of chance, where the "color walks" of William Burroughs become evidence of color's ability to itself walk. As Barthes says, the name of the color transports him.

And not only Barthes or Burroughs, but Goethe as well strikes an equally color-active tone when he cites Philipp Otto Runge on account of his focus on transparent colors as polymorphous magical substances that lead a life of their own, spiraling off into nether regions of soul and mind.[11] With transparent color "objects are cloaked with a charm," Runge writes, "that usually lies more in the air lying between us and the object than in the lighting of its forms."[12]

This reminds me of magic lanterns and the translucent colors they projected, filling the air with shimmering color. Recorded as early as 1646, such machines found color-magic a congenial helpmate for their spectacular displays, effortlessly transmuting the color on the glass slide or mirror into transparent color. Thus magic lanterns filled the centuries between Gothic stained glass and modern cinema. In my version of color history, magic lanterns took up where Van Eyck and Vermeer (1632–75) left off. The nineteenth century may have killed off the body of color, but in doing so it resurrected its spirit with the improvements made to long-existing machines that projected light through colored images— thereby entering into that same ethereal region, that "generic region," which Roland Bathes sees whenever he goes to buy a color and does so according to the *sight* of its *name* . . . think India, think Persia.

This connection between the body and soul of color by means of language was seen clearly by Marcel Proust, who frequently claims that Vermeer's painting provided him with his philosophy of writing. It is an amazing assertion: *style is to the writer what color is to the painter*, Proust's insistent point being that this art, working through layers of color and light, achieves its revelatory power through indirection and never by means of conscious confrontation, because the real treasure is inaccessible to the intellect.[13]

As a child, Proust's narrator was given a magic lantern by his parents. It would be set up on top of his lamp before the dinner hour and, "after the fashion of the first architects and glaziers of the Gothic age, it replaced the opacity of the walls with impalpable iridescences, supernatural multicolored apparitions, where legends were depicted as in a wavering, momentary stained-glass window."[14]

Proust's style is itself a magic lantern (the title of Howard Moss's marvelous book on Proust), which, in its most concentrated form, is what springs into being with the famous *memoire involontaire*, the fire ignited by the play of transparent colors with opaque ones. Philipp Otto Runge talked of rebirth along with vanishing when he tried to put words to transparent color. This rebirth is as much memory as color, memories that can never be accessed by conscious effort no matter how hard we try, as when Proust's narrator imagines real persons as characters in the stained-glass window of the local church, made not just of color but of changing color, like Gilbert the Bad changing from cabbage green to plum blue, or like the persons in his magic-lantern show bathed continuously in a sunset of orange light.[15]

Slides and cinema project the spirit of color's dying corpse, as when the glittering firmament of lapis lazuli slides off the painter's palette, to be reborn in colored air of magical polymorphous substance. Slides and cinematic images seem to have depth as well. It is this mix of depth and transparency that allows them to bathe us in sunsets of orange as we sit in the darkness of theaters, washed by color and the crunching of popcorn.

9

POLYMORPHOUS MAGICAL SUBSTANCE

Some quite other medium, you now want to say, when all along you had thought it was color, just color, good old color, useful for wrapping up reality as a gift. *Some quite other medium?* But what could it be, this curious light lightness that floats, that passes, that radiates across the valley like the breath of dying sun? What could it be? Is it a substance or is it an action? Is it something out there in the extra-personal world, or is it "merely" part of the human imagination? Or could it be all these things, and such questions are irrelevant, as color mocks our usual categories of understanding?

I choose to call it *polymorphous magical substance,* this quite other medium that that floats like the breath of dying sun, a polymorphous substance that is the act and art of *seeing.*

Although the impulse for my idea here comes from the feathers of newborn birds, said by Father Gusinde almost one hundred years ago to fill the bodies of

Tierra del Fuego Selk'nam shamans, I am powerfully reminded of the fact that this class of perception not only allows for games with reality—as evidenced by the mighty displays of conjuring exercised by these shamans, extracting from their mouths white, feathery stuff in concentrated, elastic, form, and making it disappear back into their bodies again—but that, aided by song and dream, this is perception which can enter into the bodies of persons and things to kill or heal.

With this I come back full circle to Walter Benjamin's notion that with color and with the movies one's eye is encouraged to enter into the image. And not only one's eye! More like one's entire being! Gazing at colored illustrations, the child "overcomes the illusory barrier of the book's surface," he writes, "and passes through colored textures and brightly colored partitions to enter a stage on which fairy tales spring to life."[1] And if adults in the West largely lose this ability by the time they grow up, then the movies restore it, along with the child's view of color not as a surface layer applied to a preexisting form, but as some-thing "fluid, the medium of all changes."[2] And would not the Selk'nam shaman find further comfort with Benjamin's conjecture that for the child the concern with color goes, as he puts it, "right to the spiritual heart of objects"?[3]

Let me at once admit to a two-way street here, a strange confusion of words and actions, a wondrous reciprocity of passivity and activity as one enters the image but is no less entered by it. But what the shaman supplies as regards this capacity of seeing, and what Benjamin omits, is music, along with the dreaming, that passes you into the image that enters you.

Commenting on the sense of a "mystic potence" known in the world of the Iroquois as *orenda*, being neither a god nor a spirit but a diffuse power inform-ing all things, the Native American anthropologist, J. N. B. Hewitt, son of a European trader and Huron mother, wrote in 1902 that shamans have *orenda* in abundance, as do successful hunters and gamblers. To exert his or her *orenda*, the shaman "must sing, must chant, in imitation of the bodies of his environ-ment."[4] Indeed the very word *orenda* means to sing or to chant in the earlier speech of the Iroquoian people. Small wonder then that Hewitt repeatedly returns to sound, to music, singing, and the sounds of nature as the privileged domain of *orenda* and magic.

Nietzsche would have been delighted. Didn't he say that music in Dionysian states had the capacity to intensify bodily states so that you discharge all your powers of representation, imitation, transfiguration, transmutation, every kind of mimicry and play acting conjointly? In such a state you possess to the highest degree the instinct for understanding and divining, you possess to the highest degree the art of communication, entering into every skin, into every emotion, continuously transforming yourself.[5] But listen now instead to Hewitt and note how he uses the word "bodies" here, not the word "spirits":

> The speech and utterance of birds and beasts, the soughing of the wind, the voices of the night, the moaning of the tempest, the rumble and crash of the thunder, the startling roar of the tornado, the wild creaking and crack-ing of wind-rocked and frost-riven trees, lakes, and rivers, and the multiple other sounds and noises in nature, were conceived to be the chanting— the dirges and songs—of the various bodies thus giving forth voice and words of beastlike or birdlike speech in the use and exercise of their mystic potence.[6]

The shaman's song is the imitation of the "dirges and songs" of various "bodies" of the environment. Recalling that severe winter in the Dakotas in the 1870s, the Oglala Sioux Black Elk described a medicine man by the name of Creeping who cured people of snow blindness. "He would put snow upon their eyes," Black Elk is recorded as saying, "and after he had sung a certain sacred song that he had heard in a dream, he would blow on the backs of their heads and they would see again, so I have heard. It was about the dragonfly that he sang, for that was where he got his power, they say."[7]

Gusinde gives us a nice image, too, one in which you can lose yourself with-out even trying. "They fairly pour warmth into him," he said with regard to the training of a shaman, when a handful of warmth was captured from the fire and emptied onto the initiate's head as if to remove fog from the eyes. At the same time, handfuls of warmth were poured into his mouth, so that not only can he see the spirits without interference, but so that "nothing can hinder his singing."[8]

The conclusion is inescapable. Vision and song are one and at one with the shaman's body.

This body is worth some consideration. To whom or what does it belong: to the spirits themselves, to the singer, or to the body of the song itself?

Imagine the scene written down for the anthropologist Franz Boas by George Hunt, whose father was a trader emigrated from Scotland, his mother, a Kwakiutl Indian. Over at least three decades Hunt had tried several times to

Polymorphous Magical Substance

become a shaman and had, on four separate occasions, written down this experience for Boas, who considered the least mystical and most skeptical version to be this last one written in 1925. Perhaps the most curious aspect of this text is how Hunt disappears, so to speak, and is known only by his Indian name, as if he were already a shaman capable of brilliant shape changing, one day Hunt the informant, next day Quesalid, the Indian doing his thing. That is the first and most basic level on which to start contemplating the body and the song.

It is night by the sea. A shaman is singing his sacred song out in back of the village. Imagine the tall cedars, the incessant rainfall, the mists mingling with the warmth of the sea currents, the sea churning with seals and salmon, huge cedar houses along the curve of the bay with their totem poles displaying animals emerging from the mouths of other animals and humans emerging as well, one piled on top of the other in carved metamorphoses reaching to the sky. The shaman singing is the new great shaman, Making-Alive, who has been asked to cure a sick man, son of Potlatch.

Faces blackened with charcoal, four men approach, wearing red cedar bark around their heads, necks, and waists. They are covered in eagle down. They never laugh. Hunt emphasizes this. They never laugh. They are shamans who are also Cannibal Dancers, the ultimate in Dionysian splendor, as a famous student of Boas by the name of Ruth Bennedict emphasizes. They have spent months isolated in the wild, where they became crazed, ate of a human corpse, and were then taken back into the villages as tabooed personae, reintroduced over several months into human society. Now they can throw sickness into you. One of them is called Fool.

The four shamans and George Hunt/Quesalid enter the house. A fire burns inside. The sick man lies naked. The house is very large. Other than menstruating women, the entire population enters. No one is smiling. The four shamans get a board for beating time and distribute batons for music making to the song leaders. They cover the song leaders and the spectators with eagle down. The song leaders are beating fast time, stopping and starting. Now it is quiet. The new shaman, Making-Alive, enters, singing his sacred song. Three of the Cannibal Dancers walk behind him. They walk around the fire four times.

Singing his sacred song, Making-Alive feels the chest of the sick man. He is given a basin of water. He drinks. He blows the water onto the sick man's chest, then sucks it a long time. He looks up. Out of his mouth with his right hand he takes blood and squeezes it into the basin of water. He stands, walks around the fire singing his song, and extends his left hand, opening out his fingers onto which something is stuck. Like a worm it rests there in the middle of his palm.

Fool says this is the sickness.

Making-Alive walks around the fire and blows the illness upwards. Fool tells the song beaters to beat time. Making-Alive presses his hands against his stomach and staggers around the fire as if drunk, trying to vomit. Four times around the fire he goes. He is vomiting blood. He catches it in his left hand. When he opens his hand, Fool sees something in the blood. It is a quartz crystal, says Fool, who then washes it until it shines.

"Do you not now wish to become a shaman," demands Fool, "and to let this great shaman go ahead and throw this quartz crystal into the stomach of the one who wishes to become a shaman?"

No man answers. Making-Alive presses his hands together and throws up the quartz crystal. "It is flying about in the house," he says.

Fool comes over to George Hunt. "Oh shamans!" he says, "Important is what has been done by the supernatural quartz for it went into this our friend here. Now this one will be a great shaman."

It has been said that it is vomiting, as well as fire, that provides the basis of transubstantiation in Kwakiutal thought and ritual.[9] Vomiting and fire. To which we must add music and dance and, above all, this play with flow, as with vomiting around the fire while singing and shooting out quartz crystals that have been sucked out from the body of the sick man and now in turn are vomited out with blood by the shaman so as to enter into the body of a future shaman . . . this man who wanted to be a shaman and who wrote it all down for Franz Boas on the other side of America in New York City, Franz Boas, a Jew from Germany who began the anthropology department which now houses me, too. In and out they go, these crystals, glinting in the firelight. There they go tumbling, lost up there somewhere in the roof rafters, lost forever, really, even if on occasions they descend into you. Maybe. Lost forever? What do you mean?

Now and again they lodge in a body. Then they move on again. *Flow* directly implicates not one but several bodies and energies flowing into and out of one another across borders accessed by dream, surreality, and animal visitations.

Take this other personal account Boas obtained of a Kwakiutal man become a shaman, a man known as Fool.

He describes wolves coming down the beach, vomiting foam over his body while his kinsmen lie dying on account of the holocaust wrought by the White society in the form of smallpox, reducing the Kwakiutal population by an unbelievable 80 to 90 percent between the censuses of 1862 and 1929.

"After we had stepped from our canoe," recounts Fool, "we found much clothing and flour. We took them and ten days later became sick with the great smallpox. We lay in bed in our tent. I was laying among them. Then I thought I was also dead."

Wolves came down to the beach, whining and howling, licking his body, he remembered, vomiting foam, which they put into his body. They tried hard, he explains, to put foam all over his body, continuously licking him and turning him all over. When it was all licked off, they vomited over him again, licking off the scabs of smallpox in the process.

> Then the many wolves did not leave me. Indeed, I walked among them. Indeed I became well and I lay down when the other wolf came, the one whom I had dreamed of at Foam Receptacle and who told me his name was Harpooner-Body. He sat down seaward from me and nudged me with his nose that I should lie down on my back, and he vomited and pushed his nose against the lower end of my sternum. He vomited the magic power into me . . . Now I was a shaman.[10]

To enter into every skin, said Nietzsche, thanks to music and quartz crystals, not to mention a little foam and vomit. Beating time is how Making-Potlatches-in-the-World describes this music. Otherwise it is the shaman's song. This skin of Nietzsche's is easier to enter when covered with eagle down, thanks to vomit and fire. In and out they go, these crystals, glinting in the firelight. There they go tumbling, lost up there in the roof rafters, awaiting a body. Catching the light like that, they would seem to precipitate and for a moment give body to out-of-place ephemera such as foam and vomit, like spume on the ocean wave, lost forever, polymorphous magical substance, like the feathers of newborn birds, like color, too.

10

pLasma

Music and color relate to this flow of fire and vomit in and out of the body, in and out of the image, not just as flow, but as what the filmmaker Sergei Eisenstein in his book on Disney's early animation called *plasmaticness*. "What is strange," wrote Eisenstein, "is not the fact that it exists. What is strange is that it attracts!"

He was thinking of elasticity of form, like Alice in Wonderland's body growing tall, then shrinking and falling into a lake created by her own tears. He was thinking of line drawings in which, in moving across the page, the line assumes different forms such that what is made manifest is a sort of ur-form applicable to storytelling, too—a line "which behaves like the primal protoplasm, not yet possessing a 'stable' form, but capable of assuming any form and which, skipping along the rungs of the evolutionary ladder, attaches itself to any and all forms of animal existence."[1] He was also thinking of firelight expressing this same sort of ur-form of images, similar to Nietzsche when he says that life for us means constantly transforming all that we are into light and flame. Back to the savant's savant, Isidore of Seville, who, in the seventh century AD, claimed that colors came from sunlight or from fire because the words for them were the same, *calor* and *color*.

Fluidity, such a lovely notion, then broken, staggered, stopped, and snapped into a formation, only to flow off once more. For Eisenstein this is what permeates "folktales, cartoons, the spineless circus performer and the seemingly groundless scattering of extremities in Disney's drawings."[2] Such a pity Eisenstein hadn't encountered the ethnography of the Selk'nam Indians of Tierra del Fuego where plasmaticness in the form of white feathery insides achieved exquisite rendition—all the more a pity as he invokes music along with color as when he tells us that "Disney is astonishingly blind, with respect to landscape—to *the musicality of landscape* and simultaneously the *musicality of color and tone*."[3]

But Vincent van Gogh got the musicality down without any overt music—the animality, too, in the raw energy pulsing through the lines of color plasmatically exuding from thick ribs of oil paint. "The effect of daylight, of the sky," he wrote to his brother Theo from the south of France, "makes it possible to extract an infinity of subjects from the olive tree." It was as if there was no such thing as the olive tree. It was more like a momentary artifact, a blaze of colors on their way to becoming blue flies and emerald rose beetles on their way to becoming leaves with that tinge of violet to be found on ripe figs . . . Nothing could be further from the notion that first there are forms and then we have color lying on top as a cover or a jacket. If anything, it is the other way around.

> At times the whole is a pure all-pervading blue, namely when the tree bears its pale flowers, and big blue flies, emerald rose beetles and cicadas in great numbers are hovering around it. Then, as the bronzed leaves are getting riper in tone, the sky is brilliant and radiant with green and orange, or, more often even, in autumn, when the leaves acquire something of the violet tinges of the ripe fig, the violet effect will manifest itself vividly through the contrasts, with the large sun taking on a white tint within a halo of clear and pale citron yellow.[4]

That was three weeks before he took his life. Two years earlier he had conceived of "modeling with color" as the "true drawing." We see this distinction when comparing his reed-pen drawings with his color paintings of the same subject. Here we are able to watch the transition from the world of black and white to that of color.

These black-and-white drawings can be seen as protocolor images. They teach us about the energy of color. Note how the strokes become suggestions more than outlines and how blank space vibrates with life, the life of the sun. In the early works done in the south of France, such as the *Street in Saint-Maries-de-la-Mer* on June 3, 1888, the color version is one that uses broad slabs of homogenous color in complementary opposition—yellow and violet, red and green, orange and blue—while the black-and-white drawing of the same scene is the antithesis, in that the surface is broken up by energizing, short, black strokes, striations and shell-bursts, pulsing with life.

By the time we get to the oil painting *Cypresses* a year later, the color is no longer applied in flat slabs like painting by numbers, but now brings the pulsating shell-bursts and striations of the black-and-white drawings to their ultimate rally-ing point—in color. The mountains in the background are waves of blue motion while the cypresses that dominate the picture are barely recognizable as trees, being deep green explosions, ruffles sprinkled with yellow and pink. The only form visible now is a scepter-shaped yellow moon as drawn in children's books.

Is this what Burroughs is getting at when he conceives of words as animals—a flurry of alternating language and nonlanguage that he seeks with his cut-ups and amputated lyricism so that the words, being animals, are set free? Being freed from their cages, they run across the wide landscape of snows through human events, where fantasy and power blend in the rush to the apocalypse. Their trademark is metamorphosis but also effervescence, here one moment, gone the next, swallowed up as so much word-dust by blue silence. Whenever he gets the chance, Burroughs lets the color-demon loose and, as with van Gogh, this color is not laid on top of already formed forms but creates forms we barely dreamed of, such as blue silence, that other form of musicality, along with the rush of words cut up and freed.

Perhaps that's how the Indians on the plains, in the Rockies, and in the des-erts stretching down into Mexico thought sometimes about color and animals threading their way through human extremity?

Take color in the nineteenth-century visions of Plains Indians that have been recorded for publication, in particular those of the Oglala Sioux Black Elk, whose first vision was that of horses dancing in the sky, choreographed in accord

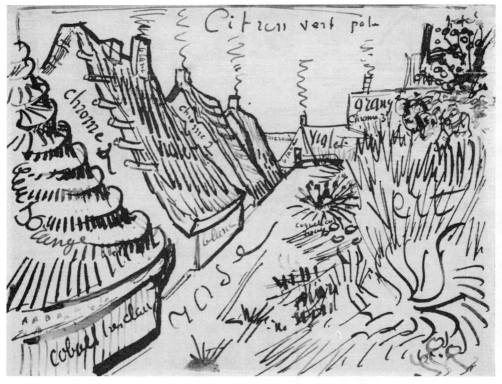

FIGURE 4. Vincent Van Gogh, *Street in Saintes-Maries-de-la-Mer*, circa 7 June 1888. Reed pen and ink on woven paper. Written left to right across this black-and-white drawing, we find:

> bleu
> orange
> cobalt tres clair
> chrome 2
> blanc
> violet
> blanc
> chrome 2
> rose
> citron vert pale
> emeraude blanc
> coquelicot rouge
> violet
> orange
> chrome 3
> vert

At this time Van Gogh wrote his brother Theo, "I am absolutely convinced of staying in the Midi, and of positively piling it on, exaggerating the color—Africa not far away." The Pierpont Morgan Library, New York. Gift of Eugene V. Thaw in honor of Charles E. Pierce, Jr., 2007. MA 6441.6. Photography: Joseph Zehavi, 2006.

with their colors, black, white, sorrel, and buckskin. Wheeling and singing, they set up slipstreams of color such that "the sky was terrible with a storm of plunging horses in all colors that shook the world with thunder." The bay horse that acted as a master of ceremonies neighed to the different cardinal points from each of which there comes a response of sound and movement within a flurry of color. When the bay neighed to the north, "the sky roared with a mighty wind of running horses in all colors, neighing back." When the bay whinnied to the east, "the sky was filled with glowing clouds of manes and tails of horses in all colors singing back." There were dancing horses everywhere. The sky was full of them. They were like the wind the way they came and went. The horses were an energy that could acquire many shapes and modes of being, what with their human voices, thunder in their nostrils, lightning in their tails and manes.[5] They changed into animals and birds of every conceivable kind, and just as suddenly vanished to be replaced by a cloud that became a teepee, the doorway of which was a flaming rainbow through which Black Elk entered to meet the Powers of the World.

I think of these horses as color, living color that, in the genocide that establishes the U.S. as a nation, is beyond color as we might normally understand the word. Instead we might borrow from these same horses with their wheelings, prancings, pivotings, and disappearances so as to become part of their shifting intensities and multisited presencings. What we confront is color as a force that triggers many metamorphoses. But if stilled, it finds its stillness in a flaming rainbow as doorway to the Powers of the World. More like a person or an animal, the color acquires a life of its own, a life that certainly qualifies for what Leiris had in mind by "the sacred," only here we are now led to ask not what color is the sacred, but instead reverse the question and wonder what is it that makes color sacred?

Given that spirited if not spiritual sense of color, not to mention the horrific character of the historic context, it is disappointing—some might say alarming—to come across standard ethnography-speak as in a book by one of the United States' most distinguished anthropologists, entitled *Indians of the Plains*, first published in 1954 by the American Museum of Natural History, in which color occupies less than one of its 150 pages:

It remains to speak of the use of color. A white background is frequent in the beadwork of all tribes, being almost exclusively used by the Arapaho, while the Cheyenne showed an additional preference for yellow . . . Colors often had symbolic meaning in art as well as in warfare and in religion. With the Dakota, red suggested the sunset or thunder . . .[6]

A rather different perspective is opened up when we turn the pages of Gladys Reichard's book on Navajo religion, in which she tells us that in each of the lower worlds a color predominated that affected the inhabitants. The first world was the red world. In it were twelve kinds of black insects, including bats. The second was the blue world. It had blue birds, swallows, and jays. The third was the yellow world. In it were grasshoppers. In the fourth were beings from the preceding worlds plus the ancient pueblo people. But when the First Man and First Woman got to their own world, the fifth, they wanted not just color but light, so they made the sun from a large blue disc of turquoise surrounded by red rain, lightning, and snakes. As for the moon, they made that from crystal, bordering it with whiteshell, forked lightning, and sacred water.[7]

Light, it seems, is made from color. Not the other way around. Color is prior to light. It exists without light. But it does not exist on its own. It comes with animal associates and its texture is decisive. To the glittering and substantial nature of the substances such as blue turquoise, rain, and whiteshell, take note of eye-catching qualities like sparkling, variegated, spotting, and stripes, each with its own mighty quotient of magical power. Color has what Reichard calls "an intimate, almost inseparable" association with shells, precious stones, and other mineral products. She enumerates: *whiteshell*, originally from seashells obtained in trade from the Californian coast; *abalone*, associated with iridescence and yellow; *jet*, a form of soft coal found in large deposits in the Southwest that lends itself readily to carving and takes on a beautiful polish. And there are others such as *turquoise, redstone, agate*, and *rock crystal*.

Reichard cites an account of the origin of the sand-painting pigments as coming from the clubbing to death of the supernatural being called Traveling Rock, who is also called The-One-Having-No-Speed. The bone became white rock; the flesh, blue pigment; the hair, black; the mouth and the blood, red; the intestines, yellow ochre; while urine, tears, mucus, and perspiration became wet spots caused by moisture oozing from rocks.[8]

Such an account does not exactly run through most people's minds when buying a box of Winsor & Newton watercolors at the stationers, although there are exceptions and they suggest, like the Navaho account, how we have by and large closed our eyes to color and to what we could see when we buy a box of paints—what we could see, and feel, and wonder, most perturbed about the dissolution of our selves, as described by Virginia Woolf, who overhears an elderly man leaning on a gate overlooking a field. A heavy man with grey hair talking to himself, wondering how light returns after the eclipse of the sun, which is the same as the eclipse of himself, feeling the nothingness of old age, when a person has the wisdom to see the unrealness of the world. The light returns

Miraculously. Fraily. In thin stripes. It hangs like a glass cage. It is a hoop to be fractured by a tiny jar. There is a spark there. Next moment a flash of dun. Then a vapour as if earth were breathing in and out, once, twice, for the first time. Then under the dullness someone walks with a green light. Then off twists a white wraith. The woods throb blue and green, and gradually the fields drink in red, gold, brown. Suddenly a river snatches a blue light. The earth absorbs colour like a sponge, slowly drinking water. It puts on weight; rounds itself; hangs pendent; settles and swings beneath our feet.

So the landscape returned to me; so I saw fields rolling in waves of colour beneath me, but now with this difference; I saw but was not seen. I walked unshadowed . . .

But how describe the world seen without a self?[9]

Not that much different, after all, from Reichard's version of the origin of the Navajo world. And always but always in Woolf's book, the play of color will be transfused into birds and their song, skittish birds that merge with trees and flowers right on the domesticated edge of nature by the sea where language itself washes up. "There is nothing one can fish up in a spoon," Woolf says about language and its relation to real life, to felt life, "nothing one can call an event. Yet it is alive too and deep, this stream."

Are these the same skittish birds and events that are nonevents that William Burroughs would, with his cut-ups, release from captivity trapped in sentences? I think so. I very much think so, and I wonder if these are not the same animals mentioned in the two years of travel between 1832 and 1834 up the Missouri and into Sioux country by Maximilian, Prince of Wied, not too long after Goethe published his color book. The prince tells us that the Mandan Indians "believe that they have wild animals in their bodies; one for instance, affirmed he had a buffalo calf, the kicking of which he often felt; others said they had tortoises, frogs, lizards, birds, and so forth."[10]

The men lived for the hunt, war, and women, spending most of their time sleeping when they weren't busy painting and preening themselves. Traders sold them mirrors, each mounted in its pasteboard case, but the Indians immediately replaced the pasteboard with a solid wooden frame that they attached to their wrist with a red ribbon or a leather strap, often carving the frame with footsteps of bears or buffaloes, or painting it red or with stripes.[11]

The color-animal mix is constant.

The body is loaded up with animals-and-color. In the portraits of men made by the prince's assistant, Karl Bodmer, we see color painted on faces and arms, hair, and clothing, along with vermillion-dyed turkey, eagle, and owl's feathers, white ermine, dyed porcupine quills, yellow-dyed horsehair, and the hair of Mandan enemies plaited into their own hair to make it longer.[12] Not only the color was striking, but its eye-catching asymmetry as well, with one half of the face yellow, the other half red, the body reddish brown with narrow stripes. At the Sioux agency, Fort Lookout, in South Dakota, Bodmer painted a sixty-year-old man, Big Soldier:

> His face was painted with vermillion, and with short, black, parallel, transverse stripes on the cheeks. On his head he wore long feathers of birds of prey, which were tokens of his warlike exploits, particularly of the enemies he had slain. They were fastened in a horizontal position with strips of red cloth. In his ears he wore long strips of blue glass beads, and, on his breast, suspended from his neck, the great silver medal of the United States. His leather leggings, painted with dark crosses and stripes, were very neatly ornamented with a broad embroidered stripe of yellow, red, and sky-blue figures, consisting of dyed porcupine quills, and his shoes were adorned in the same manner. His buffalo robe was tanned white, and he had a tomahawk or battle-axe in his hand.[13]

This blaze of intricately assembled color was offset by the cone-shaped teepees, which were made of buffalo hides scraped on both sides, making them as transparent as parchment, giving free admission to the light. In a fanciful mood we might wonder whether these be connected, the colors displayed on the bodies of the men, on the one hand, and these semitransparent dwelling places dotting the plains, on the other, the teepee's quality of transparency being that from which all colors spring and into which they die away. With equal fancy I want you to imagine what it might mean to sleep and shelter inside an animal this way, to be inside the buffalo, in this crucible of transparent color. This would make a nice complement to having wild animals inside your body. During the day, let us say, they live inside you. At night you live inside them. Such is color.

11

a beautiful blue substance flows into me

Clouds swirl along the blue ridges. You can sit for days watching the light play on the shadows of the mountains, which is maybe why William Burroughs, who drank the hallucinogen *yagé* prepared by the Indians in the foothills of the Andes at Mocoa, in the Putumayo region of Colombia, in 1953, talks so much about blue throughout his life's work from his first book to his death—as when, in that first book, *Naked Lunch*, he writes in a series of ellipses, "*Notes from Yage state:* Images fall slow and silent like snow . . . Serenity . . . All defenses fall . . . everything is free to enter or go out . . . Fear is simply impossible . . . A beautiful blue substance flows into me."

Amongst other things, he notes a blue face, a blue wall, and plants growing out of genitals.[1] No wonder he felt the room shaking. In the pharmacological appendix to the book, Burroughs assures us: "Blue flashes in front of the eyes is peculiar to Yage intoxication."[2]

FIGURE 5. William Burroughs in the Putumayo, Colombia, 1953.

The mountains drop precipitously in sheets of green and blue haze. The rivers run fast between enormous cliffs of forest. *Yagé* entwines itself in the shadows of the forest. Mashed and boiled day long, its gut-wrenching smell goes straight to your liver like one of those lightning bolts streaking along the rainbow that Shuar shamans, a few rivers south, are said to use to kill a rival. You gag. *Yagé* is alive even when just sitting there in its gourd container before you've drunk it, ominous in its muddy brown opalescence "from which colors come as from tar." I can feel my stomach churn as I write these lines—same as that nausea Jean-Paul Sartre wrote about, when passing through colors as through a magic doorway, you come face to face with reality shorn of those lovely categories with which culture so conveniently provides us for thinking straight and being straight. Sartre is a long way from the jungles of the Putumayo where even as I write, the *yagé* is being dispensed and the nausea is coming on stronger by the minute, but he's pretty well gotten it right. You can't get much more effective category meltdown than with nausea. Sartre is a philosopher, of course, not a physiologist, but then, as Nietzsche poses to us, isn't philosophy essentially an understanding—or rather, a misunderstanding—of the body?

Sartre is the anthropologist's nightmare. He is undoing the work of culture. Bolt by bolt, girder by girder, the system is being disassembled, all systems, that is, including the very idea of a system. Like Burroughs's sentences subject to the cut-up method, releasing the animals, like Burroughs's color walks decoding the very idea of a code, Sartre's nausea covers the page in wave after wave of disorientation and churning bile. Bataille's idea of the sacred as a sticky substance without clear boundaries, or of spit as a nice instance of the *formless*, amounts to pretty much the same thing, even if Sartre and he fought like cat and dog. Too close for comfort, I say.

Sartre is sick with a philosophical sickness that invades reality like spreading mucus. He is desperate for a butterfly net with which to catch the categories of thought and culture but there are no butterflies anymore, just mucus spreading across the public garden through which he walks. More like thick jelly mounting higher and higher, like flowing lava, and he shakes himself to get rid of this sticky filth . . .[3] This is the same lava that flows through William Burroughs's *Naked Lunch*. When the Sailor moved, "an effluvium of mold drifted out of his clothes, a musty smell of deserted locker rooms . . . A black mist poured out and hung in the air like boiling fur. The Sailor's face dissolved. His mouth undulated forward on a long tube and sucked in the black fuzz, vibrating in supersonic peristalsis, disappeared in a silent, pink explosion."[4]

Anthropologists spend their professional lives constructing a model of culture from the flotsam and jetsam that comes their way. Like building a watch, it can give you a sense of security to have a system and then a schedule. Yet here is Sartre going the other way, the *Naked Lunch* way, burying his nose and eyes in that flotsam, searching for a way not into but out of the system, searching for a bit of *first contact*, by which I mean a direct hit with the realness of reality.

Too close for comfort, say I. For this is definitely sacred, right up there with Bataille and his spit and sticky stuff. Sartre could be in the trance of spirit possession, maybe, or just as easily sitting in his hammock feeling the nausea come on strong half an hour after his first gourdful of *yagé*. Only he is walking in a public garden in a seaside town in France prior to World War II and, not having access to shamans, drugs, or spirits, he is forced back onto his own resources, which is his thinking about thinking. That is his *yagé*. Even more than that, he is forced to come up with a way of thinking—which means a way of using words to tell a story—that will do an end-run around language so there can be some first contact with reality. With boiling fur. How do you get it, how do you sneak past the watchful eye of the system that in categorizing holds you apart from reality?

The nausea will not leave him. In this state of first contact not only do the categories of thought and culture wobble then crash, but his body crashes as well. It is no longer an illness, he says. It is not a passing fit. It is his entire being. "It is I."

Here he is meditating, if that's the word, meditating in the garden, like Adam. He is sitting on a park bench. Right in front of him are the roots of a chestnut tree, those wide-spreading, deep green trees with their upthrusting white sprigs of flowers dotting the canopy in early spring. He is lost in thought when all of a sudden he has a vision, as with *yagé*. Categories collapse and the first to do so is that of color, specifically the color green, like the green of the sea. It turns out that color is the mediator between hard-edged categories and the nothingness (which is the everythingness) of being.

Categories collapse. Reality is no longer an object out there, over there, as in a cliché, "the green ocean," as in a picture on a gallery wall, or what you glimpse down the end of the street leading to the ocean green in Sartre's town. What happens is that like Benjamin's child engrossed in colored pictures, our friend and guide J.-P. Sartre is passing into the object in front of him. Bang! Now he's got it. Now he's in it. *First contact!* Existence has unveiled itself. It is not a form applied to things. Instead it has become "the very paste of things" that now melt, "leaving soft, monstrous masses." We have met this paste before. It is called polymorphous magical substance.

"The chestnut tree pressed itself against my eyes," he says. "Green rust covered it half-way up; the bark black and swollen looked like boiled leather. The sound of the water in the Masqueret Fountain sounded in my ears, made a nest there,

filled them with signs; my nostrils overflowed with green, putrid, odour . . .
I thought without words, *on* things, *with* things . . . This root with its colour,
shape, its congealed movement was . . . below all explanation."[5]

First contact means color contact: "I scraped my heel against this black claw: I
wanted to peel off some of the bark. For no reason at all, out of defiance, to make
the bare pink appear absurd on the tanned leather, to play with the absurdity of
the world. But when I drew my heel back, I saw that the bark was still black."

Black? That too will melt down. In fact all the colors, smells, and tastes will
melt and drag Sartre himself with them to such an overwhelming extent that he
becomes himself the black root! Even though he is to some extent detached and
therefore still conscious—still aware—of the black root, he is nevertheless "lost
in it, nothing but it." This is accompanied by a horrible ecstasy. Now he understands the nausea.

One is simply there. Those who exist let themselves be thus encountered.
"Existence," he concludes, "is not something which lets itself be thought of from
a distance: it must invade you suddenly, master you, weigh heavily on your heart
like a great motionless beast—or else there is nothing at all."[6]

And whether it weighs heavily or is nothing at all, existence as opened up by
color is certainly fugitive.

Black? The root was not black, there was something else instead of black.
Wait a minute. That can't be. He looks again at the root. Is it more than black, or
almost black?

Even though the state of color-induced meltdown means you no longer
think in accustomed ways, you can still remember some things, especially other
instances of color-initiated meltdown into nausea—like Adolphe's suspenders! They are the first thing that pops into Sartre's mind as he wrestles with the
blackness of the roots of the chestnut tree. And no wonder. For these suspenders
have a crucial part to play in the origins of the Nausea.

Let's look at them just as he saw them several weeks back in the bar of the
Railwaymen's Rendevouz, where Adolphe takes over serving at the bar when his
cousin leaves to go shopping. It was here where it all started.

"What will you have?" asked the waiter.

"Then the Nausea seized me, I dropped to a seat, I no longer knew where I
was; I saw the colours spin slowly around me, I wanted to vomit. And since that
time the Nausea has not left me."[7]

As for Adolphe, the bartender, he is in shirtsleeves, with purple suspenders which can barely be seen against the blue shirt. Sartre says these purple suspenders are "all obliterated, buried in the blue, but it is false humility; in fact they will not let themselves be forgotten, they annoy me by their sheep-like stubbornness, as if, starting to become purple, they stopped somewhere along the line without giving up their pretensions. You feel like saying, 'All right, *become* purple and let's hear no more about it.'"[8]

No doubt about it. Color is being a bother. And it gets worse.

For now the suspenders, Sartre says, stay in suspense, stubborn in the defeat of the purple by the blue. They certainly seem alive, these curmudgeonly colors. Sometimes the blue slips over and covers the suspenders completely. "I stay an instant without seeing them," he tells us. "But it is merely a passing wave, soon the blue pales in places and I see the small island of purple reappear, grow larger, rejoin and reconstitute the suspenders."

Purple gives way to blue. The blue gives way to purple. "Passing wave" seems right enough to describe this, but "continuous passing wave" would be even more accurate for this is the passing wave of nausea, when polymorphous magical substance—that paste of things—takes over like boiling fur. Which must be why our philosopher feels impelled to tell us that vision has dropped out of significance; color is something else altogether. In fact, Adolphe, like color, is animal. He "has no eyes: his swollen, retracted eyelids open only on a little of the whites. He smiles sleepily; from time to time he snorts, yelps and writhes feebly, like a dreaming dog."[9] We recall Burroughs: "The Sailor's face dissolved. His mouth undulated forward on a long tube and sucked in the black fuzz, vibrating in supersonic peristalsis, disappeared in a silent, pink explosion."[10]

Nothing can stop this nonvisual wave of color. "His blue cotton shirt stands out joyfully against a chocolate-colored wall. That too brings on the Nausea. The Nausea is not inside me. I feel it *out there* in the wall, in the suspenders, everywhere around me."

Through it all, as with the nausea of *yagé*, there is music. In place of the Indian shaman singing in the darkness of the thick night air in South America there is the phonogram playing Negro blues. It threads its way through the story, like the shaman's song in Mocoa, Colombia, stopping and starting like Sergei Eisentein's *plasma*—line drawings that, in moving across a surface, assume different forms. And here, right when we need it at the end of the story, when the Nausea is at its height, the song returns.

It returns at the point where, thanks to color, existence attains its sacred crux, where our philosopher has attained a curious state of freedom from the world by being so attuned to it. The music shows him the way forward, a way of coexisting with the Nausea, finding meaning in it and with it. But he is no singer. And the meaning, bubbling in the crucible of sheer existence, is going to be strangely put together anyway. What he can do, if he's lucky, is put the music into a story. Which is what he has done, just as I have. This we call the body of the song.

1 2

the red butterfly

In his memoir of Walter Benjamin on the island of Ibiza in the summers of 1932 and 1933, the French painter Jean Selz tells us how he took issue with Benjamin's strange ideas about language.[1] They hung out, took drugs together, told each other their dreams, and, what's more, Benjamin got Selz to begin translating his memoir of his Berlin childhood into French, despite the fact that Selz knew not a word of German. "As you can imagine," Benjamin confided to his friend Scholem in a letter, "the technique we use is not to be trifled with. But the results are nearly always outstanding."[2] This same translation gap assumed fairytale dimensions when Selz tells us how Benjamin tried to persuade him that the shape of a word resembled its meaning, adding that Benjamin would chew on a word, examining it from all sides, breaking it up into syllables to find unexpected meanings. Selz then recalled an evening in his house in Ibiza in the spring of

FIGURE 6. Walter Benjamin on the beach (with tie), seated with Jean Selz in Ibiza, 1933. Courtesy of the Walter Benjamin Archive and the Hamburger Stiftung zur Förderung von Wissenschaft und Kultur.

1933 when Benjamin came to visit and was struck by "the dominance of a certain color in a room with white walls."[3]

Bunches of roses, carnations, and pomegranates made a spectrum of reds, to which was added the bright red of a peasant woman's handkerchief made even more vivid by the light of a lamp. "A laboratory designed to extract the essence of the color red," exclaimed Benjamin. Using the German word for red, *rot*, he added: "*Rot* is like a butterfly alighting upon each shade of the color red."[4]

This was not the first time Benjamin brought in the butterfly. Some five years earlier in notes entitled "Main Features of My First Impression of Hashish," he singled out a type of philosophical vacillation as characteristic of hashish, the vacillation between freedom and indecision. He cited a line from Schiller to get this across—"the hesitant wing of the butterfly."[5]

This vacillation was intimately connected to another leading characteristic of hashish, and that was laughter. "In smiling," he jotted down in the same observation of his hashish experience, "one feels oneself growing small wings. Smiling and fluttering are related as laughter. You feel distinguished because . . . you enter into nothing too deeply: that no matter how deeply you penetrate, you are always moving on the threshold."[6]

"One feels oneself growing small wings . . ." Such is the butterflying mind, and such is the flaneur, that figure strolling the sidewalks who haunts Benjamin's mature thought, strolling right out of Baudelaire's essay "The Painter of Modern Life" as that creature of the crowd into which he enters as into a reservoir of electrical energy for which he is "a mirror," wrote Baudelaire, "as vast as the crowd itself," a "kaleidoscope gifted with consciousness."[7]

Benjamin discerned the butterfly again, two years after his first experience with hashish, as he was translating Marcel Proust's *In Search of Lost Time*. Now the butterfly was flitting among Proust's flowers and vegetation, signs of a complex social habitat no less than of densely interwoven memory-images. Proust's "most accurate insights," wrote Benjamin, "fasten on their objects the way insects fasten on leaves, blossoms, branches, betraying nothing of their existence until a leap, a beating of the wings, a vault show the startled observer that some incalculable individual life has imperceptibly crept into an alien world."[8]

Later, in Ibiza, Proust's "most accurate insights" became Benjamin's red butterfly "alighting upon each shade of the color red." Let us here recall William Burroughs's color walks, those walks which to my mind actually become color itself, color as a mobile entity doing its own walking, only in this case on the charmed island of Ibiza and in the charmed mind of Benjamin, color now not only walks but flies, flies like the butterfly as whorls of color opening and closing in light alightings. Indeed, such is insight as in-sight, light on the move as the colors on the fluttering wings lay quiet for a moment, quivering and shimmering in the petals of the flower open to the sun before the next leap in the color world.

Just as the wings open and close not in smooth flight but in hip-hop fashion, so the passage of light through the color-substance of the wings is an unpredictable journey. "We have forgotten what every butterfly 'knows,'" writes Anita Albus, "that the visual effect of colors is created by the interplay between tone and body." Like Proust's layerings, inspired by what he himself called "the varnishes of the Masters," the brilliant colors of the butterfly are due to layerings of pigment diffused through myriads of tiny scales that bend light this way then that way.

Jean Selz, the painter, paints the scene for us many years after it occurred. He takes us to sunny Ibiza, going toe to toe with Benjamin on language as they struggle with the task of translation, when suddenly he recalls the red butter-

The Red Butterfly

fly. It is a Proustian moment. In Selz's memory as memoir we flow, as it were, from language to color. First he remembers the language disputes, then, out of nowhere, so it seems, right at this point comes the memory of the color-scene, the scene of the red butterfly. Like the butterfly, we leap from an eccentric yet endearing notion of words, as when Benjamin defends his notion that the shape of a word resembles what it means, to a strange intuition about color. Thus Selz inadvertently registers the fact that for Benjamin both color and language share essential properties whereby the perceiver merges with the perceived.[9]

Recently the Ibizan poet Vicente Valero has pointed out that Selz and Benjamin were smoking opium when this red butterfly took off.[10] Selz had gone to the trouble of taking the steamer across the Mediterranean to buy opium in the red-light district of Barcelona, the *barrio chino*. Valero tells me that Selz did not realize that opium was growing all about him in those marvelously red poppies so abundant in Ibiza, where the peasants used it for their teething infants.

Benjamin was intensely interested in drugs at this time and planned to write what he himself termed "a truly exceptional book on hashish."[11] It needed drugs to make the otherwise strange connection between the word *rot* and the actual color, red, manifest. Goethe had a similar approach. Not only do magic and alchemy hover as formative influences in the background of his work, but he begins at the margins, with the fringe and outlawed aspects of so-called reality when he begins his color book by taking up what are called "optical illusions," which he sees not as illusions at all.

Selz's house stood on a steep hill in the *calle Conquista* overlooking the port of Ibiza below and the mountains in the distance. There was a soft breeze that night. The curtain undulated. With the opium inhaled from a makeshift porcelain-and-bamboo pipe crafted laboriously by Selz, it wasn't long before the town, seen through the curtain, became a film of moving tissue, wrapping itself around Selz and Benjamin and at the same time unwrapping Ibiza. "We are *curtainologists*," added Benjamin, to whom it seemed as if the curtains had become interpreters for the language of the wind.[12] Not the wind—but the language of the wind.

When it came to recording what happened that night, Benjamin recalled the scene of the butterfly felt by him as an eruption of different shades of red followed by an overwhelming sense of *numbness*. He was knocked out. "For an instant it seemed to me," he declares—in words reminiscent of Michel Leiris's question, What is the color of the sacred?—"For an instant it seemed to me that thanks to this incomparable instrument, my task consisted in discovering the sense of the color."[13]

In fact, many years before the red butterfly, the twenty-two-year-old Benjamin had all but named this sense of color when he declared that, for children, color is "a winged creature that flits from one form to the next." Color, he had declared, is part of the world of shimmering, changing moods, not the world of form, to which, in fact, it is antagonistic. Children love color because of its liveliness, shared by soap bubbles, games with folding paper, and pull-out picture books. Color "cancels out the intellectual cross references of the soul."[14]

"Everything shifts at every step." That is the world of color, and it is "the child who is allowed to join in the game."[15]

And adults? What about us?

Well, there's William Burroughs. He's an adult, but as far as I know never read a word of Benjamin. In fact, it would be hard to imagine two more dissimilar people, the one so cultured and polite, so quintessentially European, the other irascible, sarcastic, hip, and quintessentially American bad boy. But then both dressed in suits, had the same initials, W.B., and were massively curious about drugs, mysticism, revolution, film, and cut-outs as a method for producing literature no less than for writing history. And then there was color. There was so much they seem to have agreed upon. Yet it makes you laugh and roll your eyes to think of them having a conversation, perhaps on one of Burroughs's color walks starting off from the Beat Hotel in Paris.

Benjamin would have loved that. He always said that the best way to get to know a city is to get lost walking in it. After his meeting with Burroughs, he could add that the walk should be, if possible, a color walk. He may even have been inspired to write an essay about such walks. "Lost in Color," could have been the title, advancing the idea he clung to that there is an art to walking a city, same as the filmmaker's art of montage, like getting lost after several turnings, with buildings coming across at odd angles, of noise and speed alongside jostling bodies and all that stuff for sale glittering in the shop windows, in the arcades, and on the pavements in the flea markets. Burroughs would have encouraged him to throw color into the mix, but there would be no need to add that this was an art that played with history no less than with hashish as both Benjamin and Burroughs saw cityscapes through the veil of time as layered entities into which the person walking entered in an almost hallucinatory manner.

FIGURE 7. Walter Benjamin in lobster boat off Ibiza in 1933. Left to right: Jean Selz, the fisherman Tomás Varó, Paul René Gauguin, and Benjamin with glasses. This uncharacteristic photograph of Benjamin, for once out in nature and laidback, perhaps stoned or seasick or just plain sleepy, appears in the second volume of the Harvard *Selected Works* of Benjamin without any explanation other than the heading in large type "The Author as Producer," meant to announce the next section of the book. Courtesy of the Walter Benjamin Archive and the Hamburger Stiftung zur Förderung von Wissenschaft und Kultur.

I can see them now—in my mind's eye—William and Walter, as if in a black-and-white photograph by Giselle Freund or Man Ray. It looks like Benjamin has actually gotten Burroughs—normally so aloof—to bend forwards with the intensity of the conversation while Burroughs points out to him the colors shooting out on the street, not to mention the blue on a young workman's ass which, I am sure, both Freund and Man Ray would have been quick to include, along with the sudden cool wind on that warm day.

Of course the dates are wrong. Benjamin died, by his own hand, in 1940, while Burroughs took his color walks in the early 1960s. Some time travel would be involved, that's for sure, but that never troubled Burroughs because it was color that allowed him to shuttle back and forth through history like a butterfly hovering over different flowers of time. And what a good listener Benjamin would have been, hot to trot with his extraordinary ideas about lost and forgotten children's books. Yes! These two color enthusiasts were destined to meet. It was in the stars, in the constellations that Benjamin the astrologer loved so much.

For Burroughs was the one who found those lost and forgotten children's books. It was in Lima, Peru, where the Iguana sister brought him some curious books put together by an anonymous scholar. She was desperate to have Burroughs trace the originals. With the originals you held the power to influence the course of history. She must have read some of Burroughs's earlier work and admired it, for she was prepared to pay big, very big. Eventually Burroughs, being a creative type, decided to make his own "originals."

He discerned an "unbearably flawed boyishness" in the books the Iguana sister gave him to copy. They were more like color comics for which some lost color process was used to transfer three-dimensional holograms onto translucent pages such that the colors got into your body and made you ache. You could taste, feel, and touch these colors. And the contents were no less strange: fairy stories, legends, images out of Hieronymus Bosch.

"It was as if the colors in those books themselves possessed a purposeful and sinister life," Burroughs says to Benjamin. The two writers lift their eyes to gaze at the traffic lights and neon signs. Colors rise from the books, adds Burroughs, "palpable as a haze, a poisonous miasma of color."[16]

Making the "originals" took Burroughs to some strange places near the central market of Lima, which had first-rate materials: papyri from Egypt and ancient Maya codices as well as linen-based paper from the European Middle Ages. But Burroughs opted for the less expensive paper made around the time of the golden age of piracy in the eighteenth century. When it came to inks, the choice was no less exotic. The storekeeper offered him not only different colored inks, but the color came perfumed with hashish, opium, or blood.

So it seems that color walks through time as well as through space; ancient Egypt, ancient Maya, the Middle Ages . . . Take also those hourglasses containing sand of different colors—red, green, black, blue, and white—that Burroughs saw years before when smoking a joint with a seedy character in the Yucatán, Mexico, who promised to hook him up with a "time guide" that could take him back to the time before the Spanish conquest when Maya priests held sway. More terrorist than tourist, Burroughs wanted to go back to the originals so as to smash the code that the control freaks like the priests then, or the spin doctors today, have gotten control of.

The sands, explained the broker (Burroughs's term for the shaman), represented color time and color words. As the green hourglass started running and reached the level of a sign on the side of the glass, the broker administered mushrooms. Burroughs saw ancient Maya artifacts and codices. They were moving around his brain like animated cartoons as the smell of sperm and compost filled the room. A young boy accompanying him was dead to the world, fluttering in orgasmic twitchings. A green light filled the room as the boy sat up, speaking Mayan, the words curling out his mouth, hanging "visible in the air like vine tendrils."[17]

Where will this butterfly stop, if ever? In my imagination I can see them both, Benjamin and Burroughs, momentarily stilled, halfway between black-and-white and color in those photographs taken by Giselle Freund and Man Ray. Woa! The hourglass has not yet run out. Jean Selz has turned up just as we are saying goodbye. For yes! I am there too. I can see myself with an idiotic grin as time and memory pull me this way and that through the different color slides. Such a pleasure to be with these chaps as they emerge from my pages, those same pages that, in a child's book, so Benjamin assures us, with its treasure trove of colored illustrations, draws the child in so as to actually pass into the pages of the book.

Now Selz has our attention. It is getting dark. The day's color is fading, as is Benjamin. Time is running out. Selz wants us to remember his friend from Ibiza. He wants us to remember his prose as *that truly unique medium*, he says, in which poetry and the science of history merge as truth of the world. Is that "unique medium" the medium of color, I ask, the language of color? But it is getting dark. There is no reply.

As Benjamin disappeared into twilight and Burroughs wandered back to the Beat Hotel, Selz answered my question indirectly, saying that of all the people he knew, Benjamin was perhaps the only one who gave him the impression that there does indeed exist a depth of thought where historic and scientific facts coexist with their poetic counterparts, where "poetry is no longer simply a form of literary thought, but reveals itself as an expression of the truth that illuminates the most intimate correspondences between man and the world."[18]

That certainly sounds like a unique medium.

I pay the broker, who tells me next time try the black sand.

Part Two

COLOR IN THE COLONY

13

aDMINIStRatION By BLuff

Imagine a sixteen-year-old boy in 1900 in Cracow, Poland, being confined by the doctor to a darkened room on account of his failing eyesight two years after his father dies—this father whom he practically never mentions the rest of his life yet was a fabulous linguist who spent the summers talking to Polish peasants about language, much like the ailing son would do years later in the South Pacific. The sick boy's mother reads his schoolbooks to him in the darkness for several years. At times he covers his head with a blanket while being read to. Later, as an adult writing about sex and repression in the Pacific, he jots down on a notepad that he dreams of incest frequently, hates his father, and desires to go to bed with his mother, and how all of this is not repressed but is very distinct in his memory.[1] The artificial darkness imposed upon him as a youth is made worse by his fear of blindness. He comes in at the top of his class. His mother accompanies him to university and keeps on with the reading. He studies math and physics. He gets sick again and comes across a book called *The Golden Bough*, a compendium of magic and ritual in the ancient and so-called primitive worlds. He is cured.

This is a conversion experience. He discards math and physics and studies anthropology under British tutelage. En route to stupendous success in his chosen field, eventually becoming cast as the legendary father of that discipline, he keeps a personal diary during his fieldwork in the Trobriand Islands east of New Guinea. Midway through fieldwork in 1917, he writes the author of *The Golden Bough* to tell him that just as color and mise en scène are key to that work, so they will be key to his own—to his investigations no less than to his exposition.[2] At the end of the diary he keeps on and off for four years (two of which are spent in Melbourne), he grieves at the news of the death of his mother. "The world has lost color," he writes. "Truly I lack real character."[3]

After that the page is blank.

That boy was Bronislaw Malinowski. Too much of a legend now to be easily evaluated, especially as his writing straddles either side of the art-versus-science divide, we can at least look at the legend in the photographs recently resurrected in glowing and generous format in Michael Young's *Malinowski's Kiriwina*, Kiriwina being the island where Malinowski carried out his fieldwork. These photographs emanate whiteness that catches your breath, as if after all those years, crouched under his blanket listening to the words, the artificial darkness is finally swept aside by the aura of a golden bough in the heart of darkness.

Goethe says that color in its utmost brightness is shunned by people of refinement, who prefer black and white. Yet even for such people, is there not a quality of whiteness that is so stunning that it amounts to the brightest of bright colors—as manifest by those men in the colonies, pure white from pith-helmeted head down, who adopted a whiteness that covered every square inch of skin, such as workers wear in infectious-disease units or when approaching a toxic dump? The series of photographs of Malinowski captioned by him as "Introduction to the Ethnographer" show him thus dressed, radiating whiteness of such intensity that I have no idea how to explain it. Imagine a battery of spotlights shining on him, leaving the rest of the stage—for a stage it surely is—mysteriously dark in succeeding degrees of darkness, the dark skins of the almost-naked islanders passing into that other darkness of hollowed-out shadows and blurred outlines of the forest. He glows like Kurtz's ivory skull in *Heart of Darkness*. Light has chosen to condense itself into this lone figure, like sunlight focused through a magnifying glass onto a bright, burning spot.

Has to be a statement, you say. What might that be? *Administration by bluff* is what it was called by the governor of New Guinea, Hubert Murray, Oxford graduate, well read in anthropology and brother of Gilbert, the famous classicist. *Bluff* meant a few hundred European officers ruling over hundreds of thousands of Papuans. *Bluff* meant that wearing the right sort of gear was an imperial duty: "Discarding one's socks leads to the beach and the loin cloth."[4]

Bland as you might otherwise think it, epitome of neutrality or even of nothingness, white in this scheme of human values is the chromophobic extremity that ingenuity musters to box in the extremity of color. Composite of all color, it makes sense to use white to sterilize the extremity of color. White is like a sponge used to mop up color spills, same as chemical foams employed on rainbow-hued oil spills on the high seas.

Consider the spectral hue of the clerk in the heart of darkness as depicted by Joseph Conrad twenty-five years before Malinowski set foot on the island of Kiriwina—a man "in such an unexpected elegance of get-up, that in the first moment I took him for a sort of vision. I saw a high starched collar, white cuffs, a light alpaca jacket, snowy trousers, a clear necktie, and varnished boots . . ."[5] But the next white man Conrad's narrator ran into further upstream presented a quite different vision, what we might call "Murray's nightmare"—"a little fat man, with sandy hair and red whiskers, who wore side-spring boots, and pink pajamas tucked into his socks."[6]

It is perhaps not quite so obvious that white as spectral dizziness is as conducive to sexual stand-offs with the dark-hued natives as it is to maintaining colonial authority. Yet it is in such encounters, with sex rendered more awkward than usual by race and colonial hubris, that whiteness can flare to its fullest. Witness Malinowski in the Trobriand Islands, pictured in his fieldwork gear in a stand-off with Togugu'a, "a sorcerer of some repute," according to the caption in Malinowski's classic, *The Sexual Life of Savages*.[7]

Bolt upright we see Malinowski in profile, all in white. He could well be a statue in white marble, setting up ever darker shadows across the lagoon, past the coconut trees and the blurred figures of natives seated on canoes. Standing ramrod straight, hands provocatively on his hips, left leg bent, he thrusts out

his hips, tilting his body ever so slightly forwards. It is a tantalizing, tumescent posture. He is vibrating, ever so slightly, as he stares at the sorcerer, an athletic-looking man with a beautiful body who, by contrast, seems utterly relaxed, leaning in a languid fashion against a gracefully curved coconut tree, legs crossed, contemplating not so much Malinowski or the camera as some point lost in the distance.

In the photograph, the contrast between the native sorcerer and the ethnographer is a contrast of dark and naked versus white and clothed. The darkness of the native's skin fading as it does into the dark, blurred background, suggests mystery and concealment, even though the man is essentially naked. One implication might be that this man of sorcery does not even need clothes to conceal his body which thus stands revealed and concealed at the same time, and all the more magical for so being.

In seeming so deliberately beside the point, the bizarre caption, "Ethnographer with a Man in a Wig," adds to this sense of the sorcerer being clothed and unclothed at the same time, all of which can be seen as culminating in the fact that this is a picture celebrating the aura of the man in white, glowing like a star in the depths of the darkness of the sorcerer, whose enchantment ignites a flame, erotic and magical, that is the fabulous whiteness of the man in white. Could this be an instance of that "ethnographer's magic" made famous by Malinowski when he demanded that the anthropologist reveal the natives' point of view?

For here is my point of view: Is not the man in white every bit as magical as the sorcerer? Might not the roles be reversed or at least reversible, and in this regard is not the caption, "Ethnographer with a Man in a Wig," most curious? Nobody looking at the image, with the possible exception of the natives, would know the sorcerer was wearing a wig. In reality it is the ethnographer who is "bewigged," decked out in his colonial outfit, which, in its colorless purity, like a painter's untouched canvas, suggests that color shall open the doors to the art of ethnography, along the lines suggested in the letter I have already mentioned that Malinowski wrote Frazer in October 1917: "Through the study of your works I have come to realize the paramount importance of vividness and colour in descriptions of native life."

Frazer was as famous for his style as for what he wrote about, and certainly style or "voice" was Malinowski's trademark too, his singular contribution to the art of social documentary. Far from the standard view that facts speak for themselves, Malinowski writes:

In fact I found that the more scenery and 'atmosphere' was given in the account . . . the more convincing and manageable to the imagination was the ethnology of that district. I shall try to give the local colour and describe the nature of the scenery and *mise-en-scène* to the best of my ability.[8]

In a nutshell, color is the genie that lets ethnography out of the bottle. This is because there is color, and then there is "color." There is color as in this typical diary entry: "Sariba a blazing magenta; fringe of palms with pink trunks rising out of the blue sea." And then there is "color," as in "local color," meaning something more vague, more suggestive—that outer reach of words so necessary to grasp the inner nature of things. The two overlap and intertwine. Color and "color."

But then there are times when color has to be held at arm's length from what might be considered real intellectual work. Let me expand the diary entry:

Thursday 22 November 1917: Walked around the island a second time; marvelously rich coloured sunset. Roge'a: dark greens and blues framed in gold. Then many pinks and purples. Sariba a blazing magenta; *fringe* of palms with pink trunks rising out of the blue sea.—During that walk I rested intellectually, perceiving colours and forms like music, without formulating them or transforming them.[9]

"Without formulating them or transforming them." The Great Divide. Color trumps "color." The man is split. Our usual convenience. On the one side, the work of intellection, on the other, intellectual rest, which is when one lets music and color be themselves.

Would that things were this simple; that having separated these realms, they would stay separated: intellect versus rest, intellect versus color and music, and "color" versus color. To tell the truth, this last distinction is strange; the way color lends itself to this operation by which it sheds its concrete specificity and becomes a catchall for the inexpressible fire of being—as with colorful language, a colorful character, and, not to mention, "people of color." Equally strange is color's tendency to invisibility in its verbal depictions.

You don't have to read far to see that Malinowski went back and forth between color and "color," the literal versus the metaphoric meanings of the word. They merge, as in the diary passages I have cited. But they also spring apart, or appear to spring apart, one particular instance being his fieldnotes, where colors serve as an identifying tag in a heroic effort to install order into the strangeness of native life.

In his first period of Trobriand fieldwork in 1915, for instance, Malinowski would continuously check one informant against another, correcting his initial impressions, then writing "controlled" on the pages when satisfied, together with the date and the informant's name or initials written in red, blue, orange, or purple pencil. His biographer, Michael Young, notes that it would be tempting to think there is a code here, but he himself thinks the choice of color was probably arbitrary and suggests another dimension that color opens up, namely that "the notebooks became palimpsests of temporal desposits worked over in different coloured pencils."[10]

Palimpsests are layers barely discernible underneath a text or picture, suggesting an often discontinuous and illegible history of false starts, obliterations, discards, retries, sudden changes, helpful but ephemeral stagings, carelessness, and mindless oblivions. Thus palimpsests are much more in the camp of "color" than in the camp of color-as-a-code, "color" being the realm of just-out-of-reach meaning, as when Malinowski, writing in 1917 to the great Frazer in England, talks of his desire "to give the local colour." This is not a matter of blue or red, or even shimmering purples or blazing magenta, although surely the last two are edging away from color towards "color."

A dazzling idea, akin to William Burroughs's multicolored scrapbook-diary of the early 1960s, Michael Young's palimpsest proposal teases the far edge of color as if color itself is unstable and always on the move—that color can be thought of as time-travel transparencies laid one on top of the other, like Trobriand canoes painted with magical black, red, and white, gliding over coral reefs.

Just as color allows for overlap between codes, on the one hand, and palimpsests, on the other, so color provides the conditions for an overlap between fact and theory—as when Malinowski intuits that "the more scenery and 'atmosphere' was given in the account . . . the more convincing and manageable to the imagination was the ethnology of that district."[11]

This is the same overlap that reflects the move back and forth between the *diary*, the *ethnography*, and the *fieldnotes* (each written in a different language: Polish, English, and, to some extent, Trobriand, respectively). But no matter how many colored pencils or pink trunks rising out of a blue sea were invoked, the play between color and "color" was likely to be tense because the two worlds of diary and ethnography had to remain pretty much separate, on paper, at least.

Sometimes this separation could be bridged by bizarre hybrid forms, as even his love life in Melbourne became subject to natural science–type tabulation, with the construction of what Michael Young calls a "retrospective, synoptic diary."[12] Returning to the island to start his second field trip in November 1917, after thirty months away in Melbourne, Australia, Malinowski constructed a chart. Entitled "Life in Melbourne in Retrospect," it was composed of six columns which, reading from left to right, were headed SCIENTIFIC WORK / EXTERNAL EVENTS / HEALTH / N. S. / M. W. / E. R. M., the last three being the initials of three young women with whom he was in varying and conflicting degrees in love.[13]

Bizarre and unromantic, even shocking, as this chart is, does it not also present the possibility of a bold new form of ethnography? Imagine a whole book of this, page after page such that side by side with chronological charts of, for example, the great kula ring trading expeditions across the seas and the agricultural cycle of planting and of magic, we have HEALTH / N. S. / M. W. / E. R. M., as well.

Ethnography is based on fieldwork and fieldwork is personal. By imprisoning the personal in the ghetto of a private diary, the core of the experience is hidden.

But what this can mean, however, is that the disappeared self surfaces in the diary in astonishing ways—ways that splice color to "color" by means of what I call *the bodily unconscious*, which, inadvertently, Malinowski's diary manifests in a multitude of various ways, as when it assumes a body in the midst of other bodies such as the sea, mountains, and the ever-changing sky.

The eye and the body of the observer merge, and in doing so merge with what they observe.

A mere two days after his arrival in New Guinea in 1914 he could write in his diary: "Felt not too distinctly or strongly but surely that a bond was growing up between myself and this landscape . . . the purple glow in the west penetrated the palm grove and covered the scorched grass with its blaze, slithering over the dark sapphire waters."[14]

But the bond was fragile. The body drifts. Not only into landscape but into the machinery that got you there, as on the ship traveling along the south coast of New Guinea two months after his arrival:

Got up with a bad headache. Lay in euthanasian concentration on the ship. Loss of subjectivism and deprivation of will (blood flowing away from the brain?), living only by the five senses and the body (through impressions) causes direct merging with the surroundings. Had the feeling that the rattling of the ship's engine was myself; felt the motion of the ship as my own—it was I who was bumping against the waves and cutting through them.[15]

Is it a coincidence that the person-become-legend credited with "inventing" fieldwork and participant observation should be so exquisitely sensitive, so exquisitely able, or, should I say, forced to lose himself in Otherness this way? It could be your standard shamanic-speak—dying so as to transform into a spectral being.

Where is this ship that is the Self going?

Of course it doesn't work quite that way. The voyage can so easily founder. The people, with their strange customs, get in the way as much as they invite this loss of self. The merging of the body with the landscape is as much a tempting as a tedious and at times horrific experience. It is as much a defense as a joyfully accepted invitation. The pulse and texture of participant observation requires this friction. The underlining of the "I" in the diary passage I have just quoted, says it all. "I" becomes emphasized at its point of dissolution. That is what participant observation means and requires, this emphasis of the self no less than its dissolution.

The first thing we should notice is the ease, even addiction, with which color is evoked. Early on in the first diary, begun September 1914 in the capital of Port Moresby, the morning is wrapped in a light mist through which the hills appear as:

pale pink shadows projected on a blue screen. The lightly rippled sea shimmers in a thousand tints caught briefly on its continuously moving surface; in shallow spots, amid the turquoise vegetation, you see rich purple stones overgrown with weeds. Where the water is smooth, unruffled by the wind, sky and land are reflected in colors ranging from sapphire to the milky pink shadows of the mist-enveloped hills. Where the wind churns up the surface and blurs the reflections from the depths, from the mountains, and from the sky, the sea glistens with its own deep green, with occasional spots of intense blue . . . The sky spreads its blue over everything. But the fantastic shapes of the mountains continue to blaze in full pure colors, as if they were bathing in the azure blue of sky and sea.[16]

"It is," he concludes, "a mad orgy of the most intense colors, with I can't say just what strange character of festive, overrefined purity and distinction—the colors of precious stones sparkling in the sunshine."[17]

Through color, landscape comes to mime his inner states. On 14 November 1914:

I am giving in to moments of dejection. The fog induced by it is like a mist in the mountains, when it is driven by the wind, and discloses now one now another patch of the horizon. Here and there, through the enveloping darkness, there emerge remote, distant horizons, recollections; they drift by like images of distant worlds, lying at the foot of the mountain mist.— Today I feel much better. Moments of dimness, of sleepiness, as if I were in the Reading Room.[18]

Two weeks later, depressed in particular by Saville, the missionary, he wrote in the diary: "Felt sick, lonely, in despair. Got up, and covered with blanket sat by the sea on a log. Sky milky, murky, as though filled with some dirty fluid—the pink strip of sunset gradually expanding, covering the sea with a moving blanket of rosy metal . . ."[19]

As for the body's interior, take Friday, 10 May 1918: "Gray sky, silvery reflections on the sea, which is *ruffled* and *purplish*. I feel 'enervated': my eyes were smarting, I had a feeling of lightness and high blood pressure, a feeling of emptiness in the region of the heart."[20]

The inner landscape is to be continuously percolated with medicines every bit as dazzling as the pink strips of sunset: "Insomnia, (not too marked), overtaxed heart, and nervousness (especially) seem so far the symptoms . . . Arsenic is indispenable, but I must not exaggerate the quinine. Fifteen *grains* every 9 days should be just enough."[21]

This is a body prone to an almost mystical sensitivity to that other body, the body of the world.

14

walking through fire

Malinowski not only writes in his diary, but at times rereads it and then makes entries about the rereading. He ponders the relation between diary writing and what the writing is supposed to be about. His thoughts focus upon what he calls *dynamic states of the organism,* something I take to be like the "wisdom of the body" where color as metaphor takes over from color in the literal sense such that both meanings are invoked and slide felicitously into each other.

Sometimes this felicitous sliding occurs when he *hears* color . . . and is led to wonder *from where comes the color of the sea?* The color is so special:

Our shore was in deep shadow, and the air was somehow imbued with the
shadow. I looked—the shore near Borebo was bright green, the color of
a leaf just flowering in spring. Above it, a wall of white clouds, beyond it

the sea, an intense, polished, tense blue (something that lies in wait, where you feel life, as in the eyes of a living person—such is the character of the color of the sea here on some occasions)—the effect is wonderful. I wonder where that color comes from? Is that contrast between light and shadow, that absence of darkness, related to the swiftness with which the sun sets in the tropics? Or is it the strong zodiacal light, the glow given off by the sun, that illuminated that other shore with yellow light?[1]

Here self-conscious description of color-effects eases into an inquiry into the nature of color. Color does not come quietly. To invoke color head on, to face the Other Shore, bright green like a leaf under a wall of white clouds, is to perturb the practice of looking as much as what one is looking at. Ethnographic field-work can open things up, the nature of nature as much as the nature of color, not to mention the science and wonder of the shadow and its relation to colorific intensification. "Something that lies in wait," writes our diarist, in Polish, "where you feel life, as in the eyes of a living person."

To perturb looking as much as what one is looking at. The body of the writer turns in on itself in a color-activated interactivity with the environment—and this to the remarkable extent that something suicidal yet magical occurs. Early on in the diary, near Port Moresby:

Fires had been started in a few places. Marvelous spectacle. Red, sometimes purple flames had crawled up the hillside in narrow ribbons; through the dark blue or sapphire smoke the hillside changes color like a black opal under the glint of its polished surface. From the hillside in front of us the fire went on down into the valley, eating at the tall strong grasses. Roaring like a hurricane of light and heat, it came straight towards us, the wind behind it whipping half-burned bits into the air. Birds and crickets fly past in clouds. I walked right into the flames . . .[2]

I walked right into the flames . . . Back to the savant's savant, Isidore of Seville, with his *calor* and *color* breaking open the categories that would separate vision from heat, giving free rein to color as nonretinal force. In the description—if *description* be the word here and not *evocation, invocation,* or *incantation*—in the description provided by Malinowski, colors metamorphose into other colors, red into purple into dark blue into sapphire-colored smoke into black opal.

This is not smoke that is colored sapphire but sapphire on the move. You feel the change as much as you take note of the actual things being changed. The topography moves too, becoming a roaring of birds and crickets on the wing as we walk into the flames consuming our author.

Color thus facilitates a merging of the observer with the observed. In so doing, conventional conceptions of the nature of being are altered such that we, who read this passage and innumerable others similar to it that fill the diary, are pitched into another sense of what makes the real real. The human body, at least that of the young ethnographer, is lost, and lost in a way that is at times a rapture, at others, despair. Indeed there is no longer a body. It has cast off like one of those Trobriand canoes trading kula valuables, canoes shrouded in magic so as to bring the landscape as a living force into the human body, via mythology.

That is the diary. But in the *ethnographies* the body of the writer tends to get restored to what we might call Standard Western Subjectivity, nowhere more so than when dealing with *their* magic. Twenty years later, for instance, writing about the use of fire in the gardens on the Trobriand Islands in *Coral Gardens and Their Magic*, the author remains impervious to the magic of fire even though—and this surely makes the point—he realizes full well that this fire is indeed magical, *according to the islanders*, "as very sacred and important, indeed indispensable."[3]

Now a curious inversion has occurred. We are drawn close, so as to create distance. The author-anthropologist sets the stage and we readers are invited to watch. He writes or at least edits the script, putting words like a ventriloquist into the mouth of a Trobrian magician, while he, the author of this play, remains out of sight, pulling the strings.[4] It is as if Maklinowski has exchanged the magic of the diary for that of the islanders so that he can be nonmagical. Something like magic—his walking into fire, along with the wind, the crickets, and the clouds of light and heat and birds—has been replaced by magic as an ethnographic category, magic being something that they do and that he records.

Is writing about magic a way of inoculating the writer from the magic that is writing? For like fire, writing is a close cousin to crickets on the wing. All writing, that is, and not just diary writing, it being color that in the diary brings this slap-bang in our face.

This may seem a strange statement, but it is strange only because we take the conceits of documentary forms of expression at face value. For documentary uses the art of writing to conceal that art. To be blind like this is a blessing. It does all that Malinowski elsewhere attributes to magic in the Trobriands as a functional device, in this case providing confidence as to the facticity of "facts" with everything in its place and a place for everything.

Yet this is what was continually challenged by the diary writing, which found in color, more than anything else, an escape from the prison of Standard Western Subjectivity—that escape that Malinowski himself expressed, in relation to the color of the sea, as "that something that lies in wait, where you feel life, as in the eyes of a living person."

Traces of this flash through the ethnographies. They seem to provide the oxygen without which the writer would die. But the overwhelming conceit is to look professional and scientific, to be the master—of the Trobriands as much as of Anthropology.

Could it be different? Given the constraints on documentary writing and given the lack of reflexive anthropology, meaning an anthropology that turns its gaze back onto itself and its modes of self-actualization, only a despised 'amateur' would dare write differently, as did, for example, Walter Benjamin in Ibiza in 1932 and 1933, or young Tom Harrison's zestful *Savage Civilization* (published in 1937), about the people of yet another island, that of Malekula in the southwest Pacific, a beautifully Dadalike writing, all stops pulled out, eccentric no less than profoundly objective, disdainful of Western civilization and the documentary modes of professional anthropology. "The 'ethnographer's tent,' that validating image of the ethnographer's authenticity," writes Ron Edmond, "was for Harrison what the verandah was for Malinowski."[5] No matter how much a Malinowski might say he wanted to be a Conrad, or truly practice what Malinowski himself called "the ethnographer's magic," he would never allow his ethnographies to walk into fire.

To hover on the edge of their magic versus the ethnographer's magic is, I suggest, one reason why bouts of concentrated ethnographic work were followed by bouts of novel reading. "I read, read . . . and kept on reading without letup as though I were reading myself to death," reports Malinowski. To death! Indeed! He hates himself for this indulgence which he sees as threatening ethnographic work. Yet he cannot resist, despite self-admonitions such as the following, early on in the diary: "Resolved that after finishing this trash I wouldn't touch another book in NG." He writes here of his *intoxication* with the novelist Alexandre Dumas. "In the end he held me in his grip . . . I didn't stop while I was eating and I kept on till midnight. Only at sunset did I drag myself from my couch, and went for a short walk along the seashore. My head was humming . . ." Next he reads his illicit lady love's love letters, and in the next breath announces his intention: "I feel like writing the story of my life."[6]

Like diary writing, novel reading was taboo in the sense that it was part of that Other existence, tugging for expression, wanting to breathe and be openly recognized as a legitimate part of ethnography and ethnographic writing. It would be equally disingenuous to assume that first comes ethnographic field-work and after that comes the writing of the ethnography. To the contrary, fieldwork always presupposes the writing of it and is immersed in writing, no less than Malinowski's diary immerses his being in the shifting colors of the sea and sky. What died, what was continuously dying, as I see it, was the possibility if not the actual temptation to create hybrid, avant-garde forms, both fictive and nonfictive, personal and impersonal, instead of stuffing the off-screen stuff into the incommodious confines of the diary or into forbidden novel reading.

Alongside the novel addiction it is surprising to read in the diary of Malinowski's daily practice of taking and developing photographs, especially since Michael Young tells us Malinowski disliked photography and found it technically difficult.[7] Yet as I read the diary, I can sense that this man is a prowler, camera at the ready, as if in the grip of an organic compulsion. What's more, his ethnographies, more than any other I know of, are jam-packed with photographs, all of which boil down to one essential truth. To *take* pictures is synonymous with *making* pictures, and what is made again and again herein is the distanced, museum-like display: Natives Building a Canoe; Natives Weeding; Natives Dancing. *Argonauts* has sixty-five photographs. *The Sexual Life of Savages* has ninety-two. *Coral Gardens and Their Magic*, one hundred and sixteen.

While the novels provided an escape from the closeness of island life, yet can be assumed to enter into the fabrication of the written ethnography in a number of ways, photography did something similar. It created a sense of distance between subject and object that in this case could be controlled by he who adjusts the frame of the image and presses the button so as to initiate that magical process by which reality is captured in an image. But, acting against the flight into unreality or at least the escape provided by reading novels, the photographs provided his wandering mind and elusive sense of self with an anchor, something tangible, and what we might call a "reality check." It must be recalled that

Malinowski developed his photographs right there and then by himself on the island in his own tent. It is only a century later that now, with digital cameras, we can do something similar.

Such photorealism, however, must have been tantalizing in that it both encouraged yet undermined realism, showing how easy it is to manipulate such images.

That day in 1918, for instance, when Billy Hancock arrives in his boat—Billy the pearl trader and avid photographer—something exciting happens to ethnographic photography and the art of realism as Malinowski strides forth to be photographed, resplendent in his white fancy dress, bringing untold photons of brilliance to bear. Now he has changed places. No longer the photographer, he is the object of the gaze. But he mocks the gaze, as countless stories tell us of anthropological informants the world over.

Unknown until long after Malinowski died, these images "introducing the ethnographer," in Malinowski's own words, create a genre of their own, all the more mystifying for their lack of explanation. Neither diary nor ethnography, these images have yet to find a home or a category and as such are, in this mar-velously backhanded way, perfect for introducing the chameleon that is at all times and in all places the unknowable, freaky entity that is ethnography and the ethnographer. If ethnography was meant to explain the strange, it rarely found the opportunity to explain itself, the apparently nonstrange.

These weird images of whiteness-in-the-field, "playing in the dark," are per-fect not only for "introducing the ethnographer," but also for introducing color and its unsettling relation to whiteness in Standard Western Subjectivity.[8] Color pierces the chromophobic character armor holding that subjectivity apart from the body of the world. Reading Malinowski suggests that color in the tropics for the sensitive European can reorient the body as much as the mind, in the same way as the heat and the humidity do, thereby opening up what I call the bodily unconscious. I believe it is this "opening" that, like all other colonial governors, the governor of New Guinea, Hubert Murray, had, at all efforts, to forestall. If *administration by bluff* was a conscious strategy for a white minority to exercise hegemony over a black majority, it was at the same time a strategy for keeping the sense of the white body intact, no matter how hot and humid the meltdown, no matter how wonderfully disorienting the light, no matter how tumescent the standoff between the ethnographer and the man with a wig.

15

saiLing through coLor

In his fieldwork diary Malinowski gives voice to a sense of a being on the verge
of nonbeing. It is painful to read again and again how his body has become in-
ordinately sensate to heat and humidity and dreams, no less than it is dependent
upon the arsenic, quinine, calomel, iron, and streptococci he imbibes or injects
with a syringe, along with his frequent enemas, while he holds his morphine and
cocaine in strategic reserve. He lurches from the extremes of almost catatonic
mental and physical exhaustion, to hyperactive attacks of self-recrimination and
ethnographic work.

Perhaps all diary writing allows one to indulge in staged breakdowns and loss
of being, including one's own? But anthropological fieldwork has specific sets of
corrosive anxieties. Could it be that much of what Malinowski wrote about *color*
in his diary provided a comfort, a bulwark, as it were, that was both aesthetically
and therapeutically powerful? Could it be that this amounted to an immersion

not only in color but in the landscape, as if that might not only steady the nerves as much as his drugs but provide the more basic form taken by what he would later become famous for, namely the method of participant observation? For color was the flux by which he achieved this, same as what Walter Benjamin suggested was a function of color in children's books, taking them into the image—for what is fieldwork but another childhood?

Given this mimetic folding into Otherness, it is not all that surprising that in his ethnography this power of color was projected by him onto the islanders, nowhere more so than when the men were engaged in the long-distance gift giving of the sublime kula valuables that took them on arduous voyages across the ocean. Here they breathed color, they floated though color, and, as a consequence, felt the mythology of their world as impressed in reefs and mountains to be a living force in their own bodies. "The voyage which opens up the *Argonauts*," writes Harry Payne in his analysis of Malinowski's style, "is an ethnographer's voyage from a colorless world to a land of rich beauty and deep excitement."[1] To kula is to do many things, perhaps the most important of which is to sail through color—as when Malinowski describes the islanders sailing on the reef of Pilolu with the sea changing color all the time, becoming "pure blue, and beneath its transparent waters a marvelous world of multi-colored coral, fish and seaweed will unfold itself." It could be a hallucinogenic voyage, something of which we should take stock when coming across Michael Young's suggestion that Malinowski's *Argonauts of the Western Pacific* is "arguably the most influential monograph in the history of social anthropology."[2]

On the D'Entrecasteaux Islands "they will find also wonderful, heavy, compact stones of varying colors and shapes, whereas at home the only stone is the insipid, white, dead coral. Here they can see, besides many types of granite and basalt and volcanic stuff, specimens of black obsidian, with its sharp edges and metallic ring, and sites of red and yellow ochre."[3]

Isn't it always like this? Home is drab and colorless, like Goethe's, either black or white.

To sail from home is to exchange a colorless world for a colorful one. Home is scored in color that is sad and ugly, what we might call anticolor; dull greens broken up by patches of brown where seaweed grows "high and rank." But even so there are intimations of a beautified colorworld over the horizon, later confirmed as the sailors strike out to sea and the spots of emerald green "give place to a deeper sea of strong green hue."[4]

Like the sea sliding over the reef in a wash of color, the canoe itself is painted in magical paints. It is painted red, black, and white, and each one of these colors has its own, specific, magical spell chanted into it.

But is this the way to write about this canoe? Have I not fallen into the old trap of seeing color as that which fills in a form, in this case the canoe? Have I not fallen into the trap of seeing color as an add-on? Might it not be better said that without color, the canoe is less speedy, less safe, less beautiful—in a word, something less than a canoe? What effort of imagination is required *not* to see a canoe as living color—in the same way as I have said color is an animal and extended William Burroughs's idea of the color walk to mean that color itself walks?

The canoe glides over the sea. The sea is painted in magical colors too, colors that slide and flow, rising with the waves to the sky, other times depthless and translucent.

The canoe glides over the sea. The canoe is color. The sea is color. Color glides over color. Now the islanders are becoming fieldworkers, too. They feel they are strangers in a strange land. They sense the presence of foreign magic, magic that can kill, islands of people with tails, and other islands inhabited only by women. At night around the campfire on some sandbank they tell each other stories about their surroundings and destination, stories that enclose and include Malinowski. Just as Trobriand magic is practiced by speaking spells into objects, so these sailors are impregnating their anthropologist with stories of magic—or are they magical stories about magic?

He has found the perfect site for fieldwork, the heaving deck of an outrigger canoe laden with protective magic to ensure speed. And has not he himself become such a perfect site, too? Malinowski has become the receptacle, the object into whom mythology and spells are spoken "with an almost pedantic accuracy and completeness," he says, it being an easy task for a Trobriand islander to "transfer these qualities to the accounts which he is called upon to make in the service of ethnography."[5]

The color sensibility that saturates Malinowski's diary is now assumed to be part of the islanders' self-understanding, too, an assumption that can be best understood by taking into account the fact that Malinowski only seems happy in his diary when sailing, a far more effective therapy, it appears, than writing a diary or taking arsenic and enemas. "It is a precarious but delightful sensation," he wrote in *Argonauts of the Western Pacific*, "to sit in the slender body, while the canoe darts on with the float raised, the platform steeply slanting, and water constantly breaking over . . ."

> When the sail is hoisted, its heavy, stiff folds of golden matting unroll with a characteristic swishing and crackling noise, and the canoe begins to make way, when the water rushes away below with a hiss, and the yellow sail glows against the intense blue of sea and sky—then indeed the romance of sailing seems to open through a new vista.[6]

It is sailing that allowed him to escape—into color—and thereby into another world of the senses with the body suspended, open to the movement of the sea and the wind. Some readers may think it a little weird, the overwhelming amount of space he spends writing about canoes in his major anthropological book; their construction, their magic, their voyaging, and their mythology, even if it seems justified by his ostensible subject, that of the *argonauts* of kula sailing expeditions. Yet joining with these sailors was doing much more than studying the expeditions of the natives. It was an invitation to take him out of himself; to not only observe the exchange of kula valuables, but to exchange ways of bodily being, which, to my way of thinking, is one of the most significant forms of knowledge fieldwork has to offer. All that fine work society has performed over the years since we were born, orienting and adapting us to physical and cultural realities, shaping our sense of self and bodily being—all of that is shaken and, in the process, new ways of being invite us to be.

Surely Malinowski's anxiety about his body, and even more so the extreme measures he took to assuage the unknown through arsenic, morphine, cocaine, and so forth, was in good part the expression of resistance to the exchange of bodily being? Yet, in their extremity, could not these very measures act as a form of shock therapy, at first rigidifying the bodily unconscious, then collapsing it and allowing for at least the glimmer of the outpourings of an effervescence of bodily mutuality with Otherness? This glimmering that could become an outpouring was signaled in his written work first and foremost by impulses of color because color was the medium in which the bodily unconscious most easily expressed itself. His travels across the sea, in his writing, at least, were when this happened best. What is more, his diary did the same thing as these sea voyages, but in reverse. The diary was like a canoe. It took him inside himself and, as a consequence of that voyage, changed him or at least promoted and revealed alternate selves by projecting him into colored landscapes.

Such a sailing takes on stowaways and licensed passengers as well—namely you, and me, as readers. Such a sailing through color brings the reader into the realm of magic's magic, so that the reader becomes if not exactly a believer in magic, at the least its practitioner, reading being the art of letting go, of being transported into the worlds words conjure as if the words are alive, taking one into the images they form.

Is this not the same as sailing through color? To sail on shifting seas can be thought of as like sailing on a film of moving paint, yet one whose transparency gives the observer the dual viewpoint of seeing from a distance, yet becoming immersed in that which is being seen. To sail on shifting seas is to be taken out of yourself into the medium of filtered light, moving like the tendrils of seaweed swaying in the rays of the sun diffused through water. Which is medium and which is agent here, you ask yourself, seawater or sunlight?

The mountains seen from the canoe are enchanted. They serve as points—the solid colors, we might say—around which Malinowski constructs his moving colorscapes. The first thing that hits the eye on leaving the island of Kiriwina are the southern mountains which, we are told, "rise higher and higher" to appear as blue silhouettes draped in clouds. The nearest of them is known as "the mountain of taboo"—Koyatabu—and we are to understand taboo as intimately linked to the sacred as ineffable, dangerous, power, tied to prohibitions. The mountain has a slim, tilted, pyramidal shape and serves as a "most alluring beacon, guiding the mariners due south." To the right of it is the broad and bulky mountain known as "the mountain of the sorcerers."[7]

To the kula voyagers "these disembodied, misty forms" will assume "a marvelous shape and enormous bulk." They surround the sailors as "solid walls of precipitous rock and green jungle, furrowed with deep ravines and streaked with racing water-courses." Deep bays resound with what to the voyagers are the unknown "voice of waterfalls," along with weird bird cries—at which point the sea changes its color, "once more become pure blue, and beneath its transparent waters, a marvelous world . . . will unfold itself."[8]

There is a chain of being here, the last step of which is the slide from sound to color. We began with the solid but enchanted mountains. They liquefy into waterfalls, waterfalls with a voice, and end up as transparent color. We could rephrase this, saying that as the voyagers enter their new world, the mountains and cliffs are pouring myth into sparkling seas of shifting blues and greens. It is as if mythology itself is cascading into color. Or could it be even more mythic—that color, specifically transparent color, is itself thus revealed to be transmuted, liquefied enchantment—what I have in earlier chapters called polymorphous magical substance?[9]

When a flotilla of canoes comes over the horizon, polymorphous magical substance similarly spreads itself, this time as a slow smooth movement across the face of the sea accompanied by the music of conch shells, the play of color, and the clanking of cowries. "Like butterfly wings," writes Malinowski, the triangular sails of the canoes scatter across the water. Conch shells are blown in unison. As the canoes come closer still, you see them "rocking in the blue water in all the splendour of their fresh white, red, and black paint, with their finely designed prowboards, and clanking array of large, white cowrie shells."[10]

As these white, red, and black canoes come closer, so does the written text. Like what can happen watching a movie, the reader is penetrated by the image or else taken outside of himself, similar to what occurs with Malinowski on one of his canoe "outings." Anthropology has always had the potential to accomplish this startling feat by piggybacking, so to speak, on the magic of informants, which, in the case of the Trobriand Islands, is a magic of words whispered into things.

Malinowski achieves this, I believe, by sporadically blurring the distinction between himself and the islanders—and simultaneously allowing this to blur the distinction between landscape and observer. The effect of this is to solicit a magical power of language, Trobriand, English, or Polish, to engage directly with the objects into which it is chanted or whispered, traces of which can be found in the diary he kept in Poland long before he got to the Trobriands.[11]

And if in this magical use of language there lies the power of fusing the speaker with the things spoken about, there exists nevertheless the equal and opposite force of repulsion and fear—the fear of losing oneself in the object, such loss being essential, as I see it, to scientific method. *Empathy*, we can call it, but also an immersion with Otherness that makes you prone to metamorphoses of that Self you hold so dear. Walter Benjamin referred to this as the workings of what he called "the mimetic faculty," meaning that desire, need, and even capacity to become Other, a capacity he saw as at the root of language as much as dance. In making love, Jean Genet would spiral out of himself to become a turtledove pursued by a falcon. Other times he was a cobra, not merely because of what we might call a fantasy or an association of ideas or symbols, but because of the passions invested in the physical act of what was then illicit, male homosexual lovemaking *combined with* the writer's lust for making love with language that would in turn make love with the reader—"to make the reader fully conscious—as he sees love swooping down on me . . . like a falcon."[12] Nietzsche, about whom Malinowski had written sympathetically in his youth in Poland, called it Dionysian, the inability not to become Other, as much a cast of mind, character, and culture as it was of music and dance.

But when what I call blurring between observer and observed occurs in Malinowski's ethnography, it does so surreptitiously. It creeps up on you unannounced because the blurring is done in such a sneaky way. At the beginning a difference is suggested, but already the ground is being cleared for the anthropologist to claim he thinks like an islander. "Under the influence of my work," writes Malinowski very early on in *Argonauts*, "I came to regard this country within the somewhat narrow native horizon, as the distant land to which perilous, seasonal voyages are made . . ."[13] Thus, "A reader must pay close attention," writes George Stocking, "to realize from the printed narrative that Malinowski never actually sailed with a kula expedition"—except for once, early on in his stay, in 1915, when the wind blew so hard the wrong way that the islanders threw him off as the cause of their bad luck.[14] After that it was the white man's sailing boats for Maklinowski, and rowing in a dinghy in the lagoon for exercise.

Yet by the time it has sunk in that you don't really know who is being fused with nature, whether it is Malinowski or the islanders, it is too late. You don't care! You are caught up in a maelstrom of wind and beauty—as when: "It is a precarious but delightful sensation to sit in the slender body, while the canoe darts on . . . when the water rushes away below with a hiss, and the yellow sail glows against the intense blue of sea and sky."

Who is sitting in this slender body while the canoe darts on? you might ask, an anonymous Trobriand sailor, Malinowski himself, or some fictional composite? In any event, thanks to color, the author has died. The author has disappeared into the text. The extraordinary thing is that by then you don't care. Self-awareness is here no match for awareness; this hiss and glowing intensity of blueness of sea and sky.

To sail through color is to become embodied, and embodiment is the most common form of Trobriand magic—embodiment is what happens when magic is spoken as words into objects. And what are these words? They are the poetic echo of what is said to have happened long ago in the time before history, additional evidence for which is provided by striking features in the physical landscape; in the mountains, reefs, and rocky outcrops in the ocean. "Myth has not only crystallized into magical formulae but into landscape."[15]

Magic resides as wisdom in the belly of the magician from where it emerges in the form of whispered spells. Thus we could say that magic not only unites the human body to the landscape, but also unites both body and landscape to times long past. Magic achieves this thanks to an inspired, exhortatory, incantatory, secret poetry spoken into things so they may become supernaturally charged— things such as the transversals and lashings of the canoe into which magic is chanted so as to ensure speed and safety, or things such as herbs to ensure love. *Impregnation* is the term Malinowski uses, as if the words act biologically. While whispering his magic into the blade of an adze, the magician wraps a dry banana leaf around the blade, "thus imprisoning the magical virtue of the spell around the blade."[16]

The poet Sylvia Plath worked with something like this view of language, too. Let us call it embodiment. In the memoir of her childhood by the beach, the first thing she does (like Malinowski) is evoke the sea as color. She sometimes thinks that this vision is the clearest thing she owns. "I pick it up," she says, as regards this memory, "like the purple 'lucky stones' I used to collect with a white ring all the way round, or the shell of a blue mussel with its rainbowy angel's fingernail interior; and in one wash of memory the colors deepen and gleam, the early world draws its breath."[17]

Something is breathing, she says. Is it the sea? Is it herself? Is it her mother? Or all three? She is floating, floating on a sea of memories, a sea captain "tasting the day's weather" on this sea of gleaming color.

For the sailors embarked on their kula voyage, the sounds of the liquefying mountains cascading mythology into the sea of many colors is a magic binding human bodies to landscape as well as to a prehistorical force, such as breath. This slide back and forth from sound to color is what I take from Plath, too.

Sound here means not just the "voice of the waterfall" but also the fall of the human voice, which is why the American film critic, wunderkind, novelist, poet, and ethnographer, James Agee, in that strangest of strange ethnography cum poem, *Let Us Now Praise Famous Men* (likened by Dwight Macdonald to Whitman's *Leaves of Grass*), tells his readers that his "text was written with reading aloud in mind . . . that the reader attend with his ear to what he takes off the page: for variations of tone, pace, shape, and dynamics are here particularly unavailable to the eye alone, and with their loss, a good deal of meaning escapes."[18]

Thus writer and reader fuse, thanks to this capacity of language, which is why his is a *book,* Agee goes on to say, "only by necessity. More seriously, it is an effort in human actuality, in which the reader is no less centrally involved than the authors and those of whom they tell."[19] As for that *actuality,* it is where consciousness shifts from the imagined to the perception of "the cruel radiance of what is."[20]

Shifted into that *cruel radiance of what is,* there seems a chance, and a good one, at that, of becoming suspended in a sonic medium where the usual distinctions of body and mind, perceiver and the perceived, make little sense. This is the same with Plath's seashells of color evoking the breath of the sea, the breath of the mother and that of the child afloat on that sea that remains a vision — perhaps the clearest thing she owns. Color leads to breath, as with language, just as color is the result of sound, as with the mythology of liquefied mountains of taboo and sorcery falling down huge cliffs and into the ocean. Turn up the music, advises Agee, "Concentrate everything you can into your hearing and into your body. You won't hear it nicely. If it hurts you, be glad of it. As near as you will ever get, you are inside the music, not only inside it, you are it; your body is no longer your shape and substance, it is the shape and substance of the music . . . murderous to all equilibrium."[21]

This seems to be the way the canoe engages the islander as something alive, says Malinowski, as something endowed with deep love, "characteristic of the sailors' attitude towards his craft."[22]

And to which sailors is he referring? Could it be not only Trobriand sailors but sailors the world over, or at least those sailors without passports or hope who sail B. Traven's *Death Ship,* the *Yorikke,* just after the First World War? For these sailors, too, treat their ship as something alive. It tells them stories, and every piece of equipment on it, no matter how broken down or hard to deal with, is respected by them as having a soul. Like the canoes of the Trobriand Islanders, the *Death Ship,* although a steel-hulled, coal-burning, propeller-driven, leaky tub, is immeasurably ancient in terms of the magic and mythology encrusted in its proud being.

Take the winch. It belonged to pre-Flood times and was the same, in fact, as had been used by old man Noah. The goblins of that time before time had saved themselves from the flood by secreting themselves in the nooks and crannies of this ship, the worst of them finding refuge in the winch, which is why the winch had to be respected and why Stanislav, one of the sailors, had learnt to win over these goblins with noble speeches. "Heh, your Highness, once more, get your legs going, please."[23] A Trobriand canoe magician could do no better, it being precisely that time before time that is invoked in Trobriand magic and precisely this tone of respect and command that drives the magic spell.

You discern this from the first stage onwards of canoe making, when the *tokway* wood sprites have to be commanded by the magician to leave the tree trunk so the carvers can get to work hollowing out the hull. "Come down, O wood sprites, O *tokway*, dwellers in the branches, come down. . . . Come down and eat."[24]

"I don't know why, but that ship got me like a spell," declares the narrator of the *Death Ship* when he first saw her. "I was interested in the color of the hull."

I couldn't make it out. It looked as if it had been snow-white when the ship was still in her baby-shoes. That, however, must have been sometime before old Abraham left Ur of the Chaldees with his wife Sarah. I could see that at least two hundred new layers of paint had been put on top of the original white. As a result there were as many different colors painted on her hull as are known to exist. Those layers of paint made her appear twice her true size. No owner of the *Yorikke* had ever permitted all her paint to be taken off and an entirely new coat put on. Every patch of paint that was still good had been preserved so as to make the painting as inexpensive as possible. So there were a hundred square feet of sky-blue next to a hundred square feet of canary yellow . . . Were it not for the many thick coats of paint on her hull, she would have frozen to death in the cold ocean, for her blood was no longer as hot as it was five thousand years ago.[25]

Yet nothing could be further from the canoes pictured by Malinowski. Traven's sailors do nothing but work and suffer, like illegal immigrants without passports or papers in today's vicious world. They are workers, not kula voyagers, workers as in "Workers of the world unite. You have nothing to lose but your chains." Of all the different kinds of work, the most constant is painting—painting the ship's rusted, monstrous, exfoliating self. And when the ship goes under because its owners will not spend money to maintain it but drive it relentlessly to its doom, crew and all, when the *Death Ship* thus lives up to its name, then and only then will heaven open its arms and receive them regardless of their not having papers. The last words are those of Stanislav, the sailor, delirious from lack of water and exposure. As he sinks beneath the waves, he responds to the voice from above: "Aye, aye, sir. He who enters here will be for ever free of pain."[26]

My copy is old and battered. The print is small and faded. When I read these last lines, I read: "He who enters here will be for ever free of paint."

16

BODY PAINT

1916, a beach on the island of Kiriwina. The islanders are preparing to celebrate a newly built canoe. So long as we maintain our chromicidal body armor we will find it a wonderful scene, all that we have come to expect of the tropics, primal scene of color itself.

"The beach appeared bright and gaudy," wrote Malinowski in *Argonauts of the Western Pacific*, "and the lively brown bodies looked well against the background of green foliage and white sand. The natives were anointed with coco-nut oil, and decorated with flowers and facial paint. Large red hibiscus flowers were stuck into their hair, and wreaths of white, wonderfully scented *butia* flowers crowned the dense black mops."[1]

"I was the only white man present," he points out, "and besides myself only some two or three native missionary teachers were dressed in white cotton."[2]

Another scene. The villages are full of life, color, and music for about a month at the end of the dry season, when the harvest is complete. Work stops. Dancing, eating, and visiting begin.

> The men put on new and well-finished pubic leaves, apply paint to their faces, and use ornamental walking sticks or "ceremonial weapons." On very festive occasions, nose-sticks are put through the septum, aromatic leaves into the armlets, flower wreaths hung on the heads and shoulders. The dancers have a special head-dress of white feathers and with red feather topping, and they wear cassowary feather tufts in their belts and armlets. They dance holding a pandanus streamer or with a carved dancing shield in their hands. The women, who decorate their bodies with almost exactly the same ornaments, use, moreover, the elaborate and gaudily colored dress petticoats, so characteristic of this district.[3]

It is the face where chromophobes and chromophiliacs most hotly engage, as when Malinowski describes the natives' face paint as *gaudy*, a term he has already used in relation to the scene on the beach as "bright and gaudy," and when he refers to the women's "gaudily colored dress petticoats." That most lyrical and subtle of ethnographers, Kenneth Read, finds recourse to the same term where he describes the men's gear in the greatest of all festivals involving the initiation of boys into manhood where he lived in highland New Guinea in the early 1950s. "All the richness of their lives," he writes, was "played out in the flashing, gaudy colors of paint and feathers . . ."[4]

"All the richness of their lives" . . . in the gaudy colors they wear.

Likewise another sensitive and stupendously gifted writer, Laura Bohannan, describes as gaudy the socks and scarves of the rural Nigerian women amongst whom she lived as an anthropologist in the 1950s where the contrast between chromophobia and chromophilia also came into play. The women's vividly colored socks were imitations, she said, of the knee-length socks worn by the whites, which were, I presume, khaki or white.[5] How could these chaps wear anything *gaudy*, which, according to my *Webster's Dictionary*, "implies a tasteless use of overly bright, often clashing colors or excessive ornamentation (circus performers in *gaudy* costumes)"? One of its synonyms is *meretricious*, meaning "of or related to a prostitute; falsely attractive and superficially significant." We who come later can now see with an even more dreadful clarity to which side of the color bar the native belongs and why the colonies, akin to circus arenas frequented by prostitutes, could be alluring to the European imagination.

"Here we are ugly," an islander explains to Malinowski, preparing to meet his gift-giving trading partner in the kula ring of interisland exchange. But when "we make our red paint and black paint . . . our partner looks at us, sees our faces are beautiful; he throws the *vaygu'a* [precious gifts] at us."[6]

It is as if face painting transforms you from an ordinary to an extraordinary person. Small wonder it is performed for festivities and by a woman during her first pregnancy. The islanders crush young betel nut, mix it with lime, and apply it with the pestles of betel mortars. They add to their face aromatic black resin together with white lime. Voila! Red. Black. And white.

The face and body are prepared by elaborate ceremonial washing to the accompaniment of magical spells in which, in the case of a dancer, male or female, the aim of *whitening* the skin by stroking it with mother-of-pearl shell is paramount: "I smooth out, I improve, I whiten . . ." But in what sense is this *whitening*, given that Europeans were considered ugly due to their white skin with spots on it like an albino? For the islanders, whitening magic here is synonymous not so much with making oneself white as with making oneself *glowing* and *bright*, a brilliance of body further enhanced by the application of coconut oil, which produces a shining surface all over.[7]

What's more—what's very much more—face paint and body paint are impregnated with magic. Take the *talo* spell spoken into crushed young betel nut mixed with lime to produce a pigment of wonderful brightness and intensity:

Red paint, red paint, of the *udawada* fish!
Red paint, red paint, of the *mwaylili* fish.
At the one end of the aromatic pandanus flower petal
At the other end of the Duwaku
There are two red paints of mine,
They flare up
They flash up
My head, it flares up, it flashes
My red paint, it flares up, it flashes
My facial blacking, it flares up, it flashes
My aromatic paint, it flares up, it flashes.[8]

Flashing up, flaring up, color is movement—alive and stirring—as in Malinowski's description of the use of long pandanus leaves as streamers. To ensure that canoes used on the long sea voyages in the interisland trading expeditions of the kula ring are fast and safe, many magical acts and objects are involved, one of which is the attachment of two or three previously magically medicated pandanus streamers to the rigging so as to ensure speed. "The decorative effect of the floating strips of pale, glittering yellow is indeed wonderful," writes Malinowski, "when the speed of the canoes makes them flutter in the wind. Like small banners of some stiff, golden fabric they envelope the sail and rigging with light, color, and movement."[9]

Exaggerated or not, this is the color effect Malinowski paints for us. Light, color, movement . . . and speed. It is the ribbon of trembling yellow that is the key here, and to create this effect is one of the primary intentions of a great dancer as well. What is more, on festive occasions houses are decorated with these leaves, as are the *vaygu'a* or kula-ring trading valuables before they are given as gifts to one's trading partner. In their night flight, witches use pandanus streamers for speed and levitation, too.

Just after the pandanus streamers have been attached to the rigging, the magic of color is exquisitely expressed in the spell the canoe owner utters and which commences with several words, each one of which begins with the syllable *bo*, probably meaning, Malinowski speculates, *ritual, sacred,* and *being tabooed.*[10]

Abstract and speculative, this translation is brought to life as color when we consider additional shades of meaning that can—like pandanus streamers—be attached to it, for *bo* suggests the areca nut as well as the sweet-scented *butia* flower. Why the areca nut? Because, says Malinowski, in the safety of a footnote, it is a narcotic and a beautiful vermilion dye.[11] Thus we have: a sweet scent, a narcotic, and color magically endowed, contained in the one sound, *bo*, all tied together as "sacred," meaning tabooed. Could it get more perfect?

Well, yes! It could. For if we think back to the question, what color is the sacred? we see how the ethnography here enables that question by connecting color to ritual, to smell, and to the levitating effect of drugs no less than to the dancing, glowing, human body in the midst of other bodies—all immersed, so to speak, in the radiance of the "sacred," a difficult word, to be sure, but one hard to avoid as it winds itself around the sense of danger and the illicit associated with taboo. So many taboos! And so many refer to eating, which means to say incorporating aspects of the world into one's body—*incorporate*, to bring into one's body, to make part of one's body—or the exact opposite, to deliberately refrain from such ingestion as when, for example, a certain red fish is invoked in a spell—as with the face paint—then that fish cannot be eaten by the magician.

The old masters of Europe such as Jan Van Eyck or Jan Vermeer applied their pigments in layer after layer of color mixed with glazes and varnishes, many coming from colonial outposts of Europe. Yet neither aroma nor magical spells were part of the equation. Lost in translation. More's the pity. And the old masters did not paint on faces. Instead they painted onto canvas. They painted faces onto canvases.

Of course there have been throwbacks, like the new master William Burroughs, buying colors in the market in Lima, Peru, trying to make comic books with miasmatic colors that worked their way into your insides, colors that like the body painting of the magicians in the Trobriands got into your body and made you ache. You could taste, feel, and touch these colors rising from the books and, as in the Trobriands, they came perfumed—in this case with hashish, opium, or blood. In choosing aromatic colors, Burroughs manifests his affinity with the Trobriand islanders' appreciation of the magical power of properly prepared color.

It needs a crossover man like Burroughs no less than Goethe's soldier to bring out what lies hidden in Western attitudes to color. Anthropology always had the potential to do the same crossover thing but has notoriously dragged its feet in this regard, interrogating the natives' point of view, less so its own. This is what is so beguiling about the photograph "Ethnographer with a Man in a Wig," for it not only presents the ethnographic encounter in dramatic terms, but thereby clears the field with its outrageous strangeness. Who is that masked man? we might ask, referring not to the "man in a wig" but to the "ethnographer" with the man in a wig. What is he doing?

With his face painted in the manner of the Indians, Goethe's soldier may have done something similar, provoking the question: How different is it to paint a face on a canvas as compared with painting onto a face?

If the canvas mode is flat and vertical, ready for a wall to be hung upon, if the canvas mode is image magic, then face painting is *not*! It is not image magic, sometimes referred to as *sympathetic magic*, whereby the magician exploits the bond felt to connect the image with what it is an image of.

To the contrary, such color magic as that involved in face painting or that involved in wrapping objects in yellow pandanus leaves seems to me to make a different appeal to magic's magic, more suggestive of the exuberance of life, like lighting a fire, it being fire, flames, and firelight that stand behind the image, any image, as the ur-image, the ultimate, plastic, ever-changing form—Eisenstein's *plasmaticness*—as we see in cinematic animation no less than in the fluttering panadanus leaves glittering yellow like the polymorphous magical substance, or the white feather insides of the Tierra del Fuego shaman, that all along I have identified with color itself. Nietzsche would have made a good cinematic animator on this account. Didn't he say that life for us means constantly transforming all that we are into light and flame?

And have not Malinowski's Trobrianders entered deep into the cinematic image, precisely in terms of chromophobia and chromophilia? In the now classic film, *Trobriand Cricket: An Ingenious Response to Colonialism*, much energy is expended by the filmmaker in showing how the islanders have appropriated the colonist's game. Yet it is disappointing how color, so manifestly present on the screen, passes without verbal or visual comment. Early on we are shown the original game being played in England by men wearing all-white outfits. Could it be from cricket, then, that British colonial officers the world over, and Malinowski, as photographed in 1918, face to face with the sorcerer of some repute, derived their whites in such obvious contrast to the Trobriand cricketers with their lustrous body- and face-painting, dancing their way to victory?

I think I am joking, of course, yet surely this possibility is not lost on the colonized? Like Goethe's soldier recently returned from war with his face painted in the manner of the Indians, these ex-warrior Trobriand cricketers are brilliant crossover men. Here they come onto the cricket field dancing in unison and gorgeously painted up. They are great mimes. Now they are imitating birds. They run fast and swoop low, in unison, like birds diving onto the waves. The film then shows us real seabirds soaring over the sea. It is a thrilling moment to be suspended as a spectator between these two sacred moments, miming men and diving birds. Oh! Here they go again, now they are miming aeroplanes. Can you believe it! And the filmmaker retrieves some archival footage. The film switches from color to black and white, sign of age, to show us World War II planes lined up and taking off as if themselves dancing. (Maybe the planes are imitating birds, too?) Again there is this thrilling spectatorial moment suspended between the image and what the image is an image of. This time it feels tremendously strong. It is a question of waves of technologies meeting midocean, the mimetically capacious human body unclothed and painted, on the one side, the fully clothed man with the camera, the mimetically capacious machine, on the other. It is also a meeting midocean of color with black and white. The two waves coming from opposed directions meet, smash into one another, and rise up breaking and frothing. This I call mimetic excess, copying not to get the power of the other, to make love magic or win-the-lottery magic. No! None of that! It is mimesis for the sheer love of mimesis, and it occurs across the colonial divide in moments of freedom where black and white meet color—this is my point, my Goethean crossover man point—where life means transforming all that we are into light and flame.

So much for face painting. What about painting a face onto canvas? Does this obey some quite other instinct, one of preservation and fixing by means of capturing a likeness, a life captured forever in its moment of time, like photography, a funereal art first tried out as mummification in Egypt? In many ways face painting on a canvas is the complete opposite of transformation, self-transformation, and fire.

What ethnography achieves in this tradition of portraiture, however, is wonderful. Practicing participant observation, the ethnographer participates in a universe of people who paint their faces so that he will later be able to paint their faces on canvas.

It is the legend that is important, the legend that establishes Bronislaw Malinowski as the father of modern anthropology, a "messianic hero," as Michael Young explains, "who is emphatically at home with the savage, speaking his language and living (almost) as he does. This modern ethnographer descends from the missionary's verandah and pitches his tent in the middle of the native village where he stays and stays and stays . . ."[12]

And then there is the counterlegend. Take the archetypal photograph of Malinowsi's mentor, Charles Gabriel Seligman, at work on your typical colonial verandah in New Guinea in 1898, practicing neither *participant observation* nor *observation* but *testing* one by one the natives brought to him as to their color vision.

It is the legend that is important. In order to paint their faces, Malinowski had to get close as well as far. He had to be subjective as well as remote. "His eye was a camera with variable depth of field," writes Young, "a bifocal lens that combined the diarist's eye for subjective detail with the anthropologist's eye for social context. It was an essential quality of his genius as an ethnographer that he was able to combine them: to observe an act in close-up, register its unique

FIGURE 9. C. G. Seligman on the legendary/stereotypical/scapegoated colonial verandah, off of which Malinowski hopped. Seligman is in New Guinea, 1908, testing the natives' color vision using Holmgren's wools. How would Malinowski have tested on these wools? Reproduced by permission of University of Cambridge Museum of Archaeology & Anthropology (N.34989.ACH2).

properties, then draw back to apprehend its general setting, the context that gave the act its meaning."[13]

In confirmation of this double-perception Malinowski wrote a note to himself at the back of his diary: "Main thing to do, is reflect on the two branches: my ethnological work & my diary & take the clue from both. They are well-nigh complementary as complementary as can be."[14]

It is all the more surprising, therefore, that the science created out of the legend of fieldwork, and sustained to this day, basically eliminated the diary aspect and was quite magical in its insistence on the removal of the observer from the actual ethnography. This freaky entity—the disembodied observer inhabiting the pages of ethnography—is far more of a ghostly presence than any witch coursing the Trobriand skies, searching for corpses to feed on. As the "study of man," Anthropology, it seems, could not afford to study the man doing the study of man. It became less of a science for not turning its tools on itself. It became gutless.

Malinowski's diary forces us to reconsider what has been lost by that.

Deleting the observer observing by burying him in a private diary also meant the erasure of the colonial regime and its impact on the object of study. Even the sketch map Malinowski drew for his own edification of the island of Kiriwina deleted the European settlements.[15] Times may have changed. It has become fashionable nowadays, perhaps too fashionable, to plead mea culpa and evoke the colonist to the neglect of the intensive study of indigenous ways of life. Nevertheless the magical removal of the observer from the field of observation remains as strong if not stronger than ever, there being embarrassment all around, it seems, if the Self of the Observing Self is not hidden by the obligatory fig leaf.

When Malinowski got off the boat on his first fieldtrip to the island of Kiriwina, his main field site, on 27 July 1915, roads were actually being built on the island by prison labor, under the eagle eye of the assistant resident magistrate, "Doctor" Raynor Bellamy, who had studied but not completed his medical degree at Cambridge and Edinburgh and held this post on the island since 1905, ten years before Malinowski arrived. In modern parlance, Bellamy wanted to "develop" the Trobriand economy. He therefore jailed Trobrianders who did not plant coconuts and even jailed one powerful chief on charges of sorcery (sorcery was an important means of control practiced by chiefs trying to maintain the traditional economic system). There were some two hundred Trobrianders imprisoned when Malinowski arrived, and over one hundred thousand new coconut trees planted as a cash crop, undermining the traditional powers of the chiefs. The pearl trader Mick the Greek broke the chiefs' monopoly on pigs, and other traders broke their control of betel nut.[16]

Although we know from the diary that Malinowski found the colonial administrators and missionaries a severe irritation, rarely a word appears about this island reality in Malinowski's ethnographies, which, essentially, established modern anthropology. When he first landed on the island of Kiriwina, which is where he carried out most of his fieldwork over two years, Malinowski's sixty boxes were unloaded on a jetty recently completed by prison labor and taken to the house of the resident magistrate, which stood next to the police barracks, the jail, the houses of the prison warders, and a hospital.

En route to the Trobriands, on the island of Samarai off southeast New Guinea, Malinowski's informants were actually prisoners, six of whom had beaten up a missionary in German New Guinea. There were 329 prisoners serving time there between 1914 and 1915, two hundred of them for deserting European employers.[17]

Even the dead were colonized. The British administration had made the islanders stop burying the dead in the center of the village and instead place them outside. This singularly important fact—important maybe even more to the British than to the islanders—appears as an obscure note at the back of Malinowski's first essay on the island, published as early as 1916, concerning the spirits of the dead.[18]

Yet instead of an island of prisoners making roads for nonexistent vehicles, with the dead expelled from the interior of the villages—surely of ethnographic interest—Malinowski preferred to ethnographically render the place in idyllic terms, opening his most famous work, *Argonauts of the Western Pacific*: "Imagine yourself suddenly set down surrounded by all your gear, alone on a tropical beach close to a native village, while the launch or dinghy that has brought you sails out of sight."[19] This is more than a "preference." It is denial. It is also a lie, part of the "ethnographer's magic"?

"To live without other white men," he intones. Yet it is clear, writes Michael Young, that white traders were an integral part of the islands and that Malinowski spent some 40 percent of his fieldwork time living with them. In his second field trip, 1917–18, for instance, he spent sixteen out of forty-one weeks with traders, as compared with the twenty-two weeks living in his tent pitched close to the natives.[20]

This was the same man who, twenty years after his arrival on the island, wrote (in a footnote) that his excision of colonial influence was perhaps "the most serious shortcoming of my whole anthropological research in Melanesia."[21] Yet how much this was an anticolonial critique, and how much it was, to the contrary, an attempt to disarm the British Colonial Office, is hard to say. The British government was never really convinced that anthropology had anything to offer colonial administration. If anything, it was the opposite. Anthropologists were by definition suspect. Their siding with the natives could be a problem. And a problem there certainly was, as manifest by Malinowski in print with his warnings in 1929 of "black bolshevism" in colonial possessions, especially African, and hence the urgent need to widen the anthropological vision to include the effects of the colonial presence.[22]

As for the participation component of participant observation, it is clear that, unlike Goethe's soldier returned from America with his face painted, Malinowski was no crossover man. But Cyril Cameron was. A young Scotsman living on the island, reputedly with many wives, he became an important informant for Malinowski's essay on the spirits of the dead. Like the islanders he chewed areca nut and regularly hired a garden magician for his coconut plantation, which was why, according to the islanders, his trees did so much better than those of other white men.[23]

But for the anthropologist to act this way is unseemly. Yet is not the anthropologist by definition unseemly? According to the legend, he can—indeed he must—"participate," so as to be able to observe from the "inside," so to speak. Yet he must not *really* participate—not like Cyril does, for example. Unlike the missionaries, colonial government officials, plantation managers, nonindigenous traders, and beachcombers, the anthropologist lies curiously suspended between worlds and remains forever isolated. A real freak, nobody—neither the natives nor the Europeans—understands what she or he is doing (witness the highly educated Sir Hubert Murray brooding over Malinowski as a pro-German pederast—that at least is a clear and solid identity) because in the long run not even anthropologists know why they are doing what they do. Certainly they are not meant to go native and paint their faces, chew betel nut, have sex with the natives, or practice magic. Instead they are meant to transmute all that into the practice of participant observation, which enables you to tell the informants' story for them, but never, ever tell your own as an intrinsic and necessary part of that story. From Malinowski's diary we can at least see what that story could have been—his craziness, his fears, his mumbling to himself in his sad and desperate dreams, all that embedded in the real island as a colonial possession with Bellamy and roads and jails . . . and not the fake island on which, in fact, the truth was that at best he was a misfit among whites and blacks alike.

After all, what is the *field* in *fieldwork*? Surely the field begins with and forever includes the *fieldworker*? And just as surely is the field deeply ambiguous, the outcome of mutual and occasionally creative—one hopes—misunderstandings, along with false expectations? Take the shadowed face of the bewigged sorcerer,

Togugu'a, not looking at Malinowski looking at him. Is this not the field too, shadowed faces and oblique realities such that it is impossible to say from where the sorcery emanates?

Let it be noted—and let the irony be appreciated—that the famous method, if not the terminology, of participant observation derives from the study of *color blindness* by a mentor of Malinowski's, the celebrated Cambridge anthropologist and shellshock therapist, William Halse Rivers Rivers, photographed in playful action on the beach in 1898 on the island of Mabuiag, not all that far from the Trobriands (see fig. 13).

It was while studying the genetic transmission of color blindness among the inhabitants of the islands between New Guinea and Australia, long before Malinowski ever set foot in southern climes, that Rivers came to appreciate the wealth of information that could be gleaned by taking down family genealogies.[24] Indeed, with a name like William Halse Rivers Rivers, it is a little surprising that this famous *genealogical method* had not been appreciated earlier. Citing Edmund Leach, Michael Young says that it was hailed as an exemplar of the new anthropology, demonstrating "that fieldworking anthropologists were 'engaged in a science rather than in a literary exercise.'"[25]

But could not this appeal to science at the expense of literariness be not only misguided but reversed, that in asking for the histories of marriages and divorces, deaths and births, changes of residence, and so forth, going back in time as far as could be remembered, the questioner and the questioned might willy-nilly open up these and associated topics so as to discover a fountain of memories and unexpected things to talk about?

This newly minted genealogical method, potentially at least, opened up the research method to the influence of storytelling, idiosyncrasy, and wonder, it being by means of stories and chronicles that informants would respond to questions about their mother and father, brother and sister, and so forth.

It was a tragedy that this potential was rarely realized in actual ethnographic writing as storytelling. Certainly Malinowski himself soon abandoned the genealogical method as a shoddy gimmick prone to displace the more time-consuming, patient absorption of context.[26] Rivers himself, promoting the method, had stated the issue in hardly flattering terms when he said that the "savage mind is almost wholly occupied with the concrete."[27] What this hinged on was a peculiar reversal of the actual situation, it being the anthropologist, not the native, who was "almost wholly occupied with the concrete" on account of linguistic ineptitude and an underestimation of the insoluble problems of cultural translation.

The miracle is that Malinowski navigated through his bodily distress and mental despair to write us incomparable descriptions of color that, as "color," became great books with incomparably great titles, *Argonauts of the Western Pacific* and *Coral Gardens and Their Magic*. Much as he loved the outrigger canoes of the Trobriands, sailing as color on color where myth fell as waterfalls of sound transmuting into colors, he himself chose a single-hulled vessel and kept it sailing with an invisible flotation device, namely his diary, which, if published alongside his academically acceptable books, could have been called, in reference to the Trobriand color magic he taught us: *My Head, It Flares Up, It Flashes.*

17

tHe INStRUMeNt of etHNOGRapHIC OBSeRVatION

Actually it took me a long time to realize that the photograph of Malinowski in his whiter-than-white standoff with the wigged sorcerer is fake.

Maybe *fake* is too harsh. *Staged* or *theatricalized* would be more fitting. *Fake* comes out of my anger, feeling betrayed, first of all by myself.

Let me explain. All along I had been assuming that Malinowski ran around the island, interviewing people dressed in this outlandish gear, ridiculous or gorgeous, depending on your taste—flowing white shirt, white pants, light-colored puttees, and sometimes a light-colored pith helmet. The minute I put it like that, I realize how absurd it is. But for me it was not even an assumption. I was simply not aware of what I was doing. I had let the reality effect of the photographs swamp me, added to which was the fact that whiteness, after all, did seem de riguer for white men in the colonial world. Moreover, such images of Malinowski have long existed in the public domain quite apart from those glowing, whiter-than-white images recently brought to our attention in Michael Young's fabulous book of photographs, *Malinowski's Kiriwina*.

For example, there has long been circulating in public view a curious image of Malinowski in this quintessential colonial gear, fondling a make-believe phallus the size of a forearm. This image now emblazons the cover of the latest (1989) edition of Malinowski's *Diary in the Strict Sense of the Term*, made even more conspicuous by the bright orange background on which the image is set. But of course this image is not seen as bizarre, as sexed up, as comic, or as a wry comment on anthropology. It's just an ethnographer doing his thing.

Ensconsed in a group of Trobriand men on a platform, legs dangling, he sits dazzling white, this Malinowski of ours, fondling a whalebone limestick entering into a shiny dark gourd customarily used to hold the lime for chewing betel nut. The size of a soccer ball, the gourd sits in his lap. If I am not mistaken, now that my eyes have been opened, there is a faint smile on his face, as if enjoying a private joke. The practically naked chaps glowing black on either side of him similarly fondle lime sticks in the gourds sitting in their laps, though their sticks are a lot thinner than Malinowski's. Even the famous sorcerer Togugu'a is there (now wigless), sitting next to Malinowski, but now he looks stiff and unnatural as compared with the shot of him languid against the palm tree in "Ethnographer with a Man in a Wig." I rack my brains trying to guess what an average reader or browser is meant to think when viewing this in the bookstore. Certainly not *spoof*. Nor *fake*.

How suggestive it is that while we have this flagrantly sexualized-but-not-seen-as-such cover to the *diary* winking its eye at us, by stoic contrast the famous *ethnography*, *Argonauts of the Western Pacific*, displays as its first image an ever so respectable but desperate attempt to portray participant observation, this time with a black-and-white photograph not of the ethnographer's phallus but of his white canvas tent under palm trees on a beach at the end of a row of the islanders' palm-thatched huts.

In another shot in the series from which comes the cover of the diary, Malinowski's limestick and gourd has passed to the islander seated next to him, while Malinowski gazes fondly, or curiously, at the way the man is holding the stick delicately between his forefinger and thumb as it enters the opening to the gourd. In still another shot, Malinowski is seated in a row of islanders not with the gourd but this time with a briefcase in his lap. It seems like the natives can't compete with this artifact, which, unlike their gourds, requires no limestick.

One photograph has written on its reverse side, "Village scene (and Methods)." It shows a spectral Malinowski seeming to float in midair, stock still, in a sitting position, hands on knees, putteed legs outstretched. He is glowing in a soft white light catching at his few strands of hair. Beneath him sitting on the shadowed ground are some ten young people and children in neatly ordered descending height such that, like a Trobriand chief asserting rank, the ghostly ethnographer floats above them. Some method! Something insists he has to float on high, shimmering white, the effect being such that he even appears to be floating above the plane of the photograph—a spooky dream-image worthy of George Méliès, magician turned filmmaker.

Then there is another image of Malinowski complete with pith helmet and dazzling whites, all too studiously, all too ethnographically examining a necklace hanging around the neck of a Trobriander. This image, with nubile women replacing the men, appears without comment in a 1986 essay by one of the paragons of historians of anthropology, who would seem to accept and project this image as "typical Malinowski." It seems I am far from being the only naïf. Read the bland caption: "Bronislaw Malinowski with Trobriand Women."[1]

And what of the photographs placed by Malinowski himself in his own publications—such as the one deep in *The Sexual Life of Savages* (published 1929)

The Instrument of Ethnographic Observation

that I have already discussed, with "the sorcerer of some repute," and another in *Coral Gardens and Their Magic* (published 1935) showing him sitting on the raised platform of a Trobriand yam storehouse, immaculately white in his long-sleeved, flowing shirt and trousers, stock stiller than still, wearing what look like dark glasses, gazing fixedly at a group of almost naked islanders sitting alongside the platform, their skins gleaming black?[2] Inscribed by Malinowski himself as "The ethnographer with some informants . . . ," this image emits a curious yet pronounced authenticity, curious in that the authenticity derives precisely from the sharp difference between Malinowski and his seated companions, the whiter-than-white man side by side with his Others without much in the way of clothes but all the same dressed up with that fancy moniker, "informants." There he is for all the world, our ethnographer, doing his everyday thing, ethnographizing, sitting on the platform. How are we to know or even bother with the thought that this might not be a 24/7 practice?

But once the suspicion crosses your mind that this image like the photographs of Malinowski blazing white in *Malinowski's Kiriwina* are staged, and as such are wildly untrue to his everyday ethnographizing life, and once you start to look

at them with this in mind, focusing on the gestures, the facial expressions, the choreography, and the mise en scene—then you wonder how you could ever have been so silly as to have thought otherwise.

Mistakes—or rather "mistakes"—such as this teach you more about the way of the world than do attempts to spell out that way through direct revelation. What we have here inadvertently is our practicing on ourselves, if I am any guide, a type of autoshamanic conjuring; skilled revelation of skilled concealment.

More like parodies of ethnography, a cross between cartoons and spirit photography, such images seem a far cry from what came to be admiringly called, largely because of Malinowski, "participant observation." But maybe not! Maybe they represent the epitome of participant observation carried out under the aegis of dream images of possible scenarios, wild imaginings every bit as wild as the ravings we find throughout the diary? Here he is the White Man gazing into the eyes of the languid sorcerer by the edge of the lagoon; here he is again by almost-naked young women; and again sitting on a log fondling his stick-and-gourd alongside his native chums doing the same thing, all actors enjoying their dreamtime séance.

Something of this play is present in a charming and straightforward manner in a photograph of Malinowski's mentors from London and Cambridge, A. C. Haddon, C. G. Seligman, and W. H. R. Rivers, pictured at their field site on the island of Mabuiag in the Torres Straits between New Guinea and Australia some sixteen years before Malinowski set foot on the Trobriand Islands. Truly mischievous, even camp, certainly playful, this image shows five happy men, unkempt, barefoot, trousers rolled to the calf, posing for the camera not in pith helmets but in crazy-looking felt hats. They stand on the sand of a beach, palm trees in the background. Looking more like pirates than scientists, which they claim to be, only one of the five wears white, yet he looks more like a clown than a dour colonial fending off the temptations of bare feet and the loin cloth to which these rascals seem all too ready to succumb.

They are having fun with the camera, for sure, but they are far from staging ethnographers-at-work. And there is not a native in sight. Certainly not any naked ones. This is not parody. This is not a worked-out theatricalization of colonial realism. After all, these are self-confident Englishmen who fit right in. These guys are pre-Copernican in the sense that they precede the Great Revolution in Anthropology credited to Malinowski of "participant observation," and they boast no effort to fraternize with the natives, only with themselves. Yet it is the legendary "law-giver," Malinowski, who has been photographically preserved for posterity as dressed to the nines like a toy colonial official.

My critique, then, is not of Malinowski, but of myself. How could I have been taken in—especially given the fact that I myself used to wear thin cotton pajamas when I started off doing fieldwork up the Saija River on the hot and humid Pacific coast of Colombia in 1976. They kept the bugs at bay, were light, soft, and bright red.

Perusal of Malinowski's letters from the field takes us back to Joseph Conrad's split vision in the heart of darkness in the Congo; the white, starched executive in the central station versus the pajama-clad degenerate upriver. In a letter to his betrothed, Elsie Masson, in Melbourne, Malinowski described one of his rare visits to the mission station: "The three men [were] dressed in spotless white tunic coats . . . I was in ragged trousers with white socks tucked over the trousers, pyjamas coat, no tie, and a dirty coat over the pyjamas."[3]

Murray's nightmare come true.

In another letter to Elsie he described what he called his morning dress, con-

FIGURE 13. W. H. R. Rivers and colleagues on the beach in 1898. Reproduced by permission of University of Cambridge Museum of Archaeology & Anthropology (N.23035.ACH2).

sisting of "pyjama trousers and socks, the rest being exposed to the fresh air and stray mosquitoes."[4] Surprised in his tent by a European visitor by the name of Davis in May 1918, Malinowski confides in his diary that even though "unshaven and wearing dirty pyjamas I was able to maintain dignified manner. Walked with him a few steps."[5]

One of the nicknames given him by Trobrianders, *Topwegiglier*, means "the man with loose shorts," apparently, writes Michael Young, "because of his habit of hitching his trousers while trying to focus his camera."[6] What a turnaround! Instead of being photographed as the ethnographer, in this account gone as if by magic are the whiter-than-white duds and all the rest as he resumes his work-a-day outfit of oversized shorts or pajamas. There was another nickname as well, *Tosemwana*, meaning Showoff or Performer.[7]

The Instrument of Ethnographic Observation

Who, then, was this dazzling figure of fiction—this ever so nick-nameable Malinowski as photographed in the field performing fieldwork—whom Michael Young tells us placed most of the photographs of himself in the category "Intro. the Ethnographer," by which he meant "not simply to introduce himself as the ethnographer, but to situate himself in the introduction as the instrument of ethnographic observation."[8]

But to turn the instrument of ethnographic observation onto itself turns out not to be so easy. Who am I to myself? What story do I want to tell the camera, this same camera I have been using with great assiduity, taking picture after picture of the natives over two years? Here is Billy the pearl trader who likes taking pictures too. Give him the blessed camera. Let him gather pearls. Let him be the ethnographer of the ethnographer. Let him picture me as the ethnographic subject, but unlike the natives, I will be both the object and the subject. It is I who shall dictate the shot. Let us advance a little on that other game, the one called "participant observation." After all, like participant observation, parody mimics so as to gain distance as well as insight.

The closest thing to this that I know of in the anthropological canon are the migrants to Ghana from Niger in Jean Rouch's 1955 film of spirit possession, *Les maîtres fous*. Members of the Hauka cult, they become possessed by the spirits of white colonial officials and their wives. The colonial figures are thus mimicked—and parodied—with frothing mouths and frighteningly staccato movements and a staggering gait. Fritz Kramer has shown how this kind of enactment of Otherness, precolonial as well as colonial, was widespread in Africa.[9] But for the anthropologist to become possessed by the colonial officials is truly unique, a fine tribute to the spirit-possession magic of the camera, and a neat twist to the work of fieldwork.

The island was a stage, a time out of time, in which the participant observer, thanks to the camera, became the observed and, by the same token, the gaze was reversed so as to unveil the exotica and indeed the magic latent in colonial officials and missionaries as long-overdue objects of ethnographic curiosity.

And God only knows what Sir Hubert Murray would have thought of his anthropologist performing whiteness out of sight in the boondocks, alone except for the natives, the sorcerer Togugu'a and, of course, Billy the pearl trader, who left us these immaculate photographs. If it was Sir Hubert who minted that pointed principle of governance, "administration by bluff," it was Malinowski who took this bluff to heart. Not for him in these photographs the loin cloth or the soiled pajamas. No sir!

So this is my conclusion: they all seem to be enjoying this make-believe—the pearl trader and the sorcerer and especially Malinowski, whose love of irony, sarcasm, and wordplay was striking throughout his life. He switched from recording the customs of the natives to being recorded as one of those lords of whiteness who could form a magical axis with the sorcerer of some repute—as we see in the image I presented in chapter 13, *Ethnographer with a Man in a Wig*. Dark and languid, his skin shading off imperceptibly into the surround, stands the graceful sorcerer. Hands on hips, challenging him in the stance of sexual arousal, stands the anthropologist in the guise of a colonial official. Who is the more magical, the observer or the observed?

How conscious Malinowski was of this parody and to what degree it implied a critique we will never know. Certainly his diary provides abundant material critical of missionaries and colonial administrators. "Mentally I collect arguments against missions and ponder a really effective anti-mission campaign," begins one such thought late in 1914. "These people destroy the natives' joy in life, they destroy their psychological *raison d'etre* . . . No question but that they do harm."[10] Again, at the end of May 1918, towards the end of his fieldwork: "strongly unpleasant impression made on me by the missionaries: artificiality, cult of superficiality and mediocrity. *Character: 'secret society.'* In their prayers they mention the *Governor and G. in Council and legislation* . . . always 'we' for 'us,' and utilitarianism."[11] As for the colonial administration itself we find him towards the end of March 1918 speculating as to whether he could mediate between it and the islanders who see the colonial government as "a mad and blind force, acting with uncontrollable force in unforeseen directions. Sometimes acting as a farce, sometimes a tragedy—never to be taken as an integral item of tribal life. If Govt. could adopt this point of view, very well. But it cannot."[12]

And how much of his performance for the camera was drawn from the magic of mimesis and alterity he had observed in loving detail in the dance, magic, and play of the islanders? He must have been himself quite the performer anyway, to judge from one of his nicknames—*Tosemwana*, meaning Showoff or Performer.[13] To the degree he met the farce of colonial administration with his own form of farce and pantomime, it gives "participant observation" an entirely different feel from the way it has been taught to generations of anthropologists, and opens other novel and exciting ways of thinking about the work of fieldwork. One does not merely live in the village or help with daily tasks, play with the children, etc., but one acts up and one acts out. How curious, then, that this activity or way of being did not make it into the diary, but shares much in common with it. And how curious, too, that participant observation, so central to the discipline of anthropology, so revered and fetishized, included in each and every grant proposal under "method," is in fact never taught but left intangible and auratic, as if it is a secret only to be revealed to the initiated, by which time it is unnecessary and the initiated have in turn become guardians of the secret.

It would take decades of anticolonial struggle and of postmodern reformation of anthropology for *reversal of the gaze* to become a strategy, albeit short lived, of cultural self-awareness and self-analysis—a fine example of which is to be found nowadays, thanks to Tony Birch, in the Melbourne Museum, close to where Malinowski retreated for over a year halfway into his fieldwork in the Trobriands in 1917. Seated in a long glass case in the museum is a replica of one of Malinowski's patrons, that other "father" of anthropology, Baldwin Spencer, famous today for his forays into the central desert of Australia beginning at the end of the nineteenth century.

Captive in his glass case, Sir Baldwin surveys a horde of Aboriginal spears and an infinitude of boomerangs hanging in front of him from invisible threads. He is dressed in a white suit, a white tie, a white hat, and white boots. He is all scuffed up and dusted with the lightest white dust with a tinge of yellow, as if the desert blew white whiteness all over, and not what the desert really does, which is blow and glow red. Truth told, he looks a little sad. His body slumps. He has displaced the indigenous people he studied and become a trophy stuck in a glass case for all of the world to observe. And not just observe, but revere! Tony Birch's original plan formulated this nicely. But the museum people baulked. It was too much. His plan was to have an Australian aboriginal—a real, live aboriginal—stand in attendance of the diorama as guardian of a sacred site. Thus the living and the dead were to swap places, not to mention sacred sites, which in the case of Malinowski meant sacred suits—that white-on-white whiteness of soft fairy-dust-covered white suit, *that color of the sacred* that Malinowski wrought to auratic perfection in his standoff with the bewigged sorcerer of some repute years before by the side of a faraway lagoon in the southwest Pacific.

18

coLoR anD sLaveRy

One of the strangest ideas to come out of the colonial exploitation of Africa was "the fetish," a European makeshift word meant to grasp the essence of African spirituality as the worship of objects. The Portuguese slavers and traders of the fifteenth century, who invented the concept of the fetish, saw African rites concerned with trees, stones, waterfalls, thunder, figurines, charms hung on the body, charms hung in one's house, objects used for divination, and their many, many, medicines, this way—as fetishes, literally meaning *thing made* in the relevant European genealogy. Behind this label lay the Portuguese, or should we say the Christian, question: how could these people from whom they wanted slaves not see that these things were natural or made by men's hands and hence were not to be worshipped, an attitude reserved for God? Centuries later Karl Marx went so far as to say that the things we buy and sell on the market, things that we make or take from nature, have a lot in common with this fetish power, and Sigmund Freud drew attention to the visual conjuring tricks associated with sexual fetishism in the West whereby an object, famously a shoe or a corset worn by a man, garners its fantastic erotic charge from the way it both reveals and conceals the fact that women in general and one's mother in particular lack the male organ.

No wonder the fetish reeks with mystery—ours as much as theirs.

But what about color—ours as much as theirs—is it not the great fetish? Is it not a material thing with intense spiritual power? And just like the fetish, which we have hitherto reserved for *objects*, is not color the product of a colonially split world in which "man in a state of nature," as Goethe would have it, loves vivid color, while the Europeans are fearful of it? Either way, love or fear, we have something spiritual here, something that continues to influence world history.

Let me begin where so many statements on Africa begin—namely with *Heart of Darkness*—considered by many readers as the quintessential statement of colonial hubris and disillusion. Let me begin with its beginning, those sentences that connect transparent washes of light and color with tide and wind.

The day was ending in a serenity of still and exquisite brilliance. The water shone pacifically: the sky without a speck was a benign immensity of un-stained light; the very mist of the Essex marshes was like a gauzy and radi-ant fabric hung from the wooded rises inland, and draping the low shores in diaphanous folds. Only the gloom to the west, brooding over the upper reaches, became more somber every minute, as if angered by the approach of the sun.[1]

What is this gauzy and radiant fabric that drapes the low shores in diapha-nous folds? Is this not a little overplayed? Could we not simply say, "The sun was setting on the Thames?" So, what is going on with this fiery dousing of the sun? The disembodied voice, the slow, measured rhythm, the almost strange words become stranger like a hen picking up corn seed, words as objects, words as seeds—"Only the gloom to the west, brooding . . . ," all this slow winding up, laying in the pieces of a puzzle one by one, all this tantamount to saying some-thing else while taking advantage of the insinuations and echoes that come from saying one thing while meaning another; that this thrusting of fire into water, of light into darkness, concerns at its core Europe and Africa, and that this comes to rest in a thickness, a texture, a substance—as with that gauzy and radiant fabric from which color emerges as when transparent colors light up the darkening sky.

Goethe's painter friend Runge claimed transparent colors have a close affinity to fire and water and to whatever it is that makes the world anew, flare, and vanish. Contrast this with what he termed *opaque colors*, as when the narrator, known only as Marlow, comments on the European map of Africa circa 1890:

> There was a vast amount of red—good to see at any time because one knows some real work is done in there, a deuce of a lot of blue, a little green, smears of orange, and on the East Coast, a purple patch, to show where the jolly pioneers of progress drink the jolly lager-beer. However, I wasn't going into any of these. I was going into the yellow. Dead in the centre.[2]

It is the destiny of the transparent colors, says Runge, to play like spirits around these opaque colors. It is also their destiny, I might add, to bring out what I can only call the countermagic in Marlow's story.

For when Marlow got to the yellow of the center, what he found was not yellow and certainly not that fullness of a center—as in "dead center." What he found instead was a stranded Russian sailor dressed in rags, which gave him the astonishing appearance of a harlequin, "as though he had absconded from a troupe of mimes":

> His clothes had been made of some stuff that was brown holland but it was covered with patches all over, with bright patches, blue, red, and yellow,—patches on the back, patches on the front, patches on elbows, on knees, coloured binding around his jacket, scarlet edging at the bottom of his trousers; and the sunshine made him look extremely gay and wonderfully neat withal, because you could see how beautifully all this patching had been done . . . His face was like the autumn sky, overcast one moment, bright the next.[3]

The harlequin's beautifully stitched motley highlights the crazy patchwork of the colonial map of Africa. But while his body is covered with the colors of the map made bizarrely manifest, his face says something different. It suggests moody opalescent whimsy, a sign that you are going to lose yourself in this tale that, as Conrad strains to inform us, is not a tale with a secret that can be cracked open (as in his earlier story, "An Outpost of Progress") but is instead a story whose meaning lies "outside, enveloping the tale which brought it out only as a glow brings out a haze, in the likeness of one of these misty halos that sometimes are made visible by the spectral illumination of moonshine."[4]

"What saves us is efficiency," declares Conrad's narrator, Marlow, stuck in the muck of Leopold's Congo. But that thought doesn't last too long. Everything around him screams the opposite. So he breaks down, poor Marlow, another whitey takes it on the chin, leaving him the victim of morose metaphysical despair. He tries to express a big thought, "the fascination of the abomination." But no sooner has he got this out than his voice fails him, leaving it to Conrad to make one of his rare appearances as author, taking up the story: "He broke off. Flames glided in the river, small green flames, red flames, white flames, pursuing, overtaking, joining, crossing each other—then separating slowly or hastily."[5]

Marlow stops midsentence. And what fills the space, what ends the sentence . . . is color. Not just color filling already prepared forms. Not painting by numbers. Not color as a "secondary quality." But raging, ripping, tearing, color, diaphanous and ephemeral.

Green flames, red flames, white flames—pursuing, overtaking, joining, crossing, separating. This is how the "fascination of the abomination" manifests itself. It is also what George Bataille so often tried to express, "to lay out a way of thinking that would measure up to those moments . . . when the very heavens were opening."[6]

Could these flames be trade goods such as brightly colored cotton cloth exchanged for ivory—pursuing, overtaking, joining, and crossing?

Several times Marlow makes mention of a flow not out of but into the heart of darkness. This movement can seem no less self-generating and no less primeval than the mighty river Congo. "Strings of dusty niggers with splay feet arrived and departed; a stream of manufactured goods, rubbishy cottons, beads, and brass wire were sent into the depths of darkness and in return came a precious trickle of ivory."[7] As in an animated cartoon it seems that the goods move themselves. The colonized become little more than their splayfeet and, by some sort of logical but crazy connection, their feet then become the feet of "rubbishy cottons, beads, and brass wire." The humans disappear. Rubbishy cotton goods walk their way in. Ivory comes out. Who has the greater fetish, you ask, the natives or the Europeans with their ivory cut from the corpses of enormous animals so as to become false teeth, billiard balls, and piano keys? In "An Outpost of Progress," a story Conrad wrote two years before *Heart of Darkness*, the storehouse for ivory in the forest station of King Leopold's Congo is referred to by the company as *the fetish*, perhaps, Conrad says, "because of the spirit of civilization it contained."[8]

"I'd rather see it full of bone than full of rags," says one of the white men just arrived from Belgium.[9]

Yet the first thing the two new company officials in this story do to make their house feel like home in the African wilderness is put up red calico curtains, no doubt taken from the supply dropped off by the sardine-box steamer carrying "beads, cotton cloth, red kerchiefs, brass wire, and other trade goods." Otherwise such material is likely to be designated *trash*, as when Marlow in *Heart of Darkness* stands in awe one evening as "a grass shed full of calico, cotton print, beads, and I don't know what else, burst into a blaze so suddenly that you would have thought the earth had opened to let an avenging fire consume all that trash."[10]

Rags. Trash. Rubbishy cottons. Calicos. These are what the stranded Russian sailor, the harlequin mesmerized by Kurtz, is wearing, the colors of the map of colonial Africa, set awry. These are the brightly colored, cheap, and dye-fast cotton textiles first imported by the British East India Company into England in the seventeenth century, which, although suppressed by the Calico Acts of 1700 and 1720 because of pressure from wool and silk weavers, could be imported into England *so long as* they were *destined for export*—as to the colonies in the Caribbean or to Africa, where they played the major part in the African trade, notably the slave trade, and continued to do so well into Conrad's time at the end of the nineteenth century. There was considerable export of Indian "calicoes" to Spain from England, and thence to the Spanish plantations in the New World, as well.[11]

As for designating this cloth as "trash," Stanley Alpern takes strong exception, seeing such a judgment as a "patronizing myth" because "trash" signifies that Africans had either no taste or no bargaining power and that anything could be dumped on them.[12] Alpern insists that Europeans were forced to offer a wide range of quality goods for slaves, chief of which was so-called Indian Cloth. Moreover, African fashion kept on changing rapidly such that the outfitters of slave ships had to keep a sharp watch on what they carried. Africans were scrupulous in examining the goods, rejecting, for example, cloth that was either dyed or woven in France instead of India.[13] Hardly "rags."

Perhaps the situation that Conrad writes about was quite different owing to the degree of force that King Leopold could bring to bear with his 19,000 mercenaries recruited from the subject population.[14] Or was Conrad a victim of the prejudice that made bright colors anathema to men of refinement?

During the centuries of the slave trade, there existed a remarkable system of exchange as regards these "rags." Europeans bought slaves in exchange for Indian textiles, such as the famous Guinea Cloth dyed that brilliant, deep, dye-fast Pondicherry indigo from the Coromandel coast of Eastern India. Let one example as provided by Robert Harms suffice: almost 33 percent of the monetary value of the trade goods in the hold of the French slave ship, the *Diligent*, as it set out from Nantes for Whydah on the Slave Coast of West Africa in 1731 was fabric from the east coast of India. Approximately another 33 percent were the 7,050 pounds of cowry shells, a West African form of currency that also came from India, from the Maldivian islands, to be exact. What Europe itself supplied so as to acquire slaves was its brandy (constituting around 25 percent of the goods by value) and its gunpowder and guns (amounting to 14 percent). In addition there were sixteen cases of smoking pipes from Holland and ninety nine bars of Swedish iron.[15] Although at times the role of firearms in this trade must have been tremendous, the manifest of the *Diligent* and other vessels suggest that pride of place from the sixteenth to the nineteenth centuries goes to the Indian fabrics, which also served as a form of currency far into the nineteenth century when, in Senegambia, for instance, indigo-dyed Guinea Cloth was used by the French Army to buy provisions and favor in its thrust eastwards across the continent.[16] Like Alpern, Robert Harms emphasizes that "the problem was to pick just the styles and colors that were in demand along the Guinea coast that year."[17]

There was an unbelievable variety of colored cotton fabric from India that was used to buy slaves. Here is the beginning of a list in alphabetical order:[18]

allejars	usually striped red and white
baffetas	often blue or white
bajutapeaux	striped or checked; deep red, blue and white; blue and red; or flowered
birampot	red, blue, or white
brawls	striped blue and white
caffa	painted cotton, sometimes with floral designs
calawapores	striped, checked , or patterned, with red or blue predominating
calicoes	white, blue, or printed
cannequins	white cloth with red stripe at one end, some dyed blue
chasselas	striped or checked

chelloes	striped or checked, woven with colored threads
cherryderries	brown or blue or white with red or black stripes
chercolees	striped and checked
chintz	printed design, often floral
cushatees	striped blue and white or checked
cuttanees	usually striped and sometimes interspersed with flowers

Their names are beautiful to the English ear, and as astonishing as their seemingly unlimited number. Our language has been buoyed up—*chintz, cuttanees, chercolees, cherryderries*—a whole poetry of color on the tongue, short-circuited through the eye. It was a technical nomenclature, an invigorated trading nomenclature that reflected thread for thread an ancient art and craft of growing cotton, dyeing, and weaving that no European could hope to emulate until well into the nineteenth century. Some names live on, such as *chintz*. Others, such as *calawapores*, have died away, but when you try to say them, when you try to pronounce them, they return as beautiful but alien beings invested with the complexity of vivid color.

Then there were the beads. "The color range was enormous," writes Stanley Alpern, "white, yellow, lemon, orange, red, blue, green, and black, seem to have been favored as solid colors, black and white, yellow and white, red and white, green and yellow, red and yellow, and black and yellow, in combination."[19]

The slave trade thus owed much to the color trade linking the chromophilic parts of the globe, such as India with Africa. What's more, color had been used in exchange for slaves by Europeans long before. In early medieval times, slaves from Saxony and Thuringa, Brittany and Wales, England and Slavic Europe, were traded by Europeans for richly colored Byzantine cloth from the east, finely woven in rich brocades and often embroidered with gold and silver thread.[20]

Color achieved greater conquests than European-instigated violence during the preceding four centuries of the slave trade. The first European slavers, the Portuguese in the fifteenth century, quickly learned that to get slaves they had to trade for slaves with African chiefs and kings, not kidnap them, and they conducted this trade with colored fabrics in lieu of violence.

Furthermore, plenty of the slaves bought with color were put to work in the New World cultivating and processing indigo, the dye which at times in the Caribbean islands and Central America surpassed the monetary importance of sugar, even in eighteenth-century Haiti, "the pearl of the Antilles," from where it was shipped to France so as to color Napoleon's Grand Armée shipped to Haiti to fight the slave revolt. The slave colony of nearby Martinique supplied *rocou*, a plant native to that island, helping to ensure the profitability of the third leg of the triangular trade from the Caribbean back to Europe. The seeds were ground into a paste, which, when applied to white cloth, made dyes adhere more uniformly than to untreated cloth.[21]

I find it strange that what I tend to recall of European conquests achieved through trade in Africa as much as in North America is the seduction by brandy and firearms, not colors and clothes. I take myself here as evidence of the blind spot the West has in regard to color, which, to the natives of North America and Africa, comes across as no less sizzling than brandy and gunpowder.

This is not to say that color did not set aflame the European eye or soul as well. The French officers commanding the slaving vessel the *Diligent* in 1731, for instance, were on ceremonial occasions gorgeously dressed in a "blue, hip-length, sleeveless jacket over a shirt with lace ruffles on the sleeves; black breeches over crimson silk stockings; buckled shoes with red heels; a white satin scarf; and a black felt hat decorated with plumage."[22]

I especially like the red heels. But that is the color shot reserved for the ritual needs of soldiers and state ceremony, much of it based on empire, on primitivist color fantasy such as the scarlet uniforms, brass buttons, ostrich plumes, leopard skins draped over military drums, and the huge black bearskin hats of the British Queen's Coldstream Guards. The officers' bearskin hats have an eagle's feather inserted, colored red. Warrant officers have a cock's feather in theirs, while the lesser ranks have horse hair. Like sex, color is a conflagration to be held in check—restricted to the likes of soldiers striking a wild note of glory and glamour, mimicking the warriors, chiefs, kings, and wild animals of North America, Africa, and India.

Vivid color attracts the Westerner no less than it repulses. It is dangerous stuff—a highly charged fetish substance ready to explode as in that shed Marlow saw in Africa—"a grass shed full of calico, cotton print, beads, and I don't know what else, burst into a blaze so suddenly that you would have thought the earth had opened to let an avenging fire consume all that trash."[23]

Of course Marlow is sickened by the terms of trade, the rubbishy cottons being in European monetary terms but a fraction of what the ivory would be sold for in Europe. Yet it is *the rubbishy character* of the textiles that best expresses this for him and, to tell the truth, this character seems more important to him than the asymmetry of the trade. This is because to him these calicos are like addictive drugs and stand for the easy fix and pathetic superficiality that is attractive to people who, as he sees it, are not practical and efficient like him, carefully navigating his paddle steamer upriver continuously on the lookout for what lies beneath the surface. Color is for sissies.

Not so rivets, however—little marvels of sraightforwardness, simplicity, and functionality. A rivet is the antithesis of color.

Strong and functional like a rivet himself, Marlow groans while waiting by the river for rivets to fix his paddle steamer. He waits and waits.

But all that comes is color: "And several times a week a coast caravan came in with trade goods—ghastly glazed calico that made you shudder only to look at it, glass beads value about a penny a quart, confounded spotted handkerchiefs. And no rivets."[24]

As for *trash*, fast forward to the busy port of Marseilles, early twentieth century, as brought to you by the Jamaican sailor-author Claude McKay in his novel *Banjo*.

Marseilles may be bustling with rivets to spare, but there are many unemployed sailors hanging out there from the Caribbean and Africa, dancing their nights away and in no hurry to set sail. West Indian sailor Malty falls head over heels in love with Latnah. She is hard to place. It seems she speaks Arabic but it is when he first sees her dagger that he feels to its fullest measure how strange and different she is. This was not familiar to "his world, his people, his life. It reminded him of the strange, fierce, fascinating tales he had heard of Oriental strife and daggers dealing swift death."[25] Slowly it dawns on him that Latnah is Indian, meaning South Asian Indian, reminding him of the Indian coolies who worked the sugar plantations close to his seaside village. The men wore turbans and loin cloths. The women were weighted down with silver bracelets on their arms, necks, and ankles, their long glossy hair half-covered by cloth that people of African descent called coolie-red. "Perhaps," writes McKay, "they had unconsciously influenced the Negroes to retain their taste for bright color and ornaments that the Protestant missionaries were trying to destroy."[26]

Bright color indeed. Witness the main character, Banjo, himself, as introduced on the first page, walking along the breakwater in Marseilles, banjo in hand:

He wore a cheap pair of slippers, suitable to the climate, a kind much used by the very poor of Provence. They were an ugly drab-brown color, which, however, was mitigated by the crimson socks and the yellow scarf with its elaborate pattern of black, yellow, and red at both ends, that was knotted around his neck and hung down the front of his blue-jean shirt.[27]

Banjo falls for the Indian woman, Latnah, and she must feel warmly towards him, too, as we see when she gives him a present, "a pair of pyjamas all bright yellow and blue and black."[28]

Then there's that morning when he finds himself with no clothes worth showing off—"except for an American silk shirt with blue and mauve stripes, and, jauntily over his ear, a fine bluish felt that the mandolin player had forced on him."[29]

In fact the mandolin player is but the auditory aspect of color. Or is it the other way around? Certainly here music and color are not only woven each to the other, and to dance, as well, but to song—as when McKay tells us of the West African sailor-musician, Taloufa, singing with "a voluptuous voice, richly colored like the sound of water lapping against a bank."[30]

What is more, not only *color* comes from India to the descendants of the African slave trade in the Caribbean, but *magic* as well.

Could they be connected, even the same thing?

Following on his suggestion that the Indians had *unconsciously* influenced the Negroes to *retain* their taste for bright colors, McKay describes the *tricks* performed by these Indians in the British West Indies on the occasion of the annual holiday celebrating the emancipation of the African slaves in 1834. Indians performed athletic stunts and sleight-of-hand tricks, such as eating fire and unwinding yards of ribbon from their mouths, a practice that the magician Lee Siegel saw too, when he went to India in the 1980s when magicians would pull yards of brightly colored thread from their mouths.[31]

Some of these Indians were considered by the Negroes as more than sleight-of-hand artists, says McKay. They were priests and sorcerers, capable of manipulating supernatural forces and held to be even more powerful than the Obeah derived from Africa.

Worldwide, I believe, there is a significant connection between conjuring and such supernatural power, as with this self-extraction of yards of brightly colored cloth from one's mouth. We can imagine the wonder of this—streams of color being hauled out of the bottomless pit of a dark mouth—just like the polymorphous magical substance of the feathers of newborn birds that a Selk'nam shaman is reported as hauling out of his mouth on Isla Grande, Tierra del Fuego.

But the conjuring does not stop there. Not by a long shot. This mouth is worldwide and the colored streams of cloth, too, all the way from the east coast of India to West Africa, the Caribbean, and now here on this page as the image we need, the image we have found, for streams and layers of history come alive as a moment rescued from the flux of time. To read of West Indian Negro sailors in early twentieth century Marseilles remembering the Caribbean through layers of memory sedimented around an Indian woman, to feel the waves of memory radiating out from an erotic and mystical attachment to the bright-colored clothing and silver bracelets, associated with tricks—tricks as in the magic of sleight-of-hand, magic as in sorcery—is to bear witness to just such an awakening of the lost past. Enlivened by the fusion of color with the silver of women and the magic of the sorcerer, this fusion of Africa with India stretches back, "magically," we might say, "mimetically," we might say, to preceding centuries in which African men, women, and children were bought with color itself.

19

REDEEMING INDIGO

You ain't never been blue
No, no, no, child
You ain't never been blue
Till you've had that mood indigo.
"Mood Indigo," lyrics by Irving Mills

It is 1850 and the sea is but a distant memory connected by interminable water-ways. An Englishman with the improbable name of Colesworthy Grant is look-ing down on a bunch of Bengali tribesmen immersed chest high in an indigo vat. "I am puzzled to tell you what precise colour it really has," he says,

for being, like the sea, exposed to the sky, in like way its quantity and the state of the weather influence its appearance. When the beating com-mences, however, it generally presents a light green complexion. This through a variety of beautiful changes, gradually darkens into a Prussian green, and from that, as the beating continues, and the colouring matter more perfectly develops itself (the froth having almost entirely subsided), into the intense deep blue of the ocean in stormy weather.[1]

A long way from the sea, perhaps, yet so close. More than close, it encloses. The sea is change and the change is color—not color as an add-on or as an extra applied to a form, but color as that which pulls the observer into the observed, which may even include being pulled into time as in history. Why not, especially when what we are pulled into has gone and the future seems not far behind?

Is there any nature left? you ask. Is its disappearance what makes it so tempting? For the sea has long disappeared from people's lives. Now it's come back, as spectacle, something visual beyond the body, like a painting on a gallery wall. As a workspace the sea was beautiful but dangerous. It combined varieties of pleasure with varieties of pain such that both pleasure and pain were often cancelled out in place of an almost religious power, which both Conrad and Melville built their works around. Until fairly recently the sea was everywhere and a large fraction of humanity was employed by it. When I was a kid, Sydney harbor was full of working ships from all over the world and sailors and wharf-laborers could bring the country to a halt with their strikes.

As never before, world trade and shopping malls depend on ships. Yet the unions are broken, the workforce is minuscule, and the ships have departed over the horizon to remote industrial sites equipped to handle containers. Meanwhile the sailors and working-class people who lived close to the sea in the ports of the world have been pushed aside to make way for the rich who will kill for their ocean view.

I spent Christmas of 2004 in a lighthouse on a deserted island, home to wild pigs and horses off the westernmost extremity of Europe a few hours from Santiago de Compostela. The lighthouse keeper, who had two brothers working in the same profession, told me there remained but eighty lighthouse keepers in Spain and that she was the only woman. More and more the lighthouses are automated. In the U.S., I believe they all are; automated lights blinking their greetings of welcome and warning to what are basically automated vessels far out to sea. As we walked back to the lighthouse in the late afternoon, the sea alight with flickering color, she raised the fingers of her right hand between her eye and the sun setting on the sea. Between the sinking sun and the horizon there was room for two fingers only. At fifteen minutes a finger, she said, that means we have only half an hour to get the light of the lighthouse lit. These fingers are among the last sign of the human being as seafarer, fingers interposed between sea and sun as night blankets the ocean.

During the many years of the Franco dictatorship—a dictatorship essential to the U.S. as source of military bases—this island had been refuge to peasants fleeing the mainland. They had terraced the land and carved out a livelihood growing crops and raising livestock. It is said they lived better than people on the mainland. After the dictator died, the island was taken over by a relative of one of Franco's generals who expelled the peasants so as make the island into a resort. Where the peasants had built their tiny village, he built a crenellated wall a few meters high, suggesting a castle battlement. By the jetty he got workmen to construct a statue of a mermaid. But other than the lighthouse keeper, there were no human beings on the island anymore. Once I saw the new owner out to sea in a powerful cabin cruiser. It was a choppy day and his boat was pitching like a crazy thing as he circumnavigated his island.

There was life, to be sure, as with the farm animals gone wild. And there was the lighthouse keeper with her light sweeping in wide circles across the night, carrying its message of danger and comfort to the mariner. Yet all the more reason why the island seemed more dead than alive, a ghostly place inhabited by memories that I, for one, would be unlikely to access.

Nature does not so much disappear as exist in layers of such histories, with each layer written across the one before so that the earlier layers continue to be visible in a smudged-out and sometimes surprising ways. How curious that the wildness of the animals was itself probably due to this very same history whereby docile farm animals were now unapproachable, galloping in headlong flight or stock still at a distance like cardboard cutouts, a newborn foal nuzzling its mother's stomach. Through the dense undergrowth, the spiraling, burrow-like paths of wild pigs went deeper into nowhere, the beginnings of time itself, while overhead the white lighthouse kept time at a standstill. Surrounded by sea, history surfaced as prehistory.

Dialectical images such as these recast history as nature, the ideal as real. They come out of nowhere, it seems, as if by chance, making the present more present, the past more vivid, welling up within us as something alive. "There I have been," you might almost say. Yet redemption can never be final because the gap between the old and the new can never be closed. Writing worth reading is built this way, writing being a continuous confrontation with the past that evoked it. Such is the reflection of the sky in the sea. Such is indigo.

My empire for a dash of blue! In 1789 the French colony of Saint-Domingue, now Haiti and Santo Domingo, had close to 1,800 indigo slave plantations in its western province alone.[2] Not sugar but indigo was the chief export for this colony whose colossal historical resonance to the present day is, however, invariably associated with sugar.[3] By the eighteenth century, thanks to indigo, naturally lightfast and fadeproof, blue had become the uniform of work and authority.[4] Have you never wondered why our cops wear blue, other than to hide pizza stains? Napoleon's Grand Armée imported 150 tons of indigo to dye 600,000 uniforms a year. A century or more before that witnessed the invention of what has become fundamental to modern culture worldwide, as natural as the air we breathe; *denim* and *jeans* made from tough linen and cotton twill dyed in indigo: denim, so it is often said, coming from Nîmes (France) as in *serge de Nîmes*, jeans from *genoese* or *gene fustian*, *fustian* probably derived from the Egyptian city of Fustat, old Cairo.[5]

Old Cairo in our very jeans' bottom! Impossible to imagine, for the name takes us back to long before Napoleon, whose army overran Egypt, back to the European Dark Ages when the nobility was ready to sacrifice a great deal for the colors, textiles, and spices of the Orient. We are often told that European imperialism began in the fifteenth century with the search for oriental spices by such famous sailors as Vasco da Gama and Christopher Columbus seeking sea routes to get at the pepper, nutmeg, cinnamon, ginger, cloves, and saffron closed off by high tariffs imposed when the Ottoman Turks took over much of the Muslim world. The Portuguese got around this roadblock when they dropped anchor off India in 1498. Venice and the Muslim world never recovered.

What is not so commonly realized is that this trade with Europe has a far longer history than Vasco da Gama and Christopher Columbus, stretching back at least to the eighth century AD, and that it included color in addition to spices, with Baghdad, for example, becoming the center of the indigo trade. By the thirteenth century, caravan routes connecting India (hence *indigo*) and the Middle East to the ports of Venice and Genoa, Amalfi and Pisa, were carrying what today no less than back then seems quite magical: dyes and colored velvet, silk, damask (from *Damascus*), muslin (from *Mosul*), baudekin (from Baghdad), cotton (from the Arabic *qutn*), taffeta (Persian, *tafta*, meaning silken cloth, to shine), satin (*zaytuni*), and mohair (from the Arabic *mukhayyar*, meaning choice or select).[6]

Names such as *damask* or *muslin* carry with them a tremor. Exotic yet familiar, they stress the English-speaking tongue in unusual ways. Stripped of their history no less than of their place-reference, such as Damsascus in Syria or Mosul in Iraq, they have become naught but names, less than names, really, just sounds, we might say, yet for all of that, and indeed because of that, something else hovers in the aura that the sounds can, on occasion, provoke.

The tongue remembers, but you do not. Life moves on while all around you lay traces of lost eras, active in the present, hanging on the wall, covering the windows, not to mention the couch on which you sit or the dress that you will wear tonight. *Damask.* My dictionary exudes meanings from the fifteenth through nineteenth centuries: the color of Damask Rose; the color attributed to a woman's cheeks; a blush; rosewater distilled from Damascus roses; a rich, silk fabric woven with elaborate designs and figures, often of a variety of colors.[7]

Color cannot easily be separated from substance—polymorphous magical substance, we might say—from silk fabric, the face, perfume, a woman blushing, rosewater, roses . . . What's forgotten yet seems strangely familiar as something arcane and mysterious is not only the city of Damascus so far removed but the constellation of wonders designated by *damask*. You ask yourself: what happens if one tries to redeem both name *and* constellation? The name opens like a flower. This is something more than relating facts about the past, something more than reading off meanings in a dictionary.

Nor can color be easily separated from spices, another form of polymorphous magical substance. The European spice trade with the Orient meant a whole lot more than spices (a word derived from the Latin *species*). It meant dyestuffs, perfumes, and medicines, as well as condiments, a trade in which dyestuffs represented "a major portion of the overall spice trade."[8]

If historically color has been categorized as a spice, as in the phrase "the spice of life," a phrase suggestive of a "rush" that takes us out of ourselves, like a drug, it is exceedingly curious that this association with color should have been forgotten in our usual understandings of the rise of the West to economic and military prominence. Color was every bit as important as so-called spices, if not a great deal more so, and indeed could be as highly valued as gold and silver.[9]

Indeed this rush of color, like the rush of a stimulating drug such as cocaine or coffee, is there in our language and history, as with the profession of the drysalter in eighteenth-century Britain. A "vital adjunct of the textile industry," such a man dealt chiefly in dyes but also in drugs. Many dyes had medical uses and, in addition to those, the drysalter traded in pure medicines as well, such as licorice juice, talap, and quina-quina. Drysalters in fact called their wares "drugs," sometimes specifying "dye-drugs."[10] It comes as a shock to read that the first entry under "drug" in *Webster's Dictionary* today is "substance used in dyeing," the second, "substance used as medication."

The drysalter was located at the centerpoint of colonial trade. Take the marvelously named Miles Nightingale, a British drysalter in the eighteenth century, most of whose dye-drugs were imported, many from Africa, the Far East, and the New World, as evidenced in this list.[11]

indigo, from Central America and the French Caribbean islands
Cochineal, from Spanish plantations in Mexico, three crops a year of the female
    insect (70,000 of which yielded one pound of dazzling dye)
gum lac, an insect-derived resin from Bengal, Assam, and Siam
turmeric, a powdered root from Java, China, and Patna, northeast India
dyewoods, such as the red-yielding *logwood* cut down in several places in the
    New World, as by that pirate, natural scientist, and later officer in the British
    Royal Navy, William Dampier, working with runaway slaves and Indians in

the Yucatan and Nicaraguan swamps while awaiting the next piratical foray
with Henry Morgan in the late eighteenth century

other dye-rich woods, came from Brazil, Colombia, Cuba, Tobago, Jamaica, as
well as from Africa, such as Angolan *barwood,* and Sierra Leonean *camwood,*
and from Asia such woods as *redwood* from the Coromandel coast, *saunders*
from India, Ceylon, and Timor, and *sapanwood,* from Siam, the Coromandel
coast of southeast India, and the East Indies

gums, such as *gum arabic* from Alexandria, Tripoli, and Morocco, and *gum*
senegal[12]

Drysalter Miles Nightingale may have gotten his indigo from Central America
and the French Caribbean islands, but when Haitian slaves and black freemen
overthrew French rule, and when, shortly thereafter, the Spanish colonies on
mainland America fought the Spanish to a standstill, indigo production shifted
to the British East India Company such that India, now the world's most brilliant colony, reasserted what had been its sixteenth-century predominance in the
indigo trade with Europe. Yet indigo carried the seeds of revolt there too. The
"blue uprisings" on the Bengal indigo plantations just after the Indian Mutiny
of 1857 are now the stuff of legend, categorized recently as "one of the mightiest
peasant revolts in the sub-continent."[13] Ghandi's first civil actions in India, kicking off the independence movement, were on behalf of indigo workers in Bihar,
the state neighboring Bengal. As for the legend, take note of the blue elephant
deployed by the British indigo planters, many originally from the slave plantations of the West Indies, themselves often beholden to the aristocratic Bengali
landlords known as *zamindars,* collaborators of the Raj.

The blue elephant is indigo. Big and blue, it strides purposefully forward
on scrolls painted by Bengali folk artists, stamping down mustachioed rebels.
Fantastic, indeed, yet true, elephants were used as weapons of war to put down
strikers. No less fantastic, and no less true, is the demonic nature attributed to
indigo as a self-willed monster by an otherwise sober analyst of the revolt who
remarks that it was the peasants, "inevitably a marauder's first kill, who were
hurt most as the wicked weed fought, burnt and litigated its way into paddy-
fields, residential plots, county paths and the borders of village ponds—lands no
tyrant had [until then] laid his hands on."[14]

By then indigo from Bengal supplied most of Britain and some four-fifths of the world. For thirty years, from 1820, Bengal indigo was surpassed as an export only by opium, a government monopoly.[15] Money was advanced to small holders, displacing crops such as wheat, chickpeas, corn, or rice. Each factory required dozens to hundreds of laborers, tribespeople or *buna* coolies, for its preparation. Unlike indigo in the West Indies, it was not grown on slave plantations but by share-cropping tenant farmers.

Like "sugar and spice and all things nice," as my childhood rhyme has it, indigo and opium make a nice pair, a stunning metaphor of the fabulous Orient in Western eyes, a coincidence to conjure with when picturing the colonial exotic, because with opium you can enter into the image, which is to say, into the natural history of blue, elephant and all, a passage enhanced by smell—for example, the nauseating smell of indigo during harvesting and fermentation. Even snakes avoid indigo plants and, by the same token, it is said that working with indigo reduces a man's potency.[16] Given that elsewhere in Asia where indigo dye and indigo-dyed cotton fabric is in the hands of peasants and artisans, men are often prohibited from the worksite and the vat is associated magically or symbolically with the uterus and with childbirth, this allegation of impotence is significant.

According to Colesworthy Grant, sheaves of indigo plants six feet long were crushed and placed overnight in vats of clear river water, where they were steeped for ten to twelve hours, depending on the temperature of the warm night air. In the morning the water level had risen some six inches on account of the swelling of the plants, while the surface of the vat presented, he says, "a strange mottled appearance in colour—principally of purple and coppery hues, partially covered with a bluish froth."[17] Both the color and the temperature— frequently measured with a thermometer— indicated when the steeping had gone far enough.

Something quite miraculous then occurred as the fluid was drained into the lower of the two vats, known as "the beating vat." To Mr. Grant it appeared as a dull, or sometimes bright, orange, along with a "horrid odour." Spreading across the floor of the vat, the orange was "exchanged" for a "bright raw green, covered with a beautiful lemon-colored cream or froth."[18]

Here in the vat color goes crazy, overflowing its accustomed categories and cascading into other sensory realms, seriously jeopardizing the attempt of the observer to stand his distant ground and not be dragged in. Color is not only heat but texture, and not one but many textures, all exceedingly strange such as *yellow cream* and *yellow froth*.

From the remote Indonesian island of Sumba, east of Bali, we hear of the same wonderful changes in the indigo vats there—indigo vats managed entirely by specially initiated nonmenstruating, nonpregnant women, and forbidden to men—with the indigo solution dissolving and fermenting first as yellow to light green, then, as the cloth soaked in it is withdrawn and allowed to hang, the pale greenish color oxidizes to a deep blue such that the more often the cloth is soaked, the blacker-blue the final color.[19] Indeed the term there for the color produced by indigo, *moro*, designates a *range* of color from blue-black to green.[20]

Color here will not stand still. Indeed, it is not so much color that is changing here in the indigo vat, but change itself that is on view. With his innumerable experiments with pinholes of light and heating metals, Goethe reached this view of color surpassing itself, too, as when he boiled chocolate:

> we see a small circle appear, which is yellow in the centre; the other remaining coloured lines move constantly round this with a vermicular [meaning wormlike] action. In a short time the circle enlarges and sinks downwards on all sides; in the centre the yellow remains; below and on the outside it becomes red, and soon blue; below this again appears a new circle of the same series of colours: if they approximate sufficiently, a green is produced by the union of the border colours.[21]

His experiments, which seem as much playful games as laboratory science, opened up color, took "it" out of the straitjacket of the spectrum so as to release its spectrality in the same way as the vats of effervescent indigo. Witness the perceiver becoming part of the perceived. Second point: the wonder. Third point: change, flow, and heterogeneity in a constant becoming. And fourth point: a following of the trace, like a hunter, or a student, open to chance.

We may try to trap color in the vat of color categories, green, yellow, or blue, sometimes bright, sometimes dull, but it—this "it"—eludes us because it is in continuous transformative flux. We may try to trap color as an entity existing apart from the substance in which it inheres, but this thing proves inseparable from that from which it is supposedly distinct and, as if to hammer home this point, this composite color-substance keeps changing, one minute mottled, one minute blue froth, next minute lemon cream, with other composites on the way.

But the all-pervasive stench, yes! That is constant, it being smell like color that melts the barrier separating the knower from the known, this smell that is nauseating, driving off snakes and potency. This would seem even more extreme than losing oneself in the Other. It is more like "being at sea," lost and confused and on the verge of throwing up, hoping that insides become outsides. To be nauseated is to be persistently on the verge, "ontologically disconcerted" our philosophers might say, if not disconnected. On the island of Sumba this was said to be the stench of the rotting corpse.[22]

Now the indigo is ready for its beating. Stripped to the waist, tribesmen jump into the vat up to their chests so as to beat the liquid with bamboo paddles for two hours. Two hours! It looks plenty hot in the photograph I have, showing two men, probably English, in white pith helmets and spotless white duds looking down on the coolies beating the blue. Why, one of them could even be our eyewitness, Mr. Colesworthy Grant. As for the tribesmen, their chests are naked. Their ribs stick out. They are lined up in the vat to form three neat rows, arms aloft, elbows out, holding tight to their paddles. They are as near as you can get to human machines—dancing machines, dancing in stench.

It can only get worse. The surface of the vat swims before your eyes, warm stench of rhythmic chaos on the move, and intimate, very intimate with the human body in motion. Girded by a necklace of blue foam a foot high, the vat is in violent commotion:

Every conceivable variety of action is given by the men in order to make the beating perfect. They range themselves *vis a vis*, and advance, beating until within four feet of each other—then retreat to either end, generally beating in the opposite direction to their companions in front, lest by all beating in one direction, the force of so many oars together should drive the liquid—too precious to be wasted—over the edge of the vat. They will face to the right—then to the left—changing hands as they do so—then range themselves in one line, and beat from end to end,—then divide again and divide into two as at first—then form a circle, and beat towards each other—"retreating, chasing"—like the figures in a quadrille, and then travel in a circle, until the whole contents of the vat are in a whirl.[23]

As they advance and retreat along with this incandescent wave, their bodies blue, the tribesmen sing what Mr. Grant deems obscene songs and give voice to vehement cries.[24]

Here the record halts. We can go no further. Why obscene and why songs?

What might the *words* of the song mean? How do they relate soundwise and meaningwise to the vehement *cries*? Could this singing and crying be the place, we could call it "obscene," where the poetry of men at work meets the poetry of nature?

Something similar to the mysteries of the indigo vat comes across in the scene portrayed by the Baron of Aubonne, Jean Baptiste Tavernier, traveling in Bengal two centuries before Colesworthy Grant. The baron noted that the workers who sifted the indigo so as eliminate all sand, dust, and foreign matter "hold a cloth in front of their faces, and take care that all their orifices are well closed, only leaving two small holes in the cloth for the eyes to see what they are doing." Both the sifters and the clerks supervising them drank milk hourly, "this being a preservative against the subtlety of the indigo." The workers who were at this for eight or ten days or more would spit blue for some time after work. An egg placed near a person working an indigo vat would, at the end of one day, be found to be altogether blue inside.[25]

An egg! Who would have thought it? Like the canary in the mine to detect toxic gas, the egg here provides the warning. Everyday science at work. Imagine cracking open your hardboiled lunch and finding instead of a nice, smooth, all-the-same egg white, a putrid blue. Blue food! Worse still, imagine a blue yolk! No doubt chemistry can explain this diabolic penetrative power of blueness, but can it explain the chill or the unseemly mix of metaphors: the masks, the eyes, the milk, the blue spit, and the blue egg? What medley of history and horror, science and poetry, is hereby made manifest in this "subtlety" of indigo?

Small wonder that worldwide the indigo lends itself to sexual and magical ideas, such as scaring off both snakes and potency. I read that so as to cure a failed vat, the women of the High Atlas in southern Morocco spread "blackness" in the form of malicious lies so as to outdo the spirits involved in damaging the vat, a practice said to be widespread during the Madras presidency of India as well. In European and American dye manuals one finds advice such as "not to hurry her, or to work her as strong as at the first." In some third-world folklore the vat functions thanks to its intimate connection to biological reproduction. Men may be forbidden to get close, as in Ireland, in Syria, and in the famous indigo-cloth-producing island of Sumba, east of Bali, where only nonpregnant, nonmenstruating women are allowed, the indigo-making process being considered "akin to the conceiving and bearing of a child."[26] Indeed, in some Indonesian islands, a bundle of indigo cotton cloth substitutes for the uterus, in stories, at least.

You who read this are no doubt beyond such superstitions, as we like to call them, referring instead the whole seething mass of petulant color to chemistry, as this vat that is a uterus steadies itself before its next metamorphosis in which color becomes something bigger than color, in fact no longer "color" but a composite force, first dark orange, then light green shifting to dark green, which, on being stirred:

appears of a greenish or bright olive; so that I am puzzled to tell you what precise color it really has, for being, like the sea, exposed to the sky, in like way its quantity and the state of the weather influence its appearance. When the beating commences, however, it generally presents a delicate light green complexion. This, through a variety of beautiful changes, gradually darkens into a Prussian green, and from that, as the beating continues, and the colouring matter more perfectly develops itself (the froth having almost entirely subsided), into the intense deep blue of the ocean in stormy weather.[27]

Color here takes on a life of its own, a life "more perfectly developing itself," a life ever more lively such that, finally, as a product readying itself for the market, it comes to resemble the intense deep blue of the ocean in stormy weather. More than resemblance, even more than an affinity, this connection to the ocean seems one of kindred spirits. Our eyewitness does not say it is *like* the color of the ocean but, as I engage with his language, it *is* the ocean.

And the identity is not just with the ocean, if I may put it this way, but with the essence of the ocean to the extent that the blueness of the blue hauls in the entire ocean, the color here being bigger than the biggest ocean. As in some science-fiction movie, the signifier (blue) has swallowed up the signified (the ocean). No longer is the ocean exclusive home to giant serpents, whales, even dragons. Blue swallows them whole and it does so because it is inseparable from action as expressed in substance, this substance that is both liquid and plant, liquid and human. This is enhanced because of the characteristics the writer gives to the ocean, which is not just blue, but intensely and deeply blue, and is not just the ocean, but the ocean storming. Giving substance, character, and passion to the ocean in this way assures the correspondence between the color as color, as when we say "blue" or "red," and the color as something alive, flowing and moving, like polymorphous magical substance.

As viewed by the man looking down on the vat, this view brings to the fore the art of nature, the recognition of which has been occluded by modern chemistry. It is as if the feel for materials, for the delicacy of physical changes in substances, and the questions those changes pose to our own selves and relationships to nature, have been cast into oblivion. The more scientists know about nature, the less we have of a connection.

As regards this occlusion, the appreciation of color occupies a peculiar position, perhaps because it has always been defined as something "poetic" and is therefore, like love, resistant to reductions executed by scientific language. But no matter how stormy love can be, it can't come within a mile of the oceanic storm of the indigo vat. Goethe had his bubbles of boiling chocolate and the red-hot steel blade of his penknife turning blue. More mundane lovers have their rainbows with pots of gold at the end, others may even have double rainbows, mirror images of each other, but how limited these scenes of color seem when compared with the cinematic and olfactory picture Colesworthy Grant presents us of the kaleidoscopic Bengal indigo vat, so beautiful, so horrific, so otherworldly.

His is the view of the man on top looking down into the vat. It is not the view of the tribesmen dancing in the vat with blue up to their chests. The tribesmen are immersed in the sea he sees. He is not. He is looking from without. He is still, except maybe for his eyes. The tribesmen are not still. They are not voyeurs. They are part of the action and they make action. They make it with their beating with bamboo paddles for two hours and they make swirling waves with their dancing. They sing as they dance and they dance in unison. They utter sharp cries and sing obscenely, we are told. Making action like this, they are also acted upon by the action of chemistry, the oxygenation of vegetating matter by means of time, temperature, and the effects of their motions. Colesworthy Grant may be a long way from the sea, while the tribesmen are enclosed by it. Yet he is infected by them. The sea is closing in on him too. And through him, it closes in on us too. The sea has not disappeared. It is an eternal return. For are we not, in our mind's eye at least, gazing at Colesworthy gazing at them?

The tribesmen sing and dance. We can assume that this is often their custom when engaged in collective work. They bring something like poetry and ritual into the work situation. But now the work situation is different. They are working for the British, who don't dance and don't sing at work and don't get into the vat, but instead watch them as a spectacle in which the tribesmen's Dionysian performance is displaced from the performers to the ecstatic green-turning-blue liquid itself.

Where did it all go, the songs, the cries, the surging sea of green becoming blue in scenes of wonder and cruelty? How much more cruel has been the not-knowing and the forgetting, such that we could have no idea of the long march from a plant in a faraway field in the tropics to its fate in a vat and, ultimately, its fate to dye clothes? Can we retrace the steps? Is it not time for blue to exert its magic and sexuality, its fearsome impacts on snakes and potency, so as to undo that which would cast it as "color," sans history, sans density, sans song? If it could penetrate an egg and make men cough blue, this beauty that is indigo, how much more likely is it to penetrate history as a silent symbol ensconsed in a color chart? When will we cough blue?

In 1834 an oil was extracted in Germany from an evil-smelling waste product of coal and given the name of *aniline*. An intriguing substance, somewhat like the mythical philosopher's stone of the alchemists, but this time for real, it held out the promise of redoing nature from top to bottom in one grand mimesis, synthesizing just about everything that had previously been obtained from raw nature so as to create second nature. Aniline not only spawned all the colors of the rainbow within a few decades, but, as a result of the discoveries in chemical color, massively expanded the depth and reach of capitalist industry, transforming the face of the world. Yet this very same substance had been found in indigo itself a few years before and how curious it is that the word *aniline* rests on the Sanskrit name for indigo, *nila* (meaning dark blue and darkness), carried into the Arabic, *nil* or *an-nil*, thus entering into the Spanish as *añil*. Equally strange is that our eyewitness all along here is called Colesworthy. Even as he was gazing down into indigo swirling in the vat in Bengal, the German chemists in Germany and London were fabricating color from coal. Coal's worthy indeed!

There is a tortured relationship here. The new dyes that replaced the old ones not only hang onto the old name but make it even older, or older sounding, resurrecting the Sanskrit. Truly, the modern gives birth to the archaic and the proliferation of mythology. Beholden to the past by nomenclature as much as by chemical genealogy, the new colors destroy the means of production of the past, but the trace of the past is there and necessarily so, as the exotic nature that informs color in the modern and not-so-modern world. Take the *sky* blue and *mint* green of the revamped *Wall Street Journal*, mouthpiece of all that stubbornly fights against the real sky and what it means to be green.

Sure, it is long since gone, this story of blue. It no longer seems relevant, like the storyteller whose art lay in the fact that the story was embedded in the person telling it. To have blue reinstall itself in the swirling stench of purple and copper hues, in that violent mix of beauty and grand horror of the Bengali vat, not to mention in magic and sex, is this what Walter Benjamin, that avid enthusiast of the magic of color in children's books, meant when he said at the end of his life that "nothing that has ever happened should be regarded as lost to history," that the "true picture of the past flits by. The past can be seized only as an image which flashes up at an instant when it can be recognized and never seen again"?[28]

So let us add spices to the equation, the enlivened palate to the dazzled eye, mix them together as in the Middle Ages and in the feverish European demand for colonies. Throw in smell, too, as with what you get standing in an indigo vat under a hot Bengali sky—what then happens to our sense of the senses when they are blended the one with the other, let alone with such history? How can such a mix be reduced to physiology or a body out of history, a taste to taste-bud reaction, color to a retinal bleep? Does not world history enter into the innermost physiological essence of such buds and bleeps—just as world history is itself made out of the passion for such sensations?

This is what lies behind Goethe's early nineteenth-century observation that primitives, kids, and southern European women love vivid color—because color is something that gathers together all that is otherwise inarticulate and powerful in the bouquet of imagery and gamut of feelings brought to mind by the "Orient," meaning that impassioned Othering at the heart of colonization with its undertones of the faraway, adventure, and the tropics. And how fascinating and instructive that while Goethe emphasized the preference for black and white in the Europe in which he lived, it was the love of blues and reds, greens and yellows, that, along with condiments, animated Europe's aristocracy in earlier times, while indigo, so hugely important a commodity for some two thousand years, this blue that is also black and purple, became the color that supplanted color when, beginning in the fourteenth century, the aristocracy (male and female) used indigo to have their clothes dyed deep black in a widespread process of European decoloration in both Catholic and Protestant countries.

As blue, indigo crossed class lines as well, becoming the color of sailors and workers. With Napoleon it became the color of war. After the soldiers came the police, pretty much the world over, and then, in one mighty crossover, indigo went from being the color of uniforms to becoming, in addition, the uniform of the anti-uniform "casual wear," the jeans worn today by most of the people most of the time the world over, rich or poor.

Levi Strauss, the man without a first name who invented jeans in 1853–55 in San Francisco, dyed *genoese* imported from Europe with indigo. Ten years later he switched to *denim*, which even as late as the 1870s was being dyed with indigo, the cloth being so dense that it was only able to partially absorb the dye, thus giving the pants a faded color upon washing, which lent them even more prestige. In fact, when the forbears of the infamous German chemical corporation IG Farben invented an economically priced indigo-like blue in 1904, displacing plant-based indigo, manufacturers of jeans continued to provide a faded appearance by means that were no less artificial than the new color.[29] Phony old, phony indigo, who cares? For it *looks like* a living color, bearing the trace of a fermenting vat as used in the making of wine or cheese and it makes for living pants that graft themselves onto you, thanks to their faded, intimate, character. But whether bought new as faded or not faded, there is little that can compete with a well-worn pair of jeans in this regard. Faded blue, with holes in the knees and bottom, they are truly part of yourself, your body no less than your history. Only thing missing are the sharp cries and obscene songs, but sometimes there is that, too.

Indigo was the "crossover" color par excellence; from the Orient to the European ruling classes, from being one color among several in a medieval color-filled world of the wealthy and the churches in the West, to a colorless world of blacks and blues thereafter, from the ruling classes to the working classes, from soldiers and police to the uniform of the anti-uniform, from its deep blue color to all colors thanks to aniline-based dyes replacing natural dyes, from a commodity to something animate and intimate that aged with its owner—which is why indigo is the color that undoes itself as that past that "can be seized only as an image which flashes up at an instant when it can be recognized, and never seen again." That sense of color is what it would take to redeem indigo and write the color of history, something you might consider next time you slip into the blue of your blue jeans—that "intense deep blue of the ocean in stormy weather."

To slip into the blue of your blue jeans is to slip into history, not the history of this happened, then that happened—but rather what Nietzsche had in mind with his complaint that nobody had yet written the color of history. To slip into the blue of your blue jeans is to slip into a surprising and unexpected encounter with the past—old Cairo in your jeans' bottom—but without your having the faintest idea of what you are slipping into. Where might such affinities reside? How might they be awakened and in that sense redeemed?

Josef Albers spent most of his life in the twentieth century studying and teaching color, and I find him a help here for he says a color changes when a changing sound is heard.[30] Could it be, then, that not only the dancing and beating but also the sharp cries and songs of the tribesmen have a part to play in the marvelous color changes occurring in the indigo vat?

Let us extend Albers here and suggest that the most changing element in the changing sound that affects coloring is not only the vehement cries but their obscenity, because it is obscenity which radically changes the register of being.

The photograph I present of the vat is surely no less obscene than the songs are alleged to be, although in a quite different manner. In the photograph the obscenity could be said to be in the gaze of the sahibs in their breeches and pith helmets looking down on the tribesmen immersed in the vat. But there is more to it than this, as there always is with so-called obscenity. The obscenity lies in the way this gaze registers the beauty, the strangeness, and the horror of indigo vegetating, oxygenating, playing, we might say, playing with light and air and with the dancing of those strong arms and legs. This is the mixture of beauty and horror that Conrad's Marlow in *Heart of Darkness* would call "the fascination of the abomination," at which point language fails him and colored flames running across water take over.

As for that other obscenity, the songs of the tribesmen in the vat, it seems that obscene songs are often associated, perhaps the world over, with collective labor. This is what I take from the anthropology of Africa, for instance, whether it is women at work or men at work, as described by Laura Bohannan about her time in Tiv lands in Nigeria in the 1950s. Men were frightened to get too close to the women weeding together, singing their lusty songs.[31] Many years before, Evans-Prichard had tried to analyze the close association between obscenity and work, both skilled and unskilled, collective and individual, in a wide variety of African societies.[32] Although it is not clear what "obscenity" specifies in this and other writing on the topic, what is clear is that the song and the situation provide sexual license. Prohibition is suspended. "Many of them are too obscene for inclusion," noted Louise Cramer with respect to the West Indian work songs she collected in the Panama Canal Zone in the 1940s.[33] Why this link between work and obscenity exists is a matter for prolonged debate, but what I would like to propose is that we should here understand obscenity as not only transgression of sexual boundaries or rules of pollution, defined in terms of the more obvious erotic zones, but as transgression of bodily propriety more generally understood—by which I mean the sexualized body of the world, including, of course, the human body within that body. We need also to bear in mind that to transgress is not only to lift a taboo temporarily, but is also to feel its weight, charged with the conflictual and exciting currents societies muster when taboos are put to the test. Then the whole world looks different, as does the language attempting to describe this state. Hence more sharp cries and song.

To work on nature—whether it be women weeding a field while singing in Tiv lands in Nigeria, threatening, with hoary laughter, to sexually attack any man who ventures close, whether it be men in unison beating indigo in a vat in Bengal, or whether it be that select elite of magically knowledgeable women in east Indonesia working the indigo vat akin to the uterus and childbirth—is to partake sexually, so to speak, in the inner life of materials. All labor has something of this quality, this eerie intimacy with things and with motions inseparable from the thing we call mind, only we take it for granted and rarely notice it until hit with it broadside from the colonies and from other sites of manual labor where the mix of horror and the fabulous makes us sit up and take note.

Magic is sometimes said to be just this dazzling fusion of the human world with the thing world too, although the work is likely to be more involved with theater and incantation. But here in the Bengal vat, it is work, hideous and extreme, yet something beautiful and worth writing home about, no doubt. The collective nature of the work is an integral part of this too. The bodies move like one as in a chorus line in time to the music that brings the social and the natural worlds together.

It is the density and intimacy of the interaction with the inner life of the object world that astounds me, the harmonies and self-transforming movements of animating materials confined by the vat, exploding into obscene song and color. This is, I think, what it means to "redeem indigo," listening to those names, those sounds, is what I mean, sounds that trip the tongue with long-forgotten accents and meanings—such as *damask*—for, as Josef Albers says, a color changes when a changing sound is heard at the same time. To redeem is to be obscene, working with the inner realities of histories as brought forth by indigo, mother of all color.

20

OPIATION of THE VISUAL fieLD

Color is a colonial subject. Let us put aside for the moment the Great Colors such as the deep, deep blue of *indigo* from India and from the slave plantations of the New World, or the fiery scarlet of *cochineal*, its name derived from the Aztec word *nochezli*, "blood of the prickly pear," extracted from those millions upon millions of female insects crawling over Mexican cacti. Let us for the moment focus instead upon a minute fraction of the foot soldiers of color, that multitude of colored varnishes and their fantastic names that you can read about in today's textbooks for artists:

> *Gamboge*, a resin from trees in Thailand, which is a clear, bright, transparent yellow
> *Dragon's blood*, from the fruit of an Asiatic tree from Singapore and Batavia, which gives to varnishes a ruby red and dates from Roman times

Gum accroides, also known as black-boy gum or Botany Bay gum, which comes
from Australia in a golden-yellow color as well as ruby red
Shellac, from twigs of trees in India, where it is deposited by insects that feed
on the sap
Elemi, which is white, the best coming from the island of Luzon, and is called
Manila Elemi to distinguish it from inferior varieties found in Brazil,
Mexico, and the Yucatan

Leaping from the page in a sighing and a soaring of sound, these names take
you into the living interstices of the third world and beyond, to where saps run
and insects dig their way in. Together with Burroughs's aromatic inks laced with
hashish, blood, and opium, the provenience, properties, and names of these
varnishes suggest how much we diminish our sense of the world if we do not
recognize that like spices and furs, gold and silver, lapis lazuli, slaves, and feathers, the most desired colors came from places outside of Europe, *exotic* places,
we call them, meaning *colored* places.

Thanks to varnishes from the colonial world, light could be trapped and bent
through transparent or semitransparent layers that dilute, fix, and change color.
In cherishing the art of our Van Eycks and Vermeers on account of their layer
after layer of varnishes trapping light such that, like the skins of the islanders studied by Malinowski, color glows from within, might we not therefore
reserve some portion of our regard, no matter how small, for the layered history
of Western expansion into the lands of colored people, home to all manner of
bright colors and wondrous varnishes?

This love of light splayed and diffused through trapping and layering was not
restricted to artists like Van Eyck, hard at work in their studios changing the
way we see. It also came to change the way we are seen—as with the European
craze for *Indian fabrik*, one generic type of which came to be known in English
as *chintz* and which has been described by an early twentieth-century British
scholar, Maciver Percival, in terms reminiscent of Vermeer's varnishes, not to
mention Marcel Proust, who claimed with much passion that his writing style
was inspired by Vermeer's layered use of varnishes.

It was their color that made chintzes so special, and not just color but their
play with color. Maciver Percival enthused how this color-play makes and breaks
the claims of form. Color shakes itself free.

The beauty of old Indian 'painted calicoes' lies first of all in their colour, which is the first thing to strike the eye. Lovely rich tones of rose, from full crimson to delicate shell pink, purple fading to palest lilac, blue of the softest, fullest, hues, and to these there were added the originally rich green and a citron yellow, though these have faded by now.[1]

The words limp behind the color sprite. Note how the tones skip and jump from one another into one another—full crimson to delicate shell pink, then purple, fading, fading, fading, to palest lilac as we mourn the fate of rich green and of citron lost to the elements. The writer has been gotten a hold of by an extra-body experience, it seems. He could be high.

How narrow minded of generation after generation of economic historians to have seized on cotton fabric as a trade good, what Karl Marx would have called its exchange value as a commodity, to the neglect of its brilliance as a "use value," meaning the magic of its softness and the color it liberated, set loose upon the greyness of the social worlds of Europe. Because modern, factory-based capitalism got off the ground an account of cotton cloth, this is no small matter. How prophetic, then, that chintz—or should we say color—first entered the European world as a form of money!

And what beautiful money it was, being used as such in the spice trade in the islands of the Dutch East Indies. Following the Portuguese and the Dutch sixteenth-century strategy of finding ways of getting into the long-established Asian trade between Asian ports, the British East India Company swapped cottons dyed in India for spices in the Malay archipelago where, because the economies were not monetarized, cloth from India was used instead, a process repeated in Africa with the European trade in slaves. Later, in the early 1600s, it occurred to Europeans to try out the European market, which met with such success that all manner of obstacles were placed by the producers of European cloth, such as the wool industry and the silk weavers.

Of course, since the Middle Ages, the European aristocracy had had its trade routes with the Middle East, India, and China so as to acquire brilliantly colored silks and velvets. But in the seventeenth century, with the opening of the sea route to India, vivid and, most importantly, dye-fast color became affordable to a much larger segment of the European populace on account of cotton, and this to the degree that a new family of clothing words was thereby born for Euro-

Figure 16. Detail of chintz. Courtesy of the Avery Architectural and Fine Arts Library, Columbia University.

peans—words such as *dungaree, gingham, sash, seersucker, shawl,* and that ever familiar friend of the night, *pyjama,* such as Malinowski wore during the day in the Trobriands when Sir Hubert Murray, fearful of white men breaking the dress code, was not watching.

From 1600 to 1800 "India was the greatest exporter of textiles the world has ever known, and her fabrics penetrated almost every market of the civilized world."[2] To date, the history has been cast as one of *fabric.* But it could just as well be cast as one of *color*. This is why it makes sense to think of India as having a big part to play in European notions and feelings for colors in particular, for color in general, and why color, too, is a colonial subject.

It was said in the West that *from time immemorial* in India a "perfect method" for printing color on cotton cloth was employed, first explained to Europe in 1742 by a French missionary, the Jesuit Père Courdoux, then elaborated by the Dutch, from whom French and English printers subsequently learned. This learning process, such as it was, took a long time, over a century from when cotton cloth began to be exported from India to Europe. The cloth thus printed in England was called *Londrindiana*, while in France it was popularly called *Indienne*.

Europeans imitated India. In some respects their designs were almost the same: the tree of life, peacocks, snakes, birds, and bamboos, "all taken over bodily from Indian chintzes."[3] But even when some of the coloring methods used in India were learned, it is said that "their chemical rationale was not fully understood and painstaking imitation was impossible."[4]

How much of this was a question of the technology, and how much a question of attitude towards speed and materials is hard to say. The Indian method of dyeing used a millennia-old knowledge of *mordants*, the chemicals used to fix colors. This was not only to prevent colors running with water or fading in the sun. We could also think of it as a form of drawing or painting using a liquid medium instead of pencil or paintbrush. By having the mordants in certain places in the cloth and not in others, and by using wax softened in the sun so as to penetrate the cloth and keep the mordants and dyes from the waxed area, the artisan could construct not just a colored but a multicolored design of great complexity. The designs I have seen stand out not so much because of a clear outline, say of a bird or a flower—there is that, to be sure—but even more so because of what I would call a "dazzle effect" in which a rippling variegation is ceaselessly at play.

To achieve this could take months for just one piece of cloth. There were no cylinders or wheels rolling out the design so as to speed up the process. It was as if the colors demanded a meticulous, hands-on approach and this was, overall, an approach to life and work inimical to the rhythms of work inculcated by the capitalist industry of the West. At root, this attitude to speed and materials is perhaps part of a philosophy and a religion that makes for the fundamental difference in color appreciation that so struck Goethe when he more or less divided the colonizing world from the colonized world by the criterion of chromophobia. In music, no doubt, we would find analogies as well.

The speed of color printing was compared by Europeans to that of a snail inching itself across the cloth millimeter by millimeter. Entire families, writes Audrey Douglas, "were accustomed to work for months at a minimal wage to create the intricate beauties of a chintz that would prove invaluable in a European market."[5] Such slow deliberation of speed, or rather nonspeed, suggests an intimacy of the artisan with the colors, the mordants, the wax, the sun, and the weave of the cotton cloth.

Little of this, of course, gets consciously registered by the consumer, whose talent lies elsewhere, as with the "chintz room" in English homes. According to Percival, an old English house without a chintz room was like *Hamlet* without the Prince of Denmark. And, like Hamlet, there is a mysterious, moody, and conflicted aura in such a room, for chintz, writes Percival, "at once brings to mind visions of colour bright and gay, yet soft and subdued withal, of dark gleaming mahogany, honey-colored oak, walnut of mysterious grain, reflected in the polished surfaces the tints and hangings . . . in a word, all the surroundings of a typical country house."[6]

Strong stuff. What we have here is the viewpoint of a person passing into matter via color "bright and gay" such that, remarkably, the part completes the whole. The chintz—from India—comes to beautifully complement and establish the whole English country house.

This mix of "color bright and gay" with the "subdued withal" is a reminder of how wrongly we recall Kipling—east is east and west is west and never the twain shall meet—for here they blend nicely, ever so nicely, and generate in ever more subtle tones this mix, as in the gleaming mahogany, the honey-colored oak, and the walnut of mysterious grain.

Just as the house had to have its chintz room, so, we might say, the English person, as a moral entity, and the English body, as a material one, had to have their chintz rooms, too, although of course here I am speaking poetically or metaphorically. It is as if the Orient was like one of William Burroughs's color viruses, insinuating itself into English oak like the grain of the wood itself, and just as inseparable. I know of no concept that can do justice to this subtlety, for the final result is *oh so English*—the "typical" English country house—yet to achieve this perfection and splendor has to be *oh so Indian*, as well.

Everything is combined so as to become all the more separate. This I call the chromophobic law of color, with its effervescent charge not only of repulsion but also of attraction as engendered by color, no less than by the Orient. This same law is at work in the way that Indian artisans were encouraged to change their colors so as to satisfy English taste—such as changing red backgrounds for white—with the paradoxical result that the English devoured the Indian cloth as exotic and authentically Indian.

For Percival, the lovely thing at the core of this circuitry was that which "*at once brings to mind visions of colour bright and gay.*" This enthusiastic language of visions suggests an almost mystical force, one capable of propelling persons beyond the confines of the chintz room—as indeed happened in a typical country house in Yorkshire in the north of England, scene of England's first detective story in the middle of the nineteenth century, *The Moonstone*, written by Charles Dickens's good friend, Wilkie Collins.[7]

In this house, a magnificent diamond has been stolen from the young woman to whom it had been bequeathed, a diamond with a long-standing curse upon it. Known as the Moonstone, it had been torn from its sacred location in India in 1799 by a British officer at the battle of Seringapatam, the victory that allowed the British East India Company free reign in India from then on. The person or persons who stole it have never been found, although for a long time suspicion has fallen upon mysterious Indians lurking in the neighborhood.

I myself may be poorly informed, but it does seem a little strange to me to have Indians hanging about in Yorkshire in the mid-nineteenth century. Just hanging. And lurking. And, of course, mysterious. Powerful as the spooking Orient may be, there is some added juju here, that's for sure.

Here is how the juju is made manifest. Exactly a year after the theft, rich, young Franklin Blake lies in an opium-induced sleep in this typical English country house where the theft occurred. He is being closely observed by a lawyer, by the lovable head servant of the house, and by a mesmerist (a type of hypnotist)—the perfect triumvirate. It is their hope that, thanks to the opium, the young man will rise from his bed and, in a sleepwalking trance, repeat step by step his actions of a year before. For in his conscious reckoning, Franklin Blake has no memory whatsoever of what he did that evening exactly a year before.

The perfect triumvirate has a hunch that a year ago to the very hour, young Franklin, under the influence of opium slipped into his drink by the real thief, had, without being aware of what he was doing, removed the diamond from the sleeping heiress for safekeeping, a well-intentioned action which lead instead to its theft by someone spying on him. A complex story. The perfect triumvirate thus hopes to clear him of suspicion and even locate the Moonstone.

It is a terrible thing, this Moonstone. It wreaks death, madness, deception, secrecy, and malevolence. In the words of the lovable, loyal servant, "here was our quiet English house suddenly invaded by a devilish Indian diamond . . . Whoever heard the like of it—in the nineteenth century, mind; in an age of progress, and in a country which enjoys the blessings of the British constitution?"[8] It is as if the Moonstone is alive with a mind of its own.

It is not only its humongous size but its humongous color that enables the Moonstone to have a mind of its own. Its color is beauty and its color is danger, something we call sublime, even sacred, but which in your typical English country house would tend to be passed off as superstition or as "Indian"—and all the more terrible for being what we might call "repressed sublime." But why do I emphasize its color so much? To the lovable, loyal servant who saw it one year before, it is not the size but the light—the self-generated light and, with it, its color—that provides the essence of the stone, for the "light that streamed from it was like the light of the harvest moon. When you looked down into the stone, you looked into a yellow deep that drew your eyes into it so they saw nothing else."[9]

Drawing you into the image, precious stones like the Moonstone share properties with the way colored illustrations in children's books are said to affect the young reader.[10] Like the rainbow, such stones are the epiphany of color, "transparent color," which grants to precious stones the twists and turns of their fate no less than their ability to twist fate like the light that courses within. These stones live the life of color, prophecy, and mystery, as when Benjamin quotes from a story called *The Alexandrite* by Nikolai Leskov, "Look, here it is, the prophetic Russian stone!" screams the gem cutter. "O crafty Siberian. It was always green as hope and only toward evening was it suffused with blood."[11]

The overwhelming majority of precious stones came from European colonies, ex-colonies, or remote stretches of Europe's periphery of snow and tundra, such as Siberia. In their exuberance, like the stones taken from India that became British crown jewels, precious stones stand with unparalleled power as signs of the triumph of colonial plunder, precisely the history that sluices through the Moonstone ripped from its sanctuary in India.

Now, one year later, it is almost midnight. It is raining, same as it was that night one year ago when the diamond was stolen. It is quiet. The clock ticks. The

FIGURE 17. This is how I imagine young Franklin Blake's chintzed-out bed. Courtesy of the Avery Architectural and Fine Arts Library, Columbia University.

three men watch without talking while the man on the bed tosses and turns. It is like a stage upon which British colonial fantasy is ready to explode.

And how is the stage set? *It is set with chintz.* The opiated man tossing on the bed is enclosed on all sides of his bed by chintz curtains. He sleeps in a chintzed-out world. This is his own, personal chintz room, we might say. Sure, the Moonstone is a tremendous thing. But the exquisite box containing him, this chintz room, is ever much more so.

As master of ceremonies, the mesmerist half draws the chintz curtain on his side so that by placing his chair a little back, "I might let him see me or not see me, speak to me or not speak to me, just as the circumstances might direct."[12] This is the beauty of the chintz room; by adjusting one's angle of vision, one can appear or disappear at will, "as circumstances might direct." One commands as if by magic the visual field and can choose when and how to let that command become visible. Thanks to a little push from opium—and the mesmerist's uncanny influences—Indian chintz in England would seem to be the fulcrum of the visual. More than that, chintz in England provides access to the illusions of light, to seeing, and to the strange tricks of the visual field. A remarkable feat.

To be seen and not be seen, as circumstances might direct. To see and not be seen . . . Is it a coincidence that Britain's first detective novel, *The Moonstone*, set in Yorkshire and London, is seeped in and framed by India, and that what makes it such a brilliant and emphatically such a *detective* novel with its cliffhanging mix of logic and superstition is precisely this motif of not being seen seeing as well as of being able to manage when one is seen and not seen? A century later, with Poe, Baudelaire, and mid-nineteenth-century Paris in mind, Walter Benjamin would single out the urban crowd as the medium in which the detective story was born. In a crowd, too, a person can "be seen and not be seen, as circumstances direct." Poe stalks the man in the crowd. He has fog and anonymous bodies pushing and mingling in the streets of London as afternoon passes into night—against which Wilkie Collins brings us light pouring forth yellow, drawing us in. The point is neither the deception nor the voyeurism—but rather the opiation of the visual field, emblematic of the chintz effect, meaning the color effect, inducing trance states and doppelganger switchbacks of being. What better way to recover the Moonstone—with its "yellow deep that drew your eyes"—than with its equivalent, this chintz effect, whose mysteries lie far beyond any detective or detective novel?

21

sex appeaL of tHe INORĢANIC

With the first shipment of colored cotton fabric from India to Britain in the ships of the British East India Company in 1602, it seems that color was desired and despised in equal measure. What one discerns most readily in the published record are the protests by the silk and wool weavers in cities such as London and Canterbury, protecting their trades—but by no means was this simply a protest against cotton in favor of silk and wool. Color was no less at issue here. It beckoned to beauty and flair and being somebody else, something new. Color meant the Orient, in particular India, and it had to be contained.

A nice instance of the schizophrenia involved here is the colorful vilification of colored cottons—using color to dispatch color—alongside what one close student of clothing at this time has called "a generalized distrust of color in European culture."[1]

But what, then, is such "distrust"? Surely distrust implies attraction, too, a defense against attraction? This gets to the hub of the problem, the problem of color in modern and not-so-modern Western culture.

Rich and poor, Catholic and Protestant, north and south, it was pretty much the same distrust of color throughout Europe, although more marked north of the Alps. Yet it is the very monotony of blackness and colorlessness that makes the momentary spasms of color-lust so revealing.

Explosion of color is how Jane Schneider summarizes the Italian Renaissance dress, which, with a few exceptions, such as the Medici ruler of Florence and the noblemen of Venice, consisted of "parti-colored garments in which the sleeves were of contrasting colors, the pants legs also, and the body still another color. Garments, now intricately tailored, were slashed with hundreds of cuts to reveal a different color layer underneath."[2] And why *slashing*? Does not this term suggest the most powerful hunger for color release, plus the resistance it had to overcome? Hundreds of cuts! Slash away, my friend, my color-loving fiend, slash that black and get to the color.

No matter how short-lived this color explosion was, it had a far longer parallel in the sacred coloring invested by the Christian religion in the stained-glass windows of its churches. There, at least, vivid colors found a niche, to the glory of God, striking tribute to the idea that, as with children and "man in a state of nature," such color was too wild for ordinary Western man and had to remain ensconced in the sunlit color streaming through the walls of the church.

Equally revealing was the resistance to color following the arrival of Indian fabrik in England. Journalists such as Daniel Defoe demonized such cloth as a threat to the core of the nation.[3] Representing the most extreme form of "effeminate luxuries of the east," such fabrik was said to be causing a hemorrhage of bullion as well.[4] "As ill weeds grow apace," stated Pollfexen to the board of trade in London in 1696, "so these manufactured goods from India met with such a kind reception from the greatest gallants to the meanest Cook Maids, nothing was thought so fit to adorn their persons as the Fabrik from India."[5]

The virulence of these sentiments tells you just how powerful was the current running the other way, with men protecting women and gallants from the seductive power of Orient color. Certain it is that in seventeenth-century Britain, it is women who are singled out for punishment for their passion for color, as with the Calico Act of 1700 (beefed up in 1720), which prohibited "the wearing of any printed or dyed calicos whatsoever, *whether printed at home or abroad*, and even of any printed cotton goods" (emphasis added). "All Silks and Calicoes, except such as are entirely White" were prohibited.[6] The act of 1720 made it illegal to use or wear "all printed, painted, flowered or dyed calicos in apparel, household stuffs, furniture or otherwise."[7] On the other hand, such textiles could be imported and stored in bonded warehouses for re-export in order to buy slaves in Africa.

Anyone wearing the colors made possible by light cotton cloth would be fined the staggering amount of twenty pounds sterling, while informers would receive a reward of five pounds, equivalent at that time to four months' wages.[8] It is said that people wearing calicoes ran the risk of having their clothes torn to pieces.[9] Whether fact or fantasy, the image is riveting.

France prohibited colored calicos and calico printing, as did other European countries, but not Holland. Yet many European women broke the law, beginning with the wives of ministers and ladies of the French court, "passionately fond of wearing painted calicoes," but "too much" color could well mean one was a prostitute—which effectively makes the point about the danger of color.[10] Choice chintzes were smuggled into England directly from India or via Holland, like cigarettes across the Canadian border into upstate New York today, or like cocaine from Colombia.

Imagine being informed upon to your local police officer for wearing a nice, colored cotton skirt or shirt while strolling down the Broadway, or for having a clandestine fashion show behind locked doors? This sheds light on today's war on drugs. Imagine the prisons upstate full of African American and Hispanic young men found guilty of selling colored shirts. The hype against Indian color involving such inordinate penalties is the same as the current hype against drugs, especially in the U.S.

Is it that much of a surprise that in England color-work was handed over to the "untouchables"? The first color printing factory in England, printing onto cotton cloth imported from India, was set up in 1690 on the river Thames by a Catholic Frenchman who had spent time in Holland, learning from Dutch masters, before coming to England. He employed a great number of men and women, deemed "a saucy and independent lot," mostly French Catholics, and hated, as my source says, "on both accounts."[11]

The very name, *calico*, shows the same love-hate relationship to color. With the flurry of excitement for these beautiful fabrics in the 1600s, consequent to the British East India Company importing them to England, the term *calico* meant, in the trading lingo of the time, "an Indian stuff made of cotton, some-

Sex Appeal of the Inorganic

times stained with gay and beautiful colors." But nowadays, continues my *Oxford English Dictionary*, nowadays in England it refers "chiefly to plain white unprinted cotton cloth, bleached or unbleached." In short, over time *calico* has been stripped of color and anglicized. Chromophobia triumphed. How could it not, given exclamations such as the following in the early eighteenth century, attributed to one J. Roberts in the aforementioned dictionary, referring to calico as: "a tawdry, pie-spotted, flabby, ragged, low-priced thing called Calicoe . . . made . . . by a parcel of Heathens and Pagans, that worship the Devil, and work for a half penny a day."

On its etymological trajectory to colorlessness, calico here is not only un-Godly—that's pretty clear—but is subject to a process of disgust and degradation whereby it becomes something eerie and way more than a mere "low-priced thing." It's more like the sort of thing you hold gingerly between your fingertips with one hand, the other clenching your nostrils or shading your eyes. There is little reason for us to take Mr. Roberts seriously at the expense of his rhetoric, for it is precisely the rhetoric that is worth thinking about. Calico is so splutteringly goddamn awful that it effuses spiritual power. The Devil also comes colored.

Color here cannot be separated from filmy, flowing substance. This stuff from strange lands, this thing called *cotton*, held out the utopian promise of lightness-of-being, a new human body that flowed and floated in swathes of color that were, by and large, not only dye-fast but cheap as well. They were beautiful. Both sides. Awed by the "enormous quantity of very transparent muslins" being exported to Persia, Turkey, Muscovic, Poland, Arabia, Grand Cairo, and other places, Jean-Baptiste Tavernier, Baron of Aubonne, traveling in Bengal in the 1630s, went on to describe them:

> Some of these are dyed various colours and ornamented with flowers, and women make veils and scarves of them; they also serve for covers of beds, and for handkerchiefs, such as we see in Europe with those who take snuff. There are other fabrics, which are allowed to remain white, with a stripe or two of gold or silver running the whole length of the piece, and at each of the ends, from the breadth of one inch up to twelve or fifteen—in some more, in others less—it is a tissue of gold, silver, and of silk with flowers, and there is no reverse, one side being as beautiful as the other.[12]

It was color, every bit as much as the filmy flow of the cotton material in which it inhered, that excited attention. Like a law of nature, like Nietzsche's "eternal return," cotton repeatedly performed the rainbow trick, converting the women of the West into beautiful flowers. Thanks to India, Europe now had an entire climate change, a spring after millennia of grey winter.

Jules Michelet saw a species change in the women of France. "The great and fundamental revolution," he wrote in 1846, "has been in cotton prints." Whereas before a woman was restricted to wearing blue or black, "now her husband, a poor worker, covers her with a robe of flowers for the price of a day's labor. Whereas the great promenades were formerly in mourning, today they are ablaze in the dazzling colors of the iris."[13]

As far as color was concerned, cotton was extraordinarily user-friendly. Compared with silk and wool, cotton not only held color fast, but prior to cotton, colors in the West had usually been restricted to *solid* colors, often in a *somber hue*.

But now, how different the world becomes, a world of many colors and most especially a world of *light transparent colors*, doubling the transparency of the cloth itself as color and substance blend with light and lightness. What this added up to was a qualitative shift in the Western psyche, creating what today we call *fashion*— fashion being what three centuries later Walter Benjamin, in his idiosyncratic way, would perceive as the death ritual of the commodity, meaning that frenetic search for newness in consumption and in public display, which has, as its precondition, instant obsolescence.[14] Nothing is more dead than yesterday's fashion. Indeed yesterday's fashion functions not merely as an *anti-aphrodisiac*, according to Benjamin, but as "*the most radical anti-aphrodisiac imaginable.*"[15]

What this implies is that the erotic element in fashion is dependent on a life-and-death speed-up, a situation that would lead us to what Benjamin calls the "sex appeal of the inorganic," taking us into the world in the same way that Jean Genet enters into the image and undergoes animal metamorphoses, especially when sexually aroused. This is the adult equivalent, let us surmise, of Benjamin's child who passes into pictures, thanks to their color. And now, thanks to calico and chintzes and the great East India Company, now your ordinary European can do the same thing, or come pretty close to enjoying this sex appeal of the inorganic.

"Fashion prostitutes the living body to the inorganic world," is one of Benjamin's memorable statements in this regard. It is as if we have been sold, or sold ourselves, to the extrasocial world of substances and things, becoming extensions of that world, or at one with it. And Indian fabrik, meaning colored cottons, meaning color, is the exemplary instance—if not cause—of this "prostitution" of the body to the inorganic world.

It needs eccentrics like Benjamin to catch this, of course, and it is the same as what underlies my effort to present color as an animal and as polymorphous magical substance. For, as I see it, color fits uncomfortably into the bifurcation of reality into subjects and objects. That, after all, was the source of both Goethe's irritation and wonder. It was as if color had somehow fallen through the cracks of Western self-making and the everyday sense as to the makeup of the world. Nobody could decide if color belonged to the subject or the object, or whether it was visual or corporeal. Then came India. Then came the colonies. And what India supplied and what the Orient did was to potentiate this indisposition of color and allow everyman—or, should we say, everyman's everywoman—to indulge the trickster quality of color, adding to it the aura of those mysteries by means of which the West envisioned the magic, the strange gods, and the colorful rites of colored people. Such fancy had best be held in check. Restrict it to the fair sex, but not excessively, for that way lies the image of the painted woman. Keep it in the chintz room, isolated from the rest of the typical English country house. Such is the color of the sacred, like the altar, fenced off by the danger it exudes.

Part Three

cOLOr IN prOUSt

22

CROSSOVER MEN

If there was one artist who had an eye for women's fashion, it was Marcel Proust. Indeed we could think of his book on memory as not quite a novel and more like a woman's dress, memory lying in the conjunctions color and cut make with nakedness adorned, the dress being where inner and outer worlds, nature and culture, are brought together. Is it because of this hybrid—half book, half woman's dress—that crossover men like Goethe's soldier recently returned from America unexpectedly pop up in his work? Meet Mme Swann, for instance, "practically a coquette," writes Proust, meaning a high-class whore, now respectably married to multimillionaire Jewish Swann, whom she has led in a merry dance of betrayal and anguish. Well of course he's done more than his share of betrayal, too. And he still sees his mistress. But now Mme Swann has put all that behind them. Yet is there not an indefinable something that clings to her, the secret of her past that, in some perverse way, bestows nobility? It seems that her meteoric rise in society has made her an object of resentment, yet also of wonder.

For is she not, our Mme Swann, a skilled imposter in the higher ranks of Parisian society, a society Proust defined as similar in the inflexibility of its many gradations of pollution and purity to the caste society of India? And could this be why she is so often depicted as dressed in one of the greatest imposters of modern life, *mauve*, the color that almost as soon as it was invented gave birth to the rainbow of artifice?

Here she comes, on her Saturday lunchtime walk in the month of May along the Avenue des Champs-Elysées, "blossoming out in a costume which was never twice the same but which I remember as being typically mauve, then she would hoist and unfurl at the end of its long stalk, just at the moment when her radiance was at its zenith, the silken banner of a wide parasol of a shade that matched the showering petals of her dress."[1]

Is this a dress or a flower with many petals? Does it matter? What matters is that this flower brings to our imagination what sort of dress this is, making it so real it becomes something else, something unreal, same as Mme Swann herself becomes something else. Same as the fact that there is sameness combined with change, a decidedly strange state, you might say, a state we will henceforth call "mauve," making note of the fact that mauve permeates all volumes of Proust's great work and that mauve was the first of the artificial dyes, meaning aniline dyes, and gave birth to all the colors of the rainbow thereafter, being discovered accidentally by a teenager in a makeshift laboratory in his parent's house in London in 1857 while trying to extract quinine from coal under the direction of a great German chemist named Hoffman, patronized by Queen Victoria and her chemistry-loving husband, Prince Albert. What a miracle it was, this beautiful pink color from coal supplanting at one stroke the so-called natural dyes that had held sway for millennia.

Petals, yet also a shower. What we see is a continuous cascade of color, "never twice the same but typically mauve," falling and falling, mauve falling, time on the move, petals falling, it does not matter, mauve or petals, but never coming to an end, self-perpetuating pouring mauve, yet a mauve that is always changing its color, same as Mme Swann herself, wrapped in radiant mystery yet "blossoming out." As for the mauve parasol unfurling against the sky, is it not the magic wand whose task it is to orchestrate this endless surge that is color?

Is this what William Burroughs had in mind sixty years later with his color walks in Paris in which, as I have suggested, it is not the person but color that walks, color as an animal like a Swann on the edge of language?

For color to walk like this it must transcend the boundary separating nature from second nature, things natural from things artificial, itself an artificial distinction. In an elevated language, mauve was the sign of "second nature" displacing "first nature," this displacement being the sign around which Proust's work works until he finds what all along he has been looking for, Time Lost, which turns out to be the secret of art, as in artifice, wherein both nature and second nature, the natural and the artificial, distinguish themselves in their mixing such that a new type of conscious awareness regarding the bodily unconscious is born.

Barely has this, the world longest novel, begun, before mauve makes its appearance, straddling first and second nature as Proust's narrator informs us that the tearful face of his beloved grandmother, walking in the fields and gardens of Combray, was a "beautiful face with its brown furrowed cheeks, which with age had become almost mauve like the plowed fields in autumn . . ."[2]

Proust adores nature, such as these plowed fields in autumn, and it is totally in keeping that his sense of nature is acutely time sensitive—not the plowed fields, but the plowed fields *in autumn*—time here being the march of the seasons and thus the march of the colors, natural time, we might say, the clock that alters the nature of the light that comes from the sun, the same clock that reconstellates the pattern of colors from the green of summer to the russet golds and mauves of autumn and the greys of winter. What is more, as with his grandmother's "almost mauve" face like the plowed fields, color for Proust is intimately associated with women, especially their dress, and hence provides the route to Time Lost.

For it is a fact with Proust, a surprising fact, that *artifice* and *nature* mesh with each other and with *the work of memory* such that color taps into the unconscious of one's body, which is, and has to be, the unconscious of the world around us, and the basis of the magician's art, as well. This *artifice* is primarily represented by women's clothes, especially their coloring, while *nature* is evoked as flowers, hedges, and trees, special attention being paid to their coloring and texture. What the mix amounts to has been nicely put by Svetlana Alpers in her book *The Art of Describing: Dutch Painting in the Seventeenth Century*, in which she says that "the artifice of the image is embraced along with its immediacy."[3] And so it is with Proust, whose enthusiasm for Jan Vermeer was boundless, it being above all color that for Proust supplies this immediacy.

People, too, are thought of as flora—and color. Albertine's laugh has the color and smell of a geranium while Gilberte and her mother, Mme Swann, are lilacs, white and violet. Samuel Beckett, from whom I take these instances, adds that this amalgamation of people and flowers accompanies very naturally Proust's "complete indifference to moral values and human justices. Flowers and plants have no conscious will. They are shameless, exposing their genitals . . . There is no question of right and wrong. Homosexuality is never called a vice."[4]

Because it has no conscious will, the flower lies outside the realm of the useful, as Bataille makes much of in his "Language of Flowers," his idea being that flowers are the epitome of uselessness, expending their beauty for a few days or weeks, only to fall into decay and ultimately compost.[5] This can mean that the object, freed of will, is all the more free to become an object of study, quiet contemplation and understanding. Hence Proust sits all night writing with a branch of apple blossom laid by his lamp, "staring," writes Beckett, "at the foam of white corollae until the dawn comes to redden them."

When he sees the flowering apple orchards on the hills by the beach resort of Balbec, Proust's young narrator remembers the trees as all green, but now as far as the eye can see they are in full bloom with the most marvelous pink satin ever seen. Glittering in the sunlight, they set off the horizon of the sea as in a Japanese print. Through the branches, the serene blue of the sky looks almost violent. The blossoms draw apart to reveal the immensity of their paradise. A cold breeze sets them trembling. Birds settle on the branches and flutter among the blossoms, suggesting that all this has been painted by "an amateur of exotic art and colors who had artificially created this living beauty."

This "amateur" painter of exotic art and colors is Proust himself.

The scene moved one to tears because even though it appeared to be something rendered by such an artist, it also felt like it was profoundly natural — "that these apple trees were there in the heart of the country, like peasants on one of the high roads of France."[6]

Was this that "miracle of transubstantiation" of life into words to which Proust referred in the letter he wrote Lucien Daudet? The orchard is wonderful because it seems no longer a work of man but a work of man created by nature. It is unnaturally natural, we could say, but then we get caught in our wording and want to reverse it and say it is naturally unnatural. It does not matter. Or rather it matters a whole lot, and art for Proust is now philosophy as urgent, I dare say, as theology, a matter of finding which direction should be accented, this task being left to color as the loyal go-between, art and nature amounting to the embrace of artifice along with its immediacy.

Bringing his first volume, *Swann's Way*, to its end, Proust ramps up to bursting point the tension permeating his novel between the domestic interior, the artifice, on the one hand, and the immediacy of nature outside, on the other—weather, snow, night, and now the yellow leaves swirling in the Bois de Boulogne in autumn, the Bois being itself a stunning instance of nature in its crossover phase, "an artificial place," writes Proust, "and in the zoological or mythological sense of the word, a Garden."[7]

Now it is he and not Mme Swann who is walking through the garden, spellbound by color presenting itself in the double row of orange chestnut trees, "as in a picture, just begun, to be the only thing painted so far by the scene painter, who had not put any color on the rest."[8] (Our "amateur" painter once more.) Here in the Bois in autumn, color is emphasized as concussive points of isolated explosions; first the scattering of yellow leaves, then the orange trees, "with no color on the rest," followed by a single red tree shaking its hair, giving way to a pink winter hawthorn, alone of all its kind. The net effect is that "the Bois had the temporary and artificial look of a tree nursery or park" with fantastic foliage creating light such that early in the day the trees "seemed to be undergoing a change in substance, and later, too, when in the early twilight the light flames up like a lamp, projects over a distance onto the foliage a warm and artificial glow, and sets ablaze the topmost leaves of a tree that remains the dull and incombustible candelabrum of its burning tip."[9]

As for this "change in substance" of the trees touched by the sun, is this not that same substance that I have, with reference to color, called *polymorphous magical substance*? And is it that surprising, knowing Proust's scheme, that this polymorphousness of color assumes, above all, nature passing into artifice much like crossover men and mauve, which, in the case of the Bois, shall mean trees that change into dazzlingly colored women?

For the trees have become assimilated to the women of the city who stroll by them for hours each day as the hours give way to changes in color and the days and seasons likewise pass, ensuring metamorphosing effects similar to the magic lantern whose colors entranced the narrator as a child. Here in the forest the sun gilds the highest branches such that, steeped in sparkling dampness, they emerge "alone from the liquid emerald-colored atmosphere in which the entire forest was plunged as though under the sea."[10] By "a sort of grafting," as Proust puts it, the trees have given birth to a wood nymph of a "quick and colorful beauty," obliging her to feel, as the trees do, the power of the seasons and thus that happy time of the narrator's gullible youth when he would come to places where "masterpieces of feminine elegance were created for a few moments among the unconscious and complicitous leaves."[11]

I very much like this nymph created out of a "sort of grafting." She transforms people into trees and vice versa, not just people but beautiful women in beautiful clothes, not just trees but trees bursting with color and colors. Our little sylvan creature, she of "quick and colorful beauty," is she not the magic wand, the wand of color that transforms what it touches?

But now the sun is sinking. Shadows lengthen. A cold wind whips across the lake and the narrator senses that memories are richer than reality. He yearns for Lost Time, for that long ago when Mme Swann used to drive by in her horse-drawn coach, wearing a spectacularly beautiful dress in which she looked like a queen.

And how is she thus remembered, plucked from time? Why, of course! in a simple mauve hood or a little hat with a single, straight iris poking up from it. How could the people of today, he fusses and fumes, recall, let alone appreciate, the elegance of those far-off times? How could they understand or feel the emotions he had then felt on meeting Mme Swann on a winter's day when, dressed in her sealskin coat and a beret with two blades of partridge feathers sticking out, she seemed to be both outside on this cruel, cold day yet also enveloped in the artificial warmth of her apartment,

> conjured up by nothing more than the bouquet of violets crushed at her breast whose live blue flowering against the gray sky, the icy air, the bare-branched trees, had the same charming manner of accepting the season and the weather merely as a setting, and of living in a human atmosphere, in the atmosphere of this woman, as had the vases and flower stands of her drawing room, close to the lit fire, before the silk sofa, the flowers that looked out through the closed window at the falling snow?[12]

This novel is like natural-history manuals, with this difference, as summed up by mauve. Trapped in his bed in his cork-lined room, the writer cannot write without invoking weather, flowers, hawthorn hedges, seas, sunsets, orchards, and the play of light in its colorful brushstrokes. But then it is the fact and manner by which, like Goethe's soldier, such nature crosses over, that provides Proust with his justification for writing and for what he calls art, by which he means the attempt to undo the grip that habit exerts in constraining our view of ourselves and the world. For it is Proust's view that habit anesthetizes us to reality, making our lives bearable but at the cost of diminishing our sense of what life is or can be. He grabs that nettle in the hope that art shall waken us from the living dead and he does so by getting habit to dehabituate itself. There is no other way. The change cannot be imposed from without and, since habit is by no means merely mental but also physical, located deep in the body as bundles of reflexes, the whole point of which is to act outside of consciousness, is it any wonder that Proust has to find a medium such as color that can engage with that unconscious aspect of bodily being? It certainly is wonderful, not only the way he goes about it, but the more than curious fact that it is the mother of the unnaturally natural colors, mauve, that makes the embrace of artifice natural.

23

techniques of the body

What We Falsely Call Life

Not too long after Proust finished writing his novel, the famous French anthropologist Marcel Mauss gave a lecture in Paris, "Les techniques du corps,"
which translates into English as "Techniques of the Body." It made no mention
of Proust, but was aimed at what Proust meant by *habit* or something close
to it. The thrust of it was that just as French men and women, for instance,
speak a different language from English, so too their bodies "speak" a different
"language," which you notice when they walk, swim, dig a trench, sleep, cough,
bathe, whatever. And of course you don't have to compare the French with the
English to see this. You see it easily enough comparing women with men any-
where in the West—when throwing a stone or running, for instance. Anthropologists know this all too well through the intimacies of fieldwork, as in that
hilarious and embarrassing scene described by Laura Bohannan when she had
to squat down and demonstrate to her hosts in the backblocks of Nigeria in the

1950s how she defecated. The mud lavatory they had built her turned out to be quite inadequate to her "technique du corps."[1] Less dramatic but equally telling is the way you hold your back and stoop. Referring to a new found Tiv friend, Bohannan writes, "There, despite my protests that I could learn by watching, she taught me how to weed, knees straight, back bent. My muscles were aching when she finally let me go."[2] I myself went through the same ordeal when I was instructed by women of African descent on how to pan gold on the banks of the Timbiquí River on the Pacific coast of Colombia—knees straight, back bent. Even if they use steroids, sports trainers and athletes must get to know this level of bodily unconscious technique well, in order to try to enhance performance and reconfigure the intricate relationships between mind and body so that a person may swim faster, dive more elegantly, add more twists or somersaults—the point being that such "techniques of the body" are not, strictly speaking, only body, but a continuous action and interaction back and forth between those entities we designate as "body" and "mind."

Somewhat like these athletes and their coaches, Proust wants to reconfigure the techniques of the body, beginning with reading, the reading of his text. He has to plumb those bundles of reflexes that constitute habit so as to explore the fabulous world therein where history and nature silently do their best work. To accomplish this he has to get habit to "wake up" to itself, yet—and here's the rub—at the same time his is a delicate operation since something absolutely essential to the difference between conscious and unconscious force has to be preserved, something that Mauss failed to explore. Like an open secret that is known and not known at the same time, some part and some function of the bodily unconscious has to remain buried and out of sight.

Imagine, for example, walking or riding a bicycle in such a way that every step, every flexion of a muscle or movement of the knee or ankle joint is consciously processed! More than likely we would fall over, remain immobile, or shake uncontrollably. Consciousness would betray our being. Likewise Proust has to expose more through his doing than through his showing, more through getting us, the readers, to embark on a novel exercise—reading Proust being Proust—than through our being told directly what to think.

To explore habit is to explore where society imprints the body such that the artificial becomes natural. This was pretty much what Franz Boas called "culture," and so a new Anthropology was born. Such imprinting has something of the miraculous about it because it depends on the body's capacity to imitate and perfect exceedingly complex activities unthinkingly. One not only learns to walk. One walks as a Frenchman. One not only learns to talk. One talks as a Frenchman.

So it is with language, and not only the way we throw a stone, which is why, in his essay on the mimetic faculty, Benjamin invokes speed as essential to reading and writing—speed here being the unthought quality of thought, the automatic capacity a person has to relate shapes and sounds of words to what words mean.[3]

This is why speed is so important for Proust's writing. He locates a mode, a *style*, we say, or should we say a *speed*, that expands and contracts the automaticity Benjamin suggested was necessary to reading. With that comes more general awareness as to the miracle of the bodily unconscious otherwise blocked by the habitude of habit. Our body will be refunctioning itself, performing mimetic calisthenics, as it were, if the speed-based *technique* works, yet at the same time this body of ours will be made aware as to the wisdom—if I may put it this way—of remaining unaware.

Mauss did not do this. His concern was the far more conventional study of cultural differences and the changes over time in the way we use our body, not vice versa, the way our bodies use us, and this comes out clearly in his primary example, that of swimming. He heaps praise on an essay in an early edition of the *Encyclopaedia Britannica* dedicated precisely—and I mean *precisely*—to bringing techniques of swimming to consciousness, focusing on "the greatest swimmer of his age," Joseph Nuttall, who won the hundred-yards championship in 1886. Allow me to quote from the encyclopedia at length so you get the fullness of the full picture.

His wonderful leg kick and extraordinary speed powers astonished everyone, and swimmers were not slow in taking advantage of the object-lesson afforded them, and soon learnt to adopt his style. A peculiar screw movement of the leg is the distinctive feature of it. Suppose the swimmer to be lying on his right side at rest, the legs one above the other. The under leg is bent double and the left leg pushed slightly forward, and bent as little at the knee. Then the left leg is straightened with force, and the right simultaneously swirled rapidly to it, the foot of the right leg swinging as on a hinge. The lower arm is pulled down towards the hips, then the hand is turned quickly thumbs upwards, so that together with the lower part of the arm it cuts the water, the arm at this stage being bent almost double. As the arm is shot forward the hand is gradually turned palm downward, and is hollowed for the next sweep downwards. The upper arm used to be fully extended beyond the head, but now it is customary to bring it only a foot in front of the face, then pull it through the water towards the waist and recover close to the body, the arm straightening as it leaves the water. When the under arm is in a position for its stroke, the upper arm should have completed its sweep and the legs be extended ready for the kick. Breathing should be regular and timed with the stroke. It is carried on principally through the nose, and after a time a swimmer learns to inhale naturally during the recovery of the upper arm.[4]

Get it?

How strange and estranging the bodily unconscious can be when made conscious is nicely brought out in an essay on Kafka by Walter Benjamin in which he cites the following description published in 1929 by the physicist Arthur Stanley Eddington in his book *The Nature of the Physical World*. In it "one can virtually hear Kafka speak," claimed Benjamin.

I am standing on the threshold about to enter a room. It is a complicated business. In the first place I must shove against an atmosphere pressing with a force of fourteen pounds on every square inch of my body. I must make sure of landing on a plank traveling at twenty miles a second round the sun—a fraction of a second too early or too late the plank would be miles away . . . Verily it is easier for a camel to pass through the eye of a needle than for a scientific man to pass through a door.[5]

So it is wiser, concludes Eddington, that the scientist become an ordinary person and walk through the doorway instead of waiting for the scientist to figure it all out.

Surely this was Nietzsche's heartfelt counsel, too—Nietzsche, who said that all of philosophy is an understanding, or rather a misunderstanding, of the body? Here we would do well to consider the fabulous conjuring common to shamanism as *the skilled revelation of skilled concealment*.[6] For what is required here is not the exposure of the bodily unconscious as this would more than likely destroy its connections with consciousness. We would be left like that cyclist or walker, shaking in spasmodic immobility. Instead what is required is a certain quality—an art, a magic—of skilled revelation that does justice to the way the body and the mind interact so as to lay claim to ourselves as sensate and moral beings heretofore repressed and molded by conventions that, without our being aware, all the more emphatically control us. The trick for confounding this—for undoubtedly it is a trick—is to slow down or even block and divert the way by which we so speedily, even instantaneously, transform sensory knowledge into knowledge. Then we can become either more aware as to the existence of this mechanism and its mode of functioning or, perhaps, even find new life suspended in this in-between place. This is, I believe, what Nietzsche meant by a "gay science," and this is where Proust is taking us as well.

For Proust, the trick for achieving this awareness of the bodily unconscious will be a particular pausing in sensuousness, heaping sensation upon sensation. Continuously brought into play for almost 3,000 pages, this sensuous pileup duplicates the dialectic back and forth of nature and second nature—"second nature" being where the artificial becomes so grounded in our bodies and daily routines that it becomes natural—as with Mme Swann in her sealskin coat in the park in winter, wrapped warm in what comes across, thanks to the colors she wears, as the artificial warmth of her apartment.

What involuntary memory can achieve in this regard is the retrieval—the re-living—of the sensuous clustering composing actions and ideas that the intellect strips bare—as when Proust writes that even our most insignificant action at any period of our life "was surrounded by, and coloured by, the reflexion of things which logically had no connection with it and which were later separated from it by our intellect which could make nothing of them for its own rational purposes."[7] The simplest gesture, he goes on to note, "remains immured as within a thousand sealed vessels, each one of them filled with things of a colour, a scent, a temperature that are absolutely different one from another."[8] On the other hand, conscious memory "presents the past in monochrome," writes Beckett. "It has no interest in the mysterious element of inattention that colours our most commonplace experiences."[9]

And what is the claim for aesthetics-as-truth that lurks behind all this? Proust the dandy, Proust the fusspot, Proust of the interminable sentences and of sentences buried in other sentences, is actually Proust the critical critic whose primary task is to undo that which makes us biologically, makes us mentally, and makes us socially. What all that intricate scaffolding of metaphor and imagery is meant to achieve, however, is not the transmission of ideas so much as the creation of an atmosphere, an atmosphere that shall transform the reader learning a new and different art of reading, first of the text, then of the world.

His is an art that shall thus reverse the art society employs to dumb us down, the art that conspires with our bodies to create social bodies, thereby strapping us into place and forcing us to lead what he devastatingly calls "those ordinary lives which we live with our gaze averted from ourselves . . . accomplished by vanity and passion and the intellect, and habit, too, when they smother our true impressions, so as entirely to conceal them from us, beneath a whole heap of verbal concepts and practical goals which we falsely call life."[10] Above all, this technique of his meant "the abrogation of our dearest illusions, it meant giving up one's belief in the objectivity of what one had oneself elaborated . . ."[11]

As practiced on himself—or, should we say, on his narrator—Proust's technique allows the bodily unconscious to surface, only to disappear. Yet having once surfaced, it cannot remain the same as it did before, because now a new reckoning has been established in the contract between the wisdom of the mind and the wisdom of the body, which can, so it seems, afford only brief interludes of access by the intellect.

This new reckoning is when our self-consciousness expands into consciousness of the world at large such that *we know what not to know*, which is what Nietzsche counsels in *The Gay Science;* "how we nowadays learn as artists to forget well, to be good at *not* knowing!"[12] And by *art*, of course, he meant philosophy as well—to the very considerable extent that life, like a work of art, is really made up—witness this: "for all of life is based on semblance, art, deception, points of view, and the necessity of perspectives and error."[13]

Much the same for Proust, whose art is a bear hug with life-as-art, so as to change that reality. How does this work, this use of art to engage with the art by which we unconsciously live? Having provoked the reader's self-awareness as to the bodily unconscious, he then proceeds to cancel it out by leaving a thick trace of not knowing, like the wake of a ship plying troubled seas. This wake where seagulls dart and flying fish play is where the interminable sentences bubble such that sensuousness passes into mind wondering about itself, about love, about custom, and why people are what they are.

Eventually, in fact and as the overarching story the book has to tell, this bubbling wake results in a work of art—*In Search of Lost Time*—an art in which forgetting is every bit as important as remembering because, finally, the art of not knowing has been mastered as an essential feature of the more general attitude towards life and nature as the mastery of nonmastery.

It seems to me perfectly in keeping with this skilled revelation of skilled concealment that this undoing of ourselves is tied to sleep or, rather, to *awakening*, a crossover state, carrying sleep and dream into the day, which, given Proust's nocturnal habits of writing, would not be day but night.

For if ever there was an advocate of sleep as the most important aspect of a person's life, it was Proust. Not dreams, but sleep. And this is totally of a piece with his emphasis on the body, the sleeping body, not the sleeping intellect. One cannot properly describe human life, says Proust, "unless one bathes it in the sleep into which it plunges night after night and which sweeps around it as a promontory is swept by the sea."[14]

The world of sleep is the world of the body into which we travel like wanderers in outer space. Sleep is where we are remade, "in the organic and now translucent depths of the mysteriously lighted viscera." In that world we "traverse the arteries of the subterranean city," so as to embark upon "the dark current of our own blood as upon an inward Lethe meandering six-fold, tall solemn forms appear to us, approach and glide away, leaving us in tears."[15]

To embark upon "the dark current of our own blood as upon an inward Lethe" is to do something more than journey into the subterranean city of our inner consciousness. For this is a journey *in sleep* when this being that is myself exists no longer. Body and soul have formed another configuration. Insofar as these distinct versions of myself are both distinct and yet "me," this is thus a journey that corresponds nicely to the maneuver that articulates and disarticulates the bodily unconscious with the wide-awake world. It is also a journey that reminds us that consciousness is capable of many planes of absorption and self-absorption, including daydreaming and reverie.

We may not be aware of the journey we nightly make. We may be only partially aware. And we may not be aware in the manner in which Proust's narrator is aware. Yet to the extent that Proust has hit upon a strange truth of the body-in-sleep, we are indebted to the artist not merely for the power and grace of his figurative language, but for a new science of a new reality that requires this figuration, this "poetic" language, so that readers can experience what they knew without knowing it. This is not to say there is the real reality that science knows best on the one hand, and on the other hand a poetic version of it that helps makes the reality communicable to the layman. Not at all. This reality of the sleepwalker is the poetry essential to life, as essential as the "dark current of our blood."

Merely to express this journey as a substantial truth of our selves and our bodies is to jolt the reader into a new awareness. *Could this be me?* you ask, *me asleep?*

Sometimes Proust sees sleep as death, or as the imposition of an alien being within us. But awakening is a *resurrection*, or, to take a less dramatic but telling parallel, it is the recognition of something forgotten, "similar to what occurs when we recall a name, a line, a refrain we had forgotten."[16]

Could Michel Leiris have had something like this in mind with his bizarre question that I paraphrase as What is the color of the sacred? With this question was he not performing a trick that would facilitate what he saw as a primary aim of the sacred—to develop self-understanding? And was he not adamant that this task was in effect the Proustian one of scrutinizing one's memories, mindful of the fact that the relevant plane of memory is not accessible to conscious recall? Here is what he said: "If one of the most 'sacred' aims that man can set for himself is to acquire as exact an understanding of himself as possible, it seems desirable that each one, scrutinizing his memories with the greatest possible honesty, examine whether he can discover there some sign permitting him to discern the *color* for him of the very notion of the sacred."[17]

Insofar as this journey is akin to Proust's journey to the subterranean city of the sleeping body, what are we to make of color's place and function? Why did Leiris seize on color in relation to the sacred as the key to this journey into the unknown that is the Self, which Proust insists is not one Self but many, and as changeable as the weather is colored?

Benjamin reports on the surrealist poet with that lovely, indeed surreal, name, Saint-Pol Roux. He retires to bed about daybreak and fixes a notice to his door:

POET AT WORK.

And "Breton notes, 'Quietly. I want to pass where no one has yet passed, quietly!—After you dearest language.'"[18]

Take that other poet at work, namely Marcel Proust's narrator. Now he is awakening in a strange room. We already know from him that sleep in strange rooms is an effective means for breaking habit, and now we know that the strangest room of all is our body, especially when asleep.

He feels himself to be a dual creature, like a moth emerging from a chrysalis.

Half immersed in the bed clothes, half outside them, this is also the duality of awakening being half asleep yet half awake. His eyes feast on color while his lower body, under the blankets, requires not color but warmth, which, as he emerges from the bedcovers, will soon be resupplied artificially, as he puts it, by the fire in the fireplace, just as natural color will be displaced by artificial color.

Delighted by the delicacy of the pink-and-golden morning supplied by the few strokes of color on the leaves outside his window, he becomes disturbed by the violent red wallpaper of his room, sprinkled with black and white flowers. Eventually he adjusts, noting that these artificial flowers "succeeded only in striking me as novel, in forcing me to enter not into conflict but into contact with them, in modulating the gaiety and songs of my morning ablutions; they succeeded only in imprisoning me in the heart of a sort of poppy . . ."[19]

Disarticulation and rearticulation of the wisdom of the body with that of its echo in our conscious awareness seems especially prone to a color-dependent process that involves playing off the natural with the artificial—the leaves outside shot with streaks of color against the startling red, black, and white flowered wallpaper inside.

Because artificial things are not so much the opposite of natural things but instead are things that grow out of nature, forever imbricated in it, and because artifice is not only an imitation of what we take to be nature, but an imitation with a difference—note the violence of the red in the wallpaper—the artificial lies uneasily over that which it imitates. Proust acknowledges this uneasiness when he remarks how what is at first a *conflict* becomes *contact*, thanks to two highly significant ritual and bodily efficacious acts; first his singing, and second his washing himself, the net effect of which is to mightily activate the wallpaper such that its flowers imprison him in their artificial hearts.

The method is colored. Not just colored, but color itself, color in action, we might say—as when Proust states such an art has to be *a new and distinct material, of a transparency and a sonority that were special, compact, cool after warmth, rose-pink.*[20] What color achieves here is to further remind us that whatever rules and principles may be necessary for this art form, even more important is the question of the medium with which—and within which—one works. At first this medium that is color-in-action seems external to the writer, and as such can be manipulated. Initially it is either outside or inside and the relationship is antagonistic. Ritual of the body intervenes, conflict gives way to contact, and this contact swarms over the body enclosing it, indeed imprisoning it, in the artificial heart of the poppy readjusting the unstable boundary separating nature from artifice.

As such, this medium cannot be easily named or sorted into categories. Note its *transparency*, but also its *cool-after-warmth,* summed up as *rose-pink*. In defining method here, color is preeminently polymorphous magical substance, transparent cool-after-warmth rose pink, and therefore this continuous cross-over, this crossing over, between nature and second nature, flowers and women, back and forth, as with mauve—and as with the flower-patterned, colored coverlet wrapped around his invalid Aunt Leonie on her bed, there in the village of Combray where, if memory is our guide, it all began.

24

an hour is not merely an hour

You can start, as most critics do, with the mother not being allowed by the father to kiss the little boy to sleep, this little boy who would thus have suffered a thousand cuts and more had it not been for the colored images moving across his bedroom walls projected from his magic lantern. Or you could start, as I do, with Aunt Leonie, who makes her appearance right after the narrator's first encounter with the *memoire involontaire* thanks to his biting on "one of those squat, plump cakes called *petites madeleines* that look as though they have been molded in the grooved valve of a scallop shell" that his mother gave him on page forty-five of the first volume.[1]

For his aunt's room is the world in which this novel breathes.

This is the room of the bodily unconscious.

Proust describes this room:

just as in certain countries entire tracts of air or ocean are illuminated or perfumed by myriad protozoa that we cannot see—enchant us with the thousand smells given off by the virtues, by wisdom, by habits, a whole secret life, invisible, superabundant, and moral, which the atmosphere holds in suspension; smells still natural, certainly, and colored by the weather like those of the neighboring countryside . . .[2]

Above all note the habits, but also the wisdom—the wisdom of the body—its invisibility as much as its secret life, which the "atmosphere holds in suspension."

Let us switch from space to time as a way of being in this room—in which case an "hour is not merely an hour." Instead it is "a vase full of scents and sounds and projects and climates, and what we call reality is a certain connection between these immediate sensations and the memories which envelop us simultaneously with them."[3]

To get this notion of time across, the author surely lived up to his statement, "an hour is not merely an hour." And of all the enveloping memories, it is the one leading him to his aunt that is the most important. For *is she not in fact Proust himself*, the guardian of that chamber of sensations that will be recruited thereafter to break the safe that is habit?

In cracking this safe, Proust had to do far more than specify sensations and their associated memories. He had to be "climatological" as well. This is because he needed to work in concert with the artwork in the body that is the world that is more like the "sense of sense" that corresponds to no particular sense organ or sensory modality. Instead it is a "sense of being in the world," whether that state of being lies in an apparently inert object, such as the flowered coverlet over his long-suffering aunt's bed, or is an actual human being, such as his aunt, thus covered.

Such "edge sensations" are what trigger the memoire involontaire as much as do discrete sensations, like the taste of the petite madeleine. "Polluted" by their histories and their situations, such sensations have, purely as sensations, somehow in our culture escaped easy categorization or signification—sensations such as the stiffness of the folds of a napkin felt while eating dinner in a restaurant by the sea, the sight of the sea at that very moment, the speed of the wind, looking forward to lunch, or wondering which of the different walks at Combray we might take.

Let us rub our lips along the starched stiffness and smoothness of the fold, let us unfold the fold that is the Self. There are plenty of them; the napkin, already mentioned, which in turn is like the towel the narrator used to dry his face that day of arrival at the sea, and, many years later, this napkin at the meal at the sumptuous party in the Guermantes palace in Paris as the Great War grinds on close by. Let us unfold the fold. What do we find, side by side with these other, earlier folds brought out of hiding in the folds of time? Why, we find this: "the plumage of an ocean green and blue like the tail of a peacock. And what I found myself enjoying was not merely these colors but a whole instant of my life on whose summit they rested . . ."[4]

Aspects of life we take for granted, such sensations may on occasions feel at home in a strangely magical world as aspects of ourselves long since forgotten in childhood, when our bodies and the world were one—which is why Proust can play with the idea that objects are not dead and that they can even look back at you, which is one way his translator, Walter Benjamin, citing Proust, defined "aura."

Proust invokes what he calls the Celtic belief that the souls of dead persons who were emotionally close to us pass into an animal, plant, or inanimate object, where they lie imprisoned until, perhaps, one day, by chance, they will be resurrected if we recognize them. "It is the same with our past," he continues, locked in things that no amount of conscious effort can restore to us until, by chance, we encounter that memory and have it restored to us.[5] Surely he had himself in mind when he remarked elsewhere that certain people like to believe that "objects retain something of the eyes which have looked at them"?[6] But what gives this magic its force, as I read him, what makes the aura auratic, is the poetry—I can think of no other word—intrinsic to the "edge sensations" that linger like dust and cling like moss to the situations that one day may be recalled and hence restore Time Lost. "A name read long ago in a book," writes Proust, "contains within its syllables the strong wind and brilliant sunshine that prevailed while we were reading it."[7]

To evoke strong wind and brilliant sunshine within the syllables of a name is to evoke at the cellular level of our existence not so much a sensation as what I call a "sense of sense," corresponding to a stream of human existence and capability buoyed up not by visual images but by what Proust, when he tells us that "an hour is not merely an hour," refers to as projects and climates. This wind blows through all of the search for Time Lost. It is the *invisible vagabond, the presiding spirit of Combray.*

Proust's translator, Walter Benjamin, called it *the weight of the catch*, meaning the proto-imageric realness that precedes actual images in the workings of memory—the classic scene being Proust's first rendition of the memoire involontaire when his narrator feels a tumult of sensations before he envisages in his memory the precise details of his aunt Leonie's bedroom and then the village of Combray spreading out through the window before him as if looking through a zoom lens.

> I feel something quiver in me, shift, try to rise, something that seems to have been unanchored at a great depth; I do not know what it is, but it comes up slowly; I feel the resistance and I hear the murmur of distances traversed . . . I can just barely perceive the neutral glimmer in which the elusive eddying of stirred-up colors is blended . . .[8]

No wonder Benjamin referred to this zone beyond the image and beyond conscious recall as *the weight of the catch*, implying an invisible weight—the drag—fishermen feel when hauling in the net they have hurled into the sea, in this case the Sea of Time Lost. And Proust's sentences, adds Benjamin, "are the entire muscular activity of the intelligible body; they contain the whole enormous effort to raise this catch."[9]

This "muscular activity of the intelligible body" is equivalent to the *presiding spirit of Combray*, the *invisible vagabond* that is the wind that *crosses* the paths that the narrator's family walks each afternoon in the summer, choosing either the Guermantes Way or the Méséglise Way. To cross the path of human choice and human intention is the way of this wind, this vagabond wind. What we are aware of, if we care to reflect, which is not often, are the effects of this wind as they take on curious undulations. "I saw a single gust of wind," remarks the narrator, telling us of his walk along the Méséglise Way, "coming from the farthest horizon, first bend the most distant wheat, then roll like a wave through all that vast expanse and come to lie down murmuring and warm among the sainfoin and clover at my feet."[10]

Weight of the catch, says Benjamin; *invisible vagabond*, says Proust. Rolling wavelike through the wheat, this bottom-most layer of the memoire involontaire is situated, like color, beyond any image, but we need an image so as to bring it to consciousness. This is why the way we talk of color is so confused, our language for color being like a net we use to catch the wind. What we get instead is the weight of the catch, not the catch itself. That comes later, if at all, translated into an image such as that wave rolling across a wheat field at right angles to our walk along the Méséglise Way. And when the connections are all firing, you may for a moment as brief as a flash of lightning escape Time and hence Death itself.[11]

What this brings about in turn is just as extraordinary.

For you then enter into the essence of things such that your own essence undergoes a sea change—the same as what Benjamin and Burroughs formulate about color as having the power to pass us through the image into that other world where death has no dominion. Here one can tack back and forth through history, like Burroughs with his Mayan shaman dispensing mushrooms and hourglasses filled with colored sands. Choose your color!

Taking mescaline, hashish, and opium, Walter Benjamin saw these colored sands, too, or something pretty close. But for him the effect of the Mayan shaman in Burroughs's story, with the hourglasses of different colored sands, was achieved largely by an amalgam of the Jewish kabbalah, Marxism in its more active, anarchist mood, and, above all, Marcel Proust's *In Search of Lost Time*.

In fact Burroughs's leap into the past parallels Benjamin's philosophy of history. "In order for a part of the past to be touched by the present actuality," Benjamin wrote in the last decade of his life in "File N," "there must be no continuity between them."[12]

This also parallels Proust's definition of reality as bound not merely to memory but to a montage of memories as *slices in time* laid on top of one another—a *now* overlaid by a *back then:* "what we call reality is a certain connection between the immediate sensations and memories which envelop us simultaneously."[13] With Proust this is normal everyday reality, if only we could see it—if only our everyday language made it easy for us to talk about it that way.

With Benjamin this is the montage of memories that flashes up at a moment of danger, meaning especially in political crisis. "The true picture of the past flits by," begins one of Benjamin's famous theses on the philosophy of history. "The past can be seized only as an image which flashes up at the instant when it can be recognized and is never seen again." This has Proust's fingerprints all over. The image Benjamin has in mind is that of the memoire involontaire, grafted onto a Marxist vision of world history and revolution. It is an image that can affect, if not alter, the deepest layers of one's being where habit reigns, such that bodily dispositions are transferred to another register altogether—from homogenous empty time to "time filled by the presence of the now" blasted out of the continuum of history.[14]

This unexpected, abrupt, and tearing change of pace is of a piece with *awakening*—as when in "File N" Benjamin comments: "Thus, in Proust, the importance of staking an entire life on life's supremely dialectical point of rupture: awakening. Proust begins with an evocation of the space of waking up . . . The realization of dream elements in the course of waking up is the canon of dialectics. It is paradigmatic for the thinker and the binding for the historian."[15]

And that is why Proust wrote in bed, wrote all night, and slept all day.

25

cardiac fatigue

"For a long time I went to bed early. Sometimes, my candle scarcely out, my eyes would close so quickly that I did not have time to say to myself: "I'm falling asleep." And, half an hour later, the thought that it was time to try to sleep would wake me . . ."[1]

These sentences open Proust's novel.

First sleep, then awakening—awakening because in his sleep he has the thought that it is time to go to sleep—in a time and place when people were intimate with fire and candlelight, flame being that protean entity that could dynamically assume any form, what Sergei Eisenstein called "plasmaticness," the fluidity that I myself link to color as the epitome of polymorphous magical substance.

Yet while this space of waking begins Proust's novel, it is also the case that shortly thereafter we are plunged into a rather different and recurrent permutation of it—the space of cardiac fatigue, the space of the invalid—where the anticipation of death, on one side, and memory, on the other, now engage in a fight to the finish, where both shall triumph. I take this space of cardiac fatigue to be *the space of death*, that tabooed space with more than its fair share of lingerings, anticipations, and unevenness in its mix of fears, awakenings, and backtrackings. To the degree that it can be harnessed it is an amazing place from which to write, and this is what Proust does at the beginning of his book with his aunt, as well as at the end of the novel where he joyfully describes himself as privileged because he writes as a half-dead man, a gymnast with Time's machinations.

This space of death is what we enter in his aunt's room, the room of the bodily unconscious—as remembered—the sort of provincial room, says Proust, "just as in certain countries entire tracts of ocean are illuminated or perfumed by myriad protozoa that we cannot see—enchant us with the thousand smells given off by the virtues, by wisdom, by habits, a whole secret life, indivisible, superabundant, and moral which the atmosphere holds in suspension."[2]

This is the realm of the organic as spirited decay. It is the realm of death or, rather, dying—as when Sigmund Freud, at the height of his creativity, posits the overriding importance of a "death instinct," "to return to the quiescence of the inorganic world."[3] Nietzsche said it best: "Let us beware of saying that death is opposed to life. The living is only a form of what is dead, and a very rare form."[4]

With regard to smell, notoriously the effluent of decay at its spirited best, and notoriously the fast track to deep memory, the smells in this room of Aunt Leonie are "colored by the weather," as manifest in the changing odorscape of the surrounding countryside no less than in the seasonal variation of jams and flowers. Colored by weather, remembrance now comes full circle to focus on the most significant object in this space of self-willed invalidity, namely the "central, sticky, stale, indigestible, and fruity smell of the flowered coverlet" over the aunt's bed.[5]

To be colored by weather, as by this coverlet, to be afloat on a perfumed ocean illumined by myriad protozoa, is to be the reader of this work—a work whose writer bears an uncanny resemblance to the invalid aunt under her flowered coverlet. She has something loose in her head, she thinks, and must therefore speak softly. Nevertheless she cannot stop speaking because she believes it is beneficial for her throat, just as Proust cannot stop writing those endless sentences turning in on themselves, just as, no doubt, he has something strange going on in his head, too, not to mention his aunt's fervent belief that such nonstop muttering could reduce her fits of breathlessness, this being Proust's infirmity, too. We learn, moreover, that like Proust, or at least his writing, she attributes to "the least of her sensations an extraordinary importance" such that she cannot keep them to herself, just as she keeps reminding herself not to forget that she did not sleep.

For these reasons I believe that if it is the body that lies at the heart of what Proust called the memoire involontaire, defining it therefore as something more than a memory-picture, then, strange as it might seem, the collapse of the body can be an overwhelming stimulus to such heightened recall. I suggest this is how we might read *In Search of Lost Time*, as a book of cardiac fatigue, dedicated to the adjudication of those celestial scales that emerge when one of Proust's main characters, Bergotte, the writer, is dying of kidney failure, the illness that in real life killed Proust's mother.

Gazing at a patch of yellow in Vermeer's *View of Delft*, a painting he thought he knew well, the dying Bergotte noticed for the first time some small figures in blue. He then saw the pink color of the sand, and, most significant of all, "the precious substance of the tiny patch of yellow wall," at which point his dizziness accelerated and he fixed his gaze on the yellow patch like a child upon a yellow butterfly that it wants to catch.[6] On the point of collapse, eyes fixed on the "butterfly," Bergotte said to himself: "That's how I ought to have written. My last books are too dry, I ought to have gone over them with a few layers of colour, made my language precious in itself, like this little patch of yellow wall."[7] At which point there appeared a celestial pair of scales. In one pan lay his life, while in the other was the "little patch of wall so beautifully painted in yellow."[8]

This of course is Proust's own notion of writing, "making language precious in itself" through a Vermeer-like layering of transparent color. But as we shall see, the trick here is not only writing as an analogy to painting. It is also an obsessive referencing of color in the text alongside the use of transparent colors such that, through transparency, there is eventually a successful approach to the search for Lost Time. These are big ideas.

When it came Proust's turn to die, he saw, in his mind's eye, a Vermeer painting. He dictated a last sentence: "There is a Chinese patience in Vermeer's craft."[9] Well, at least that's the story.

All his writerly life Proust was thus "dying," inspired in so many different ways by this deathbed sentiment—in its "active" phase of "spirited decay" continuous within us, from day one within us as bodily unconscious. If he was not exactly dying like Bergotte, he was at least existing in some sort of deathlike space analogous to death in the same way as insomnia is akin to sleep, dying for oxygen, dying of allergies or fear of whatever it was that closed down his lungs, an invalid living on borrowed time such that while he had all the time in the world, lying in bed, it was if he had none at all. Walter Benjamin felt that Proust's syntax "rhythmically and step by step reproduces his fear of suffocating" and that it was possible that it was his art that caused his asthma as much as the other way around.[10] This brings writing and the body together in unexpected ways.

In Search of Lost Time can also be thought of as a book defined by falling asleep as another sort of bodily collapse. Not sleep itself. But falling, and failing. Instead of dreams, the labored cycles of insomnia. "It is finished," Proust announced to his devoted maid, that other celestial scale, Celeste Albaret, whom he called to his bedside to announce that he had just written *The End*. "Now I can die," he said.[11] He could just as well have said, "Now I can sleep." And what was the finishing point, the point of finishing, apart from his imminent death? It was that at the end, he could now begin! It was the end, in other words death, that gives Proust's narrator, Proust's alter ego, the license to become a writer and begin his great work, all 3,000 pages of toil buoyed up and charged with this newfound confidence.

How strange is that! Only at the end of the book can the writer begin to write it!

This epiphany takes place as a result of an astonishing flood of involuntary memories triggered by a clanging fork, the stiffness of the napkins, and the misstep on the cobblestones at the grand party he attends in the palace of the Guermantes in the heart of Paris. The epiphany owes much to the fact that the narrator is now experienced enough with life's ups and downs to take philosophical and moral stock of such memories. But that is not all. Something new has entered reality, and that is that he has simultaneously suffered an acute disturbance to memory in *not* recognizing his old friends, who have aged so much in his prolonged absence from Paris during the war. Those aged faces, those opaque eyes, the rambling speech and twisted frames present one picture placed on top of another, older picture of those friends that is actually a memory-picture but one not accessed until that very moment. The early picture refers to the vigor of youth when one was far from death and decay, and far from the corpses and damaged bodies littering the trenches of the Great War.[12]

So on the one hand we have this bouquet of involuntary memories, this embarrassment of memory-riches. On the other hand we have alongside that another, new form of involuntary memory—so different from the *petit madeleine!*—the embarrassment due to a malfunctioning of memory due to the physical decay of his friends making it—at first—impossible to recognize them. And it is not the recognition that is important so much as the double image that results of them here and now on the road to decay and death compared with back then.

It is then the *combination* of these two distinct memory-effects that doubles *the weight of the catch*. Heavy with spirited decay and cardiac fatigue, the pre-imageric zone now overflows with an abundance, ensuring that the man who wants to write is, finally, on the write track.

And what was this track? For Benjamin it was the magnificent but futile attempt to recuperate "experience" otherwise lost because of the way people shield themselves from the shocks and starts of modern life even by imitating them as Charlie Chaplin makes much of with his white face of shock and terror—no! this is not just a clown's face—his discombobulated walk, and his body jerking explosively on the assembly line because he is out of synch with his mind and his understandings while the objects he is meant to work on work on him. Against that Proust tried to slow down the assembly line, "Taylorism," and "scientific management." He tried to slow down the speed of the speed machine to a snail's pace of meditative mastication. The stimulus shield was to be disarmed—if only this once—by having his readers rework the bodily unconscious through learning to read in a different way than before.

In describing Proust's work as "the reference work . . . the mandala of the entire literary cosmogony," Roland Barthes paid scant justice to the possibility that we could have both the cult of the author *and* what he called "the death of the author" in the one and the same work. This, however, is achieved in Proust because of what I have called "cardiac fatigue," meaning a type of death from which the prose flows as if from a spring, and because of what Barthes made famous as "the death of the author," meaning the preeminence of language itself over the author such that from that death the reader is born.[13]

Nietzsche perceived this issue long before when, at the end of his preface to *The Geneology of Morals*, he spoke to the unique value of writing aphoristically as that which could reassert the practice of reading as an *art* (his emphasis), "something that has been unlearned most thoroughly nowadays."[14]

And so it is with Marcel Proust. Having found a way of cheating on time through involuntary memory, he also found a technique—we call it *style*, that transparent cool-after-warmth rose pinkness—that takes us not to writing but to reading. To read Proust is to be recalibrated psychohistorically in somewhat the same way as watching a film in slow motion or listening to his aunt in Combray under her flower-colored coverlet. The process of perception is prized apart. Minute particulars are so meticulously displaced into unexpected patterns that they disarticulate stimulus from response. And into the gap thus opened, new worlds emerge.

What unfathomable mystery lies in reading no less than in writing! To read Proust is to bear witness to what he called "making language precious in itself." If Benjamin saw the mighty labor therein as the exception that proved the rule, testimony to the impossibility of otherwise restoring "experience" in Modern Times, then the first experience to be reinstalled by Proust is the experience of reading—those endless sentences (that "Nile of language, which here overflows and fructifies the regions of truth," according to Benjamin), that frenzied grammar, interminable parentheses, massive asides and no less massively baroque descriptions of hawthorn hedges, dinner parties, and the endless well of falling in and out of love no less than in and out of sleep. For this, Proust lost many readers.

His first volume was rejected by publishers on the advice, amongst others, of André Gide. But those readers who stayed the course or were attracted from the outset must have felt that they were being estranged from their own bodies and social surroundings and hence were being taught to *be aware differently* in much the same way as when you first learn to walk or swim or learn your body again after suffering a stroke, all of these being activities which require a surfacing of the bodily unconscious only to relax and let it subside once more. Reading a sensitive ethnography such as Kenneth Read's *The High Valley*, Laura Bohannan's *Return to Laughter*, Pierre Clastres's *Chronicle of the Guayaki*, not to mention Malinowski's *Diary in the Strict Sense of the Term*, can do something close to this, too, as you imagine and imbibe other ways of being and feel the difference from your own.

Let us combine these two modes of estrangement, the body and ethnography, by returning to the famous essay on techniques of the body by Marcel Mauss. Swimming is his first example, the one that cracks the ice, so to speak.[15] Polynesians do not swim as we Frenchmen do, he blurts out on his first page, and French kids today swim differently than he does, what with his swallowing water and spitting it out as he goes along like some sort of steamboat. In fact, this technique of the body is not all that dissimilar to the form of this essay.

I learned to swim when I was seven or eight. Before that, I was frightened of water. I remember big boys at the harbor pool in Sydney threatening to throw me into the deep-water end when I couldn't swim. I also remember a time of mounting panic as, unable to swim, I hung onto the shoulders of a man as he breaststroked across a river. The more he tried to reassure me, the tighter I clung. I thought his words were lies, an adult conspiracy as to the nature of being.

Later I learned to float and then swim, and thought nothing of it until one day, maybe twenty years later, swimming way out in the Pacific off a Sydney surf beach, I looked down, seized by panic as the strange thought hit me that swimming was actually some sort of miracle and there was no good reason why I wouldn't just sink to the bottom of the ocean there and then. Those twenty years had effectively concealed from my conscious self the wisdom of the body as an instinctual machine able to work in synchrony with the water, where the fish in me had asserted itself and the specific gravity of the various mediums— that of the water versus the human body, the dead weight of the head versus the buoyancy of the chest and the abdominal cavity and so forth—had found their interactive genius. All this had passed unnoticed until that fateful day twenty years later when the achievement burst into consciousness because of what seemed like its imminent collapse.

Which takes us back to that other imminent collapse of cardiac fatigue. Proust alienated the body in much the same way as my learning to swim became, twenty years later, to seem like a divine intervention that at any moment could be withdrawn. But Proust did this through writing, or, should we say, the pro-duction of reading. His method lay in *actualization*, not *reflection*, said Benja-min, adding that "none of us has time to live the true dramas of the life that we are destined for . . . There has never been anyone else with Proust's ability to show us things. Proust's pointing finger is unequaled."[16]

But what sort of *pointing* and what sort of *actualization*? I think it is as myste-rious as the conjuror pulling the rabbit from the hat because, along the lines of my swimming example, the awareness at stake here involves becoming aware of what you were already aware of without knowing it—precisely William Bur-roughs's understanding of why he writes, which is to tell people what they knew without them knowing they already knew it. As with my swimming example, some sort of shock or at the least a "system failure" sets off the alarm and the organ of consciousness tries to take over.

Yet it cannot. Not for long and only in a limited and crippled capacity. Burroughs's extraordinary intention must fail. To be good at not-knowing is the true knowing. Skilled revelation of skilled concealment is a wheel that spins without rest. The point is the effort *and* the failure, which is why, in my opinion, Burroughs adores the cut-up form with its transgressive sex, macabre humor, and truncated lyricism in which, as grammar suicides, color takes over, as animal.

To be aware differently thanks to actualization in Proust is an effect achieved by him having his style—that transparent cool-after-warmth rose pinkness—mimic his theory of memory in that what is evoked in words seems to not only exist on the page, but it seems to draw you in as well. The memoire involontaire is merely the capstone, the flamboyantly fantastic concentrate, of what is diffused throughout the work as a whole, as an all-encompassing bodily disturbance transporting the self to where it had been long ago, memories so complete that for the second they lasted "they not only force our eyes to cease seeing the room which is before them in order to see the railway bordered by trees or the rising tide, they even force our nostrils to breathe the air of places . . ." [17] Could it get more visceral than this, where in remembering, you actually breathe in the air of long ago? Likewise, the positioning of the body, especially in sleep, can act as a scheme, a module, or an analogue that transports the sleeping self to far-off times and places. Here, the limbs, or rather their position vis-à-vis each other, do the remembering.

But then there is the converse, that other colored thread running through the tapestry that is the prose. This is the thread of self-conscious questioning and intellection that this author can never, ever resist, like a dog in a cartoon smelling an old bone rooted in the soil. The net effect of these two moments in Proust, immersion and intellection, is to make the sensation evoked ever more sensate, nowhere more so than when he distinguishes between two types of coloration that correspond to two types of memory. There is *voluntary* memory, which is like a bad painter whose tints have lost their freshness, and then there is *involuntary* memory, which surges with living color, as when he suddenly hears the name "Guermantes" spoken in a particular way, which "brings back to me that mauve—so soft and smooth but almost too bright, too new—with which the billowy scarf of the young Duchess glowed, and, like two inaccessible, ever-flowering periwinkles, her eyes, sunlit with an azure smile." [18]

The writer's technique replicates what it is he is writing about. He enacts his theory. He is striving for words that mulch the in-between zone, neither body nor mind, but something basic to both, like dust floating in sun beams. Herein lay the key to that "*miracle of transubstantiation*" of life into words to which Proust referred in a letter he wrote to Lucien Daudet. For this insight I am indebted to Gerard Genette, who goes on to say that this miracle was posed by Proust as "a kind of cast, of transparent unity." "I suppose it is what is called the Varnish of the Masters," wrote Proust.[19] "This 'varnish' is not a superficial glaze," adds Genette, "but a diaphanous depth of color itself."[20]

What did Proust mean by this phrase, "the Varnish of the Masters"?

He means Vermeer, in whose time to paint a painting was, materially speaking, a massive undertaking. Think of architecture and engineering. Think of building a house or even a church as equivalent undertakings to making a painting. Unlike words, pigments were rare, and the number of colors available to the painter was few. Above all were the varnishes—meaning glazes applied in multiple layers of different thicknesses used principally as a way of playing with color, with depth, and with radiance. In keeping with their trickster character, such varnishes were not only transparent but, depending on their mixing, were usually colored as well. They could transform colors and make new ones. Using a badger brush, a painter such as Vermeer could make a deep green by applying thin layers of a transparent varnish named "yellow lake" onto an opaque blue surface and thereby create a laurel wreath around the head of a girl. Varnishes can achieve a luminosity or "shine-through" effect that is often compared to a stained-glass window that cannot be achieved by direct painting with opaque paint of the same color. It was this that transfixed Bergotte at the moment he died. You notice a painting by Vermeer, most of whose paintings are small, shining at you with a subdued luminosity from the moment you enter the gallery, no matter how far away it might be.

Along with luminosity, varnishes produce depth. Luminosity is like a stained-glass window alerting us to the miraculous. Depth, however, is not quite so easy to describe. Combined with luminosity and with color change, "depth" suggests transformation, especially on the part of the traveling eye of the perceiver moving into the painting. Suddenly, as it were, we find ourselves back on the familiarly defamiliarizing terrain—Nietzsche, Virginia Woolf, Genet, Benjamin, shamanism, and all that crew—entering into the image, thanks to transparency applied layer after layer, transparency that is both transparent and colored.

Transparent color is but another name for polymorphous magical substance, that metamorphosing medium midway between body and mind, not visual but colored—which is pretty much where Goethe feels comfortable and why he stands out in the history of Western thought, much beloved for this reason by Nietzsche as "Dionysian." Goethe's painter friend Phillip Otto Runge put his finger on it while on the Baltic island of Rugen. When asked by Goethe to write down his thoughts on color, Runge chose to dwell on what he called *transparent colors*, which he saw as something if not exactly sacred, then certainly spirited and spiritlike, playing like fire above solid colors so as to render visible things otherwise obscured. In *Heart of Darkness* these spirits assumed the movement of flame on water, where human speech gives up the ghost for one terrible reason or another. Yet in Proust it seems at crucial points like the opposite; that words thrive where the body collapses, for it is there that the wisdom of the body most easily breaks into speech.

26

what is the color of the profane?

William Burroughs has his differently colored hourglasses that, with the aid of a Mayan shaman, a sexy boy, and hallucinogenic mushrooms, flip him through time into prehistory so as to break the code of the priests living off the sweat and toil of the peasants. Burroughs wants to destroy not just a particular code but the very idea of a code, which he sees as the instrument of mind control. Burroughs is a *profane* writer.

But does not Proust break code too? Is he not therefore also a *profane* writer in that he sabotages the notion of the sign? For Proust, signs are false, like camouflage, there being a fundamental "discord between our impressions and their habitual expression."[1]

The way it works is like this: There is the "interior Proust" sitting inside dwellings, reading books or making out with Albertine. And there is the "exterior Proust" going on walks in the countryside around Combray. The two poles of inside and outside mark out the space of meaning in which signs function, such as the view walking along the Méséglise Way of a roof, or the glimmering of the sun on a stone, or the smell of the road. Such sensory signs punctuate and frame Proust's anxiety about writing and one day well in the future will provide the solution to his writing hang-up. Sensory signs stop him in his tracks, he says, because they bring him sensuous pleasure "and also because they seem to be concealing, beyond what I could see, something which they were inviting me to come take and which despite my efforts I could not manage to discover."[2]

Signs have a doubleness to them in that they not only bring pleasure but also block perception, shading into something that might be sinister as well. They emit a sense of unfathomable fullness, which, if allowed to swell forth, can rupture and overwhelm habitual modes of perception and interpretation. No sooner has the author meditated upon this vexing nature of sensory signs than, walking once more along the Méséglise Way, he happens by chance (so he says) to spy through a window a young lesbian couple whom, before falling into each other's arms, spit on the photograph of the recently deceased father of one of them, the talented musician by the name of Vinteuil who doted on his daughter and whose music not only brought Swann and Odette together but runs through the entire novel as a silver thread of unsurpassable beauty and mystery.[3]

Returning home from yet another walk late afternoon in the environs of Combray, the narrator sees the twin steeples of the church of Martinville and suddenly feels the joy of the revealed sign, the gathering surge premonitory to the memoire involontaire. Only this time the surge is cruelly aborted as with equal suddenness he recalls how his mother would not come and kiss him goodnight.

> The region of sadness I had just entered was as distinct from the region into which I had just hurled myself with such joy only a moment before, as in certain skies a band of pink is separated as though by a line from a band of green or black. One sees a bird flying into the pink, it is about to reach the end of it, nearly touching the black, then it had entered it.[4]

To enter this band of green or black would be almost but not quite the end of color as well as almost but not quite the end of our mother through her profanation. The intensity of the sacred prohibition of incest is scored in this vision of light and color by the ethereality of flight from pink to black—or is it green?—a

What Is the Color of the Profane?

flight marked by a peculiar tension, riding the edge of blackness before disappearing into it.

Sexual pleasure for Proust, the author, as well as for several of his main characters, could only be achieved or was preferably achieved through acts of defilement. Walter Benjamin was told in Paris by Maurice Sachs, whom Edmund White regards as an unreliable witness, that Proust got to be called "the rat man" in one male brothel because he got sexual pleasure from watching mice in cages devour one another, while other times the rats were pierced with hat pins.[5] (How do you get rats to devour one another?) Proust's most exhaustive biographer, Jean-Yves Tadie, seems to accept these stories and other similar ones, as well.[6]

If we look at the novel we see that Proust has one of his central characters, Baron Charlus, chained and whipped for pleasure in the male brothel—that "Temple of Shamelessness"—set up by the Baron's onetime lover, the tailor, Jupien. Then there is Swann, after whom one whole volume is named. He is only capable of being satisfied sexually by common street prostitutes of whom he enjoys an endless stream. He seems to desperately need the risks this can involve. Many times right before meeting his beloved Odette, for instance, at the dinner parties regularly put on by the Verdurins, he would be sexually engrossed with a prostitute in his carriage outside the very house where Odette was waiting for him. Many times he would thus arrive late, once so late that Odette had already left, and Odette, whom he eventually gets to marry, was herself a prostitute, albeit upper class. Swann, it appears, can only love defiled women.

Watched by gigolos in the male brothel of Le Cuziat, Proust himself would spit on photographs of his mother and father.[7] This "logic of profanation" thus conceived by Julia Kristeva holds that the mother is maintained in her holiness only by finding pleasure in defiling her or at least images of her. It is the logic that Georges Bataille explored in his elucidation of transgression, as where Kristeva cites him: "This wish for limitless horror reveals itself in the end for what it is: the true measure of love."[8]

But "logic" is not exactly what Bataille had in mind for the energy of the sacred, split down the middle into its pure and impure halves. More to the point, he had in mind something like flying through color, skating with considerable and considered tension along the edge of blackness before disappearing into it. Kristeva herself went on to call such flight "the abject," a principal aspect of which is the blurring of categories such as sacred and profane, my body and my mother's, as they willy-nilly bleed into one another and as such constitute the zone of becoming I call the bodily unconscious as well as a specific quality of verbal fluency whereby words blur with things and don't simply represent them.

Such blurring is what Bataille had in mind when he referred to the sacred as a fearsome sticky substance without clear boundaries. Bataille's notorious interest in the *informe* or formlessness, one example of which was spit, is precisely this assault on the primacy of code's primacy. Such an assault amounts to a slippage into things, of language "blurring" into that for which words stand, although blurring hardly seems the appropriate word here, given that we are in the presence of contagious magic and blurring suggests a negative, unproductive, somehow weak or crippled existence instead of a bodily enhancing, world-enhancing, exciting language expanding one's sense of being.

To spit on your mother's photograph is just that assault on form Bataille had in mind. In spades. It calls attention not to the tortured gyrations in the form of the sacred, split between the pure and the impure, but to the white heat of the meltdown of the categories themselves into polymorphous magical substance. Such are the writer's familiars. They too follow the logic, the "logic of profanation," which is not so much a logic as a flying along the edge of meaning where pink gives way to green (or is it black?). To fly through color along the edge of blackness is neither pleasure nor pain. It seems to me it would be a mix of the two, and something more, like what Irving Goldman suggested was experienced by the Cubeo Indians of the Amazon imbibing their hallucinogens, a religious activity undertaken for the power of the experience.[9]

We must not forget that this spat-upon mother is an image, a defaced image, of the real mother. Photographs come in for a lot of comment in Proust's novel and do so, in my opinion, precisely because they are so powerful mimetically, by which I mean that photographs seem to be such wonderfully faithful depictions of whatever it is they are depicting. But there is one thing more real still, and that is the act of despoliation. For the magic of mimesis is most powerfully accomplished by negation, as when the image, especially a portrait, is pierced or spat upon. Then the image flares into the fullness of being. Then the image seems no longer to be merely an image but fuses with and becomes one with what it otherwise merely represents and Proust's dream of the "miracle of transubstantiation" of life into words is fully, which is to say sexually as well as intellectually, realized.

In those days the photos were in black and white. It was Proust who gave them color, the color, as Leiris might say, of the sacred.

Part Four

COLOR IN COAL

27

CReature of the Lightless Depths

> . . . a creature of the lightless depths, where life as we know it on the surface
> cannot exist, brought light and color with him as colors pour from tar.
> WILLIAM BURROUGHS, *The Western Lands*

"Your remembrances of before and after are in black and white," a friend told Primo Levi, while "those of Auschwitz and of your travel home are in Technicolor."[1]

Being a chemical engineer, Levi was made part of the Chemical Komando that constructed the synthetic-rubber factory known as Buna set up at Auschwitz by IG Farben, the largest chemical corporation in the world, making everything from toothbrushes to the gas used for the final solution. By World War II, Farben had plants all over the world and, in conjunction with the secrecy and the anonymity inherent to business corporations, presented a new model of empire, a chemified world imperium, portrayed by Thomas Pynchon in *Gravity's Rainbow* along these lines: "Oh, a state begins to take form in the stateless German night, a State that spans oceans and surface politics, sovereign as the International or the Church of Rome, and the Rocket its soul. I. G. Raketen,

Circus-bright, poster-reds and yellows, rings beyond counting, all going at once."[2] Welcome to Fritz Lang's film *Metropolis*, the corporate city-state where technology is the basis of power, the engineer works hand in hand with the administrator, and the masses labor unseen far underground, as in the city where I write these lines. Like the bodily unconscious, this empire is molecular in the micro-infinitude of its swarming through the everyday, from your toothpaste to your Siemens-based electronic surveillance.

The year in which *Gravity's Rainbow* is largely set is one year before the Nuremburg trials of Nazi war criminals in which IG Farben directors were largely absolved by the five U.S. judges fearful of the Soviet advance and desperate to conserve all those wonderful things that Joe Dubois, the U.S. government prosecutor, enumerated when he stated that IG Farben had "visited every American home, with dyes, plastics, fabrics. If Farben did not make your bathroom fixtures, your shaving mug, or even your razor, your wife surely owes much of her prettification—from Easter hat to silk stockings—to I.G. Farben."[3]

Too potent a symbol of the marriage of business and chemistry with the Third Reich, the name was erased after World War II and Farben underwent a clumsy change of outward identity, breaking up into its constituent pieces. Amazingly, the old guard was found largely innocent of running Farben's slave-labor camps—let us call them by their real name, *extermination camps*—and were soon reinstalled in management positions in the chemical industry, as happened with Nazi rocket scientists taken to the U.S. to continue their work there so that the U.S. could continue to defend democracy.[4]

To Joe DuBois' list you can add synthetic oil and rubber, explosives, life-saving drugs, gas warfare, and, of course, color film, as in Primo Levi's *Technicolored* memories. One of Farben's constituent parts was AGFA, which in addition to Technicolor film made poison gases for World War I, such that the German army, unlike the Allied forces, never had to set up a chemical-warfare service.[5] Charged by the U.S. government for his proactive role in the Third Reich, one Farben director testified: "I wanted to see my child, or some fish or game I had caught, in color—to see it in all its beauty. And we succeeded."[6]

There is an emotionally capsizing parallel here to Colesworthy Grant looking down at the men dancing captive in the indigo vat as it changes color like the storming sea. More than an analogy, there is a historical connection as well. It was indigo, with its Sanskrit-derived name, *nila*, meaning blue, that provided the name for the substance in coal tar—*aniline*—that spawned mauves, reds, yellows, greens, and blues, and, with them, modern chemistry. There was still another connection with indigo since *aniline* was first discovered in the indigo plant six years before it was discovered in coal tar.

Aniline allowed the chemist to remake nature as never before. Yet as the mimetic elixir of the modern, the very name of the founding piece of chemistry harks back to the ancient Sanskrit name for indigo, *nila*, meaning blue. Surely such a coincidence, or rather a chain of coincidences, is but a pretty footnote in the grand march that is science?

Or is there some other connection that means everything and nothing, an uncanny logic binding the ingenuity of nature to that of mankind, as with poison gas and color photography; an accord, if you will, between nature and power by which the Bengali indigo vat was moved, so to speak, from the colonies to Auschwitz in German-occupied territory in Poland? What seemed to Colesworthy Grant beautiful, wondrous, and disturbing in Bengal now blasted the human imagination beyond repair. Or so you would think.

In acknowledging his friend's observation as to the Technicolored nature of his memories of the camp, Primo Levi went further. He called it an "adventure." This is difficult to understand. Maybe the translation is off, but that, too, would be significant. Maybe Levi and the doctor really mean the camp *plus the trip home*.[7] The *adventure* then would refer to the horror plus the release, death and despair leading to freedom, poetically equivalent to the extraction of color from coal *as colors pour from tar*. At least in Levi's own, individual case, there was this release from captivity, followed decades later in 1987 by what seems to be his suicide, but the unremitting feeling I get of Levi in his major account of the camp is that depicted by William Burroughs as "a creature of the lightless depths, where life as we know it on the surface cannot exist, brought light and color with him as colors pour from tar."

Or maybe that creature of the lightless depths is not the prisoner Levi but IG Farben, which, in February 1944, set him to work at Auschwitz, bringing light and color as colors pour from tar? By 1943 Farben had 334 plants and mines across Germany and Nazi-occupied Europe. Almost half of Farben's 330,000 workforce by 1943 was conscript or slave, like the indigo plantations of the New World.[8] But this figure of 330,000 is a gross underestimation because it does not include what the accountants would call "turnover," meaning the continuous infusion of prisoners to take the place of the dead and dying. By that same year of 1943 Farben's death gas, Zyklon B, was in routine use in Auschwitz and

Farben had invested heavily there for the construction of the Buna-Werke plant, thirty-five kilometers square, designed to make synthetic rubber, synthetic petroleum, dyestuffs, and other byproducts of coal.

As for the name, *Buna-Werke*, it cannot pass unmentioned that in Bengal in the mid-nineteenth century, the men immersed in the indigo vats were known as *buna* coolies.

The size and appearance of the Auschwitz Buna plant in a frequently presented black-and-white aerial photograph is like something out of science fiction, such as Fritz Lang's *Metropolis*.[9] Long rows of buildings stretch out parallel to one another on a fuzzy sludge floating between air and earth. Slender chimneys stand out against the sky while to the right are massive, potlike structures that today we associate with cooling towers of nuclear plants. Filling in blank space between the buildings are elevated tracks like train lines several stories high. Long shadows are cast such that some buildings project a double of themselves as fretwork onto the whitish ground while others appear as hollow-faced enigmas. There is nothing Technicolored here but it is certainly fantastic. Do all chemical plants present this forbidding specter, and why do we call them *plants*?

Primo Levi said it was as large as a city. "Within its bounds not a blade of grass grows," he said, "and the soil is impregnated with the poisonous saps of coal and petroleum, and the only things alive are machines and slaves—and the former are more alive than the latter."[10]

Dampness, mist, and mud. An area encircled by stagnant fish ponds. Heavy clay soil and frequent rain. Such was the lay of the land at Auschwitz. Between 1941, when ground was broken for the construction of this plant, and 1943, two years later, more than two million captives passed through Auschwitz Camp I, of whom many were destined to work for Farben. At least one-half of the thousands of prisoners building Farben's Buna-Werke plant along with Levi died, at a rate of around thirty-two per day. Those who were too weak to work but did not drop dead on the job were taken away and gassed.[11] Although not one ounce of rubber was produced at Auschwitz, elsewhere, in partnership with other corporations such as Degussa and Degesch, Farben managed to fulfill its role in making the gas Zyklon B, used to kill prisoners. One ton could kill a million human beings. But then Zyklon broke down within three months and had to be continuously replenished to meet demand. Farben also made methanol in Auschwitz Camp IV to burn the corpses, although the fat from the bodies burning in large pits within the camp and outside in the woods was used for this purpose as well, described in minute detail by the Jewish prisoner and for three years crematorium attendant, Filip Müller.[12] Normally such a crematorium worker would himself be killed by the SS within a few months.

Zyklon B replaced carbon monoxide pumped from running motors in mobile vans as the Nazi gas of choice for killing Jews. The story goes that it was hit upon accidentally when the deputy commandant of Auschwitz, in the absence of the commandant, Rudolf Hoss, locked some Soviet prisoners of war and Communist functionaries in a cellar in 1941 and killed them with this gas, which until then had been used as a pesticide.[13]

A pesticide? How decidedly poetic, especially as regards the extermination of Jews portrayed throughout their plagued history as insects and parasites in need of extermination. How deep this portrayal went can be seen with Kafka, a Jewish writer famous for one story in particular, the prophetic story of a man who woke up one day to find himself a bug and whose family turned on him in repulsion and killed him.

This image of the Jew as vermin was realized with theatrical flair in the gas chambers in Auschwitz, where the victims were told not that they were being murdered but that they were being deloused. They were told to undress. They were given soap and a towel. Phony metal showerheads were installed. Notices urged them to be clean and remember the number of the hook from which their clothes were hung. Other signs said "Wash thoroughly because cleanliness is health." "Don't economize on soap."[14] In fact, according to one source, the official Nazi term for the use of gas was not death but "decontamination."[15]

A cyanide-containing pesticide, Zyklon was the outcome of research conducted under the supervision of an outstanding Jewish chemist named Fritz Haber, a charming "mastermind" who was forced to flee the Nazis in 1933 despite his having deconverted from Judaism at twenty-four to become not only Christian but a pillar of the German state in its alliance with the chemical industry. There is a photograph of him being married in 1917 to his once-Jewish wife in one of Germany's most famous Christian churches—the Kaiser Wilhelm Memorial Church in Berlin. Proudly he stands smiling in the uniform of a Prussian officer with a spiked, steel helmet and sword. Some twenty years later the children of his sisters and cousins died in Hitler's camps, gassed by Zyklon B. He received the Nobel Prize in 1918 for what is called "fixing" nitrogen from the air, paving the way for artificial fertilizers and a plentiful source of explosives for the Kaiser during the First World War. "Without this effort, German military capacity would have been exhausted by the spring of 1915 for lack of munitions, and the German people would have been starved for lack of fertilizers."[16] Working with Carl Bosch, who later became chairman of IG Farben, Haber made a fortune from his nitrogen-fixing discovery. He also provided the science behind Germany's use of chlorine gas in World War I.[17] His wife shot herself dead after a party at their house, some say in opposition to her husband's role as the czar of gas warfare, others say because he was unfaithful and a bully at home. The next day he took off to the eastern front to supervise the use of chlorine gas against the Russians. From an early age and throughout his life he suffered repeated nervous breakdowns and was frequently in sanatoriums.[18] Son of a dye merchant, young Fritz did not last long in his father's business. One report has it that they argued a lot, the young man trying to convince the older that synthetic chemicals would replace natural dyes, another that he wasted his father's money trying to profit from selling chlorine to combat a cholera outbreak which ended "too soon."[19]

This is not only history as biography, but history as myth and allegory, at once real and fantastic, at once black and white and Technicolored—as is Zyklon B, with which Fritz Haber had much to do.

Zyklon means *cyclone*, an odd name for what was, at first, aimed at lice. But then were not the humans against whom it came to be used also categorized as lice? And did not the substance come to acquire the fullest meaning of the cyclone? Indebted to mythology, advertising hype here became a self-realizing act, as did that story written in Prague about the bug. By undoubted coincidence and the cleverness of advertising wordplay, *Zyklon* was also the acronym of its main ingredients, compounds of cyanide and chlorine.

The prussic acid more technically called *hydrocyanic acid* used in its manufacture came from the waste in making sugar from sugar beets. Here's another name to ponder, the *prussic* in *prussic acid*. What does it mean, insofar as such names have a meaning or a logic? It is said to refer to the intensely blue Berlin blue or Prussian blue, discovered in Berlin in 1704 by heating dried blood, replacing the *naturally occurring* blue dye *aquamarine* because it was cheaper. In 1782 the great Swedish chemist Carl Wilhelm Scheele produced an acid from this Berlin blood that he therefore called Berlin blue acid or blue acid, *Blausaure* in German and *prussic acid* in English. Later this was called *hydrocyanic acid* from the Greek, *kyanos*, for blue. Scheele himself died from prussic acid because it was so toxic.

Truly, the naming of these powerful substances follows an uncanny logic. The zigzag logic of myth and mayhem traced through chemical odysseys in *Gravity's Rainbow* is barely able to keep up with this reality.

And wherever we turn, it seems color is there before us, even in the concentration camp and the sweetness of sugar. In fact, prussic acid or Blausaure is a synonym for Zyklon B, as comes across clearly in the agonized memoir of Kurt Gerstein, the SS's leading decontamination expert, ordered into action by Adolf Eichmann.[20]

Getting the beets, raising the capital, obtaining the patent, manufacturing the "stabilizer," and organizing the marketing of Zyklon B—all required many different companies and complex networks of alliances shifting and changing over time. To focus on *Degussa* or *Farben* or *sugar beets* is to clutch at straws, as Kafka would be the first to point out. The reality is one of an infinitude of little cogs, each pretty much minding its own petty business, looking forward to the next paycheck. And this is why we seize on the stark simplicity of icons, such as the name *Farben* or the name *Zyklon*, as we try to make sense of the fact that business as usual led step by wretched step to terror as usual.

IG Farben has come to symbolize the monstrous potential of modern technology. Hitler needed Farben, and once he was in power, Farben seemed to go out of its way to ensure the aims of his Third Reich. In assessing Farben's role here, we should ask, however, if there is any major industry in the world today that would not go along with the war machine of the state? Surely Farben—and the role of the chemists—is not an isolated case? In fact, by harping on Farben's diabolic role, do we not run the risk of making it easier for current industries to escape criticism? Try Halliburton and its role in the War Against Terror.

When I think about the role of color in all this, I ask myself how we who come after can possibly do justice to the poetry in technology that outstrips both poetry and technology? It is said there can be no poetry after Auschwitz because of its unspeakability and the knockout blow it delivers to God. But I think this assertion refers us to something else as well, to the mind-numbing property of the poetry that in fact does exist not in nature but in second nature, as with the blueness not of the blue sky but of prussic acid as a world historical force. This is lyric poetry gone wild and, what is more, it is a poetry not only of language but of a force instilled into the interaction of man with nature, and emerging from that interaction.

When I try to reconstruct by what bizarre set of accidents and logic in the natural world and in Western European culture an acid has been blessed with the name of Berlin blue and prussic acid, I am forced to ask if chemistry has not given us a new way of thinking about history, composed of nature and of man's domination of nature through naming as much as through technical ingenuity. "But let us also not forget," writes Nietzsche, "that in the long run it is enough to create new names and valuations and appearances of truth in order to create new 'things.'"[21] Likewise I am forced to ask how one's mind can possibly contain the ironies of the terrible associations that resulted in Zyklon B or the larger-than-life Fritz Haber who fell out with his dad trying to profit from chlorine in a cholera outbreak and years later pioneered gas warfare using chlorine—this same fellow who perfected an insecticide to kill lice that was later used by his employers, Farben and the German state, to kill his kin; this same fellow who rejected being Jewish to become Christian and was hounded out of his job, property, and home for being Jewish? And so it goes, as with the very name *Zyklon* meaning cyclone, and becoming all the more sinister, scientific-sounding, and bureaucratic by the addition of that *B*, which surely must takes its place alongside the phony showerheads and Kafka's *K*.

28

as coLors pour from tar

To carbon, the element of life, my first literary dream was turned, insistently dreamed in an hour and

a place when my life was not worth much: yes, I wanted to tell the story of an atom of carbon.

PRIMO LEVI, *The Periodic Table*

Farben, a German word meaning colors, changed reality. Replacing natural dyes, the new colors provided the basis of modern chemistry and hence the modern world. It took a European country without colonies, namely Germany, to initiate and perfect a chemical revolution displacing the raw materials provided by European colonies. One form of color colonization, as, for example, the British in India, was thereby replaced by another, as the chemistry of artificial dyes paved the way for our Brave New World of plastics and explosives. Derived from coal, of which Germany had plenty, the colonization of nature now began in earnest as the chemists got down into molecular structure itself.[1]

Yet how is one to tell the story of this without colonizing nature still further? If only things could speak, and speak for themselves. "I wanted to tell the story of an atom of carbon," said Levi. What stories they would tell, fairytales and ghost stories like we've never heard before. For that is where the story of carbon can take you, carbon, "the element of life," now better known as I write these lines as that which is going to kill us off through global warming. Element of life, indeed! What stories they could tell! Nothing compared with what they are going to tell! To date, this story has been occupied territory called the domination of nature, but—who knows—if the storyteller got it right, then might not something else emerge?

Therefore, if it is poetry that does the hard work, combining the manmade with the natural so there is no longer much of a difference, the poetry to which I refer and defer being the join, then I shall abjure the stepwise story, this happened then that happened, and try as best I can to nudge some of the things-in-themselves into speech such that they manifest their disjointedness no less than their joint.

- *Chemistry* is as old as mankind and the mud of the river Nile from where, so it is said, the word no less than the art enters the language as *alchemy*, originally referring to the art of dyeing cotton cloth. As an artisinal pursuit until the late eighteenth century, mixing this and that, using fire, distillation, and the magic of scrolls and books, not to mention the magic of spirits, most especially the spirits of the dead, chemistry promised a good deal, including the sense that it was an occult art prone to pacts with the devil. The secrets of nature could be gotten by unnatural means. Man could become a god, but at a cost—an extraordinary idea when you come to think about it, an idea that had to be dismissed as nothing but superstition, although why it should have existed is not clear.

- I would guess that for millennia artisans worldwide had their secrets involving a mix of the practical skills of craft with what is often called superstition. It is not always easy to separate these two aspects. People who worked with leather and silk, pottery and metallurgy, glass and animal husbandry come to mind, as do herbalists, healers, midwives, abortionists, and witches, all implicated with spirits and astrology as well as with plants and the magic of the human body and its secretions. Love potions are surely among the oldest artisinal crafts, just as hunting and sailing, too, require magic in addition to practical experience. Miners following the veins of mineral in the bowels of the earth rely on detailed knowledge, to which they have added a cornucopia of magical beliefs and rituals, including the exclusion of women from the mine. Blacksmiths beating at the forge have secrets they share only with the fiery metal, and all of these activities blend the supremely practical with the magical. From the stance of the year 2008 as I write these lines, it is hard to be sure how those artisans might have distinguished between science and art or science and magic, the natural and the supernatural. The more important boundary, provoking much art, was the elusive one between good and bad magic.

◆ Artisans interact with the thing world. A vital component of this interaction is often phrased as reproduction and not only as production—*reproduction* meaning *biological reproduction*—by which I refer to fierce taboos at the worksite or operant on the tools and materials used (plants, animals, minerals, human bodily substances and secretions, etc.). These taboos concern prohibitions on sexual intercourse, on the mere presence of women, or of men, and especially of pregnant or menstruating women, as in the fabrication of indigo and of indigo-dyed cotton cloth in the accounts I have registered from Indonesia and India. Where might we go with this? What dropped out of the world picture when conception, childbirth, death, and sex were deleted from mankind's interaction with the material world via chemistry and the gimcrackery of atoms and carbon rings?

◆ First published in 1604, one hundred years before the discovery of Berlin blue, Christopher Marlowe's *Tragical History of Doctor Faustus* concerns a German scholar who sells his soul to the devil so as to unlock the secrets of nature and conquer the world, very much including the fabled Orient from where the richest colored fabrics and dyes came. *Faustus* can be read today as an old-fashioned morality play, and no doubt even in Marlowe's time it was a delight for its exaggeration. But the images and the language endure. The devil may have been banished to the world of fable and children's literature, but the poetic truth of selling one's soul to the devil is probably more relevant today than it was in 1600, for now it is an everyday occurrence and technology can be truly apocalyptic. Who needs the devil when you have MBAs and AK-47s, his favorite calling cards?

◆ *Faustus* has a message for us. Nature can be manipulated, big time. This is a common way the church and historians of religion have talked about witches and magicians. They are said to have the hubris to insert themselves into the inexorability of the world so as to bend it to their selfish desires—make rain, make love, make gold, confuse opposing armies through hallucinations, whatever. To achieve this, *Faustus* envisions a world alive with animated beings, not deader-than-dead things, and these beings can be entertained and seduced by the magician's charms.

♦ Could cooking provide the elementary model of chemistry? I am thinking of the witches in Macbeth:

> Round about the cauldron go:
> In the poisoned entrails throw [*they move leftwards about the pot*]
> Toad, that under cold stone
> Days and nights has thirty-one
> Sweltered venom sleeping got,
> Boil thou first i' th' charmed pot!
> *Says the first witch, then all chime in:*
> Double, double toil and trouble;
> Fire burn and cauldron bubble

And for central Africa in the 1930s you can read some more about the connection between cooking and chemistry magic in a celebrated anthropological book describing witches gathered around the cooking pot into which, under the direction of the chief witch, they drop in the spiritual equivalents of human body parts.[2] Mere stories, of course. Myths. Legends. Call them what you will. You can see the anthropologist taking notes as his informant relates what people tell each other about witches. Could be true.

♦ And does not storytelling add to this its own chemistry, the chemistry that belongs to the artisanry of experience? "The lower Leskov descends on the scale of created things," wrote Walter Benjamin in his essay on the storyteller, "the more obviously does his way of viewing things approach the mystical." What Benjamin meant was that storytelling sought, at least with Nicolai Leskov, to link the sacred and the profane, the heavens above with the depths of the earth below. Thus, the "perfect artisan has access," he states, "to the innermost chamber of the realm of created things."

- To the chemistry of cooking and storytelling add discovery of new colors. Before mauve was discovered, dyes were "disclosed like magician's secrets and presented like cookery recipes."[3] After mauve was discovered, this was even more true. In his tours through England in 1859, demonstrating to the public his discovery of mauve, Henry Perkin drew the chemical sequence on a blackboard:

  - you start with one hundred pounds of *coal*
  - from which you get ten pounds, ten ounces of *coal tar*
  - from which come two and one-quarter ounces of *aniline*
  - and then, finally, one-quarter of an ounce of *mauve,*
  - one pound of which can color two hundred pounds of *cotton*

  He then displayed a container with nine gallons of water illuminated by a magnesium lamp. Into this container he dropped one grain of mauve. Within four seconds the container turned mauve.

- Other conjurers pull a rabbit from a hat or a dove from their sleeve. With mighty shamans as his avatars, Perkin went further in the practice of skilled revelation of nature's skilled concealment and what he did on stage was to inadvertently display not just an overlap between science and magic but their essential similarity. For had not science, in besting nature, become even more magical than magic? "Science had got the better of nature," writes the author of a book on mauve, "and nowhere did this belief carry more conviction than in the field of colour."[4]

- The spirits of the dead, with whom Marlowe's Dr. Faust wished to work, may today be little more than metaphor, but then have not coal and petroleum taken their place? Are not coal and petroleum the most basic of all spirits of the dead, being the spirits of the forests and swamps that went under long before the first magician?

  The miracles that magic will perform
  Will make thee vow to study nothing else.
  He that is grounded in astrology,
  Enrich'd with tongues, well seen in minerals,

Hath all the principles magic doth require . . .
The spirits tell me they can dry the sea,
And fetch the treasure of all foreign wrecks,
Aye, all the wealth that our forefathers hid
Within the messy entrails of the earth.[5]

- *Within the messy entrails of the earth.* Modern chemistry was born from
  the waste products of the coal used to drive the Industrial Revolution
  of coal and iron ore. Prior to coal it was wood that supplied the heat for
  blacksmiths working iron, lead, copper, gold, and tin, although even in the
  Middle Ages some coal was used by smiths and by limeburners making
  cement, and there was an intimate connection even then between the use of
  coal and the weapons industry.[6] Wood also supplied ash and charcoal from
  which were derived gunpowder, glass, and soap. The tar from the sap of
  trees was used to caulk ships.

- But when they ran out of trees the British colony of America became a
  main supplier until the Revolutionary War of 1775. It is hard to imagine
  timber being shipped all the way across the Atlantic so many years ago (in
  wooden ships caulked with wood tar, of course).

- Once that supply was cut off, other sources of energy had to be found
  and made to substitute for wood. Thus coal was ushered into history, and
  stories like Kafka's "The Bucket Rider" came into being—along with the
  fantastical stew of residues resulting from a curious new process, the *distillation of coal.* But back to Kafka's coal story for a moment, a story we can
  read as about man's dependence on coal, so desperate, it seems, that hallucinations are easily provoked. But that's not really Kafka. Instead the story
  concerns the hallucination that is coal, standing in the way animals do in
  his stories for the human world.[7]

- As for that fantastical stew at the bottom of the vat where coal was being distilled by the new process, why! that stew became the basis of industries that were, so it is said, more important than James Watt's steam
  engine.

- You get a sense of the novelty and of the thrill of the unknown if I relate that the first account of coal distillation was reported as early as 1667, followed thirty years later by an article in the *Philosophical Transactions of the Royal Society*, "An Account of Making Pitch, Tar, and Oil out of a blackish stone in Shropshire."[8]

- *Jack Tar.* Shipping was key to most everything. No wonder that British slang for the sailing man became Jack Tar. As he sailed the seven seas in his eighteenth-century tar-caulked and pitch-bottomed ship to bring back color and spice and all things nice, the residue left over back home from the distillation of coal on Jack Tar's rainy island became the elixir that would provide not only the colors of the rainbow but the pot of gold at the rainbow's end as well. Before that could happen, however, there had to be light, as provided by the spectral glow of coal gas streetlamps in major cities from around 1800 onwards.

- *Dreamworld of capitalism made even dreamier by coal gas.* Combined with the cheap "luxury" goods made available by the Industrial Revolution, coal-gas lighting provided an enchanted atmosphere for what Walter Benjamin perceived as the dreamworld of capitalism, meaning Paris as capital not only of France but of the nineteenth century. "Gas has replaced oil as gold has dethroned woodwork," writes one observer of the café scene in Paris in 1857. Another refers to the coal-gas light as a "luminous aureole." Others spoke of the diaphanous quality of its light and how it revolutionized the nightlife of cities with a festive air that "clearly betrays the oriental character of this form of lighting."[9]

- *The story is told.* In 1843 the great German chemist Justus von Liebig, much admired by Karl Marx and Friedrich Engels, directed his assistant, the great Hofmann, to analyze a bottle of light coal oil given him by a former student who owned a tar distillery near Frankfurt am Main, one of the first such factories on the continent. The former student had distilled tar into three fractions: *light coal oil*, used for waterproofing paper and cloth, *creosote*, for preserving wood, and *pitch*, used as asphalt.[10] In this little bottle of light coal oil lay the seeds of a mighty industry, wrote the historian J. J. Beer in 1959.[11] Not too long before Hofmann held this little bottle in his hand, Goethe had the dispirited Dr. Faust in pretty much the same situation:

> This phial fascinates me, like the sight
> Of soothing moon when, deep in forest ways,
> Our very thoughts are silvered with the light
> You I salute, you flask of virtue rare
> That now I hand me down with reverent care;
> In you I honour human wit and art.
> The very spirit of the opiate flowers,
> You distillation of the deadly powers.[12]

- Faust might not have been able to literally see the future in concrete detail, but he was correct with regard to the deadly powers of what he—and Hofmann—were holding in their hands. An interesting character, Goethe's Faust brings out the demonic potential of modern science because he is able to discern the "poetic" side of chemistry, and this he is able to do because he is invested in a world "deep in forest ways," illumined by the silver light of the moon. These forest ways are those of pre-Christian European shamanic eras and correspond to a world in which things most of us today would consider mere things are instead held to possess something like a soul or a mind such that we might, like Faust, say "I honour human wit and art" in them.[13] Thus does Goethe—our philosopher of color—have this shamanic-scientist in the making, our natural philosopher, Dr. Faust, span the arts and sciences, as did Goethe, seeing them as one and unified. This is why Faust is able to feel and express terrible danger in the beauty he senses in his hands, this "very spirit of the opiate flowers."

- It is said that as a youth, Goethe was fascinated by alchemy. Using *liquor silicum*, a type of glass that melted on exposure to air so as to become a clear liquid, he tried to make a substance called *virgin earth* that could give birth to other substances from its own womb. He was nineteen years old at the time. Goethe's alignment with alchemy was lifelong and informs his color theories, especially in relation to the interplay of light and darkness.[14]

- As Faust sensed, from this phial came a new world heralded by amazing colors, one after the other. Who could believe that such intensity of color could come from tar? "The colorific intensity of some of these dyes is extraordinary," wrote a clutch of chemistry professors in 1878 in Yorkshire, one of the most famous coal-mining counties of England where *The Moonstone* is set. "One ten-millionth of a grain of 'magenta' or 'fuchsin' gives a perceptible color to a drop of water."[15] The first dye was the new color in 1856 that came to be called mauve, followed in 1859 by a cherry red given the name of *fuchsin*, after the fuchsia flower. In 1860 a black was developed, and then, unbelievably, around 1862, violets, greens, and blues were made from fuchsin, while poppy and scarlet reds were developed soon thereafter.

♦ *A new color?* I find it strange that mauve is described as a *new color*. The very idea of a *new color* suggests that the product of men's hands exceeds their imagination of color. The very idea of a *new color* is testimony to placing a big fat question mark in what was until then a relatively secure relationship of subject to object. Now it gets confusing. What is this color? That is one question. And it leads to another. What is color? Is it in nature, in our mind's eye, in a vat in a factory, or in some combination thereof? And what of the naming of the new? Walter Benjamin floated the concept of the "optical unconscious" as that which exists in nature but of which we were unconscious until revealed by the camera. It would be part of the revolutionary movement. Can we use this idea and talk hence of a "colorifical unconscious"?

♦ In his patent, the discoverer of this color called it *aniline purple* and also *Tyrian purple*, in deference to the regal color in the Old Testament. It was French dyemakers who gave it the name of *mauve*. They ignored the patent and what they made is said to have been even more beautiful than Perkin's biblically endorsed *Tyrian purple*.[16] Thus does the creation of men's hands cut across and put into question our most cherished boundaries. We name it and now see it "out there" in the world.

♦ Mauve was discovered accidentally when young Perkin was mucking about with coal tar under the direction of Hofmann, who had set him the task of extracting quinine from aniline. The fabrication of drugs, not colors, was what was on the tar-research agenda; drugs such as quinine, caffeine, and morphine. Coal-generated color was a fortuitous byproduct, first of the search for light, as in gas lighting, and then of the desire for drugs. Once discovered, these dye-fast mauves, scarlets, greens, and bright yellows took center stage for a while, but it was not long before the old links to the world of medicine reasserted themselves. Dyes led to spectacularly successful treatments of incurable illnesses, such as syphilis and certain bacterial infections, from the late nineteenth century on, while also opening new fields in bacteriology and cell biology with the use of stains derived from aniline dyes such as Congo red and methylene blue.[17] Like the microscope, color made the invisible world visible.

• The *drysalter* of previous centuries for whom dyes and medicine belonged in the same box was made anew. Only this time around there was an added buzz in the air, as if drugs and colors were designed to bring out the sizzling magic of each other since both were derived from this new and mysterious chemical process expanding the bubble of discovery. At the same time as mauve was discovered, Karl Marx hit upon the fetish character of the commodity as the key to understanding not just the modern economy but the way we who live under capitalism unconsciously formulate its animism. Just as aniline dyes came later to stain the basic unit of the human body, the cell, and its constituent parts, such as the nucleus, cytoplasm, and chromosomes, so Marx broke capitalism down to its basic cell, which he called *the commodity*. He enlarged upon the manner by which the commodity seemed endowed with magical properties, as if it had a mind and will of its own.

• Color gave a buzz to product. For example, car companies spend enormous amounts of money on getting the colors just right, the exterior, the interior, and the interior's interior where all the secrets lie. Like the caffeine and morphine built into its origin story, artificial color expressed the commodity's intoxication, fulsomely. The color that came from tar was thus more than a commodity. It was the "commodity's commodity," by which I mean it provided the commodity with what anthropologists call *mana*, the mystery that grants power to magicians, chiefs, and kings. Trying to demystify the claims anthropologists made for mana, Claude Lévi-Strauss called it *oomph*, so maybe we should too—not commodity fetishism but commodity oomph?

- Marx himself regarded *labor* as the unique commodity on which the capitalist system rested because labor was the one commodity that could be made to create more value than needed for its reproduction. Much the same could be said for color.

- Textiles occupied an enormous part of the mid-nineteenth-century European economy. One has to think small in order to grasp this bigness. Not bridges or ships or buildings or guns, but what millions of people put on their bodies. Then came the new color. "In a business as susceptible to fashion, where the desire for variety is insatiable . . . the greater the variety of textiles and the cheaper their price, the louder arose the clamor for something new, something stunning, in the line of color."[18]

- Like mana, the new color could be standardized. The magician and the king have their formulae, which compose their rites, gestures, and special languages. Similarly the chemists have their formulae. But now we engage a paradox that defines the modern world, the paradox of *standardized newness*. "Actually, however, the artificial colors came not only to surpass the old dyes in fastness, clarity, and variety, but they were perfectly standardized so that the exact color could be reproduced repeatedly with absolute certainty."[19] A similar paradox occurs with the mix of *brilliance* and *fastness* to be found with these new, standardizable colors. Before then, dyes were elusive, like the weather. They were classed as *fugitive*, like escaped prisoners. Now they could not escape as they had before under the impact of sun, rain, or the passing of time.

- It has been said that the world changed fundamentally with the invention of the camera, the lithograph, and the other methods of mechanical reproduction of images around the midpoint of the nineteenth century. Before then there had been a mere handful of pictures. But now reality could be duplicated as image on a massive scale, and was no longer so real. Color from tar was invented at the same time as the camera, and amounted to a similar mechanical reproduction of reality that surpassed reality. What follows is only a cliché-laden glimpse into what is meant here: "The desire on the part of the fashion industry to delight the eye of the customer with a riot of color not only stimulated dye research, but also had the effect of greatly beautifying the daily life of man [adding] new dimensions to man's esthetic creations."[20] Another source adds: "Dyes . . . totally changed the way the world looked."[21]

+ Imagine the world of a person who all his life could see only black and white, but was one day given color vision. This seems pretty much what happened. It was as if a painter had been let loose, turning the black-and-white world into a modern world splashed with color.

+ Marx paid close attention to chemistry. He sensed that it would provide the key to the transformation of nature by man and of man by nature. He was delighted to find in chemistry what he took as confirmation of Hegel's laws of logic, as applied to human history. Chemistry and human history, the same law.

+ In letters to Engels, Marx pays homage to Perkin's mentor, Hofmann, as well as to Hofmann's teacher, Justus von Liebig, whose father was a dry-salter and dealt in colors, as did Fritz Haber's father. It seems as if the new chemistry followed chains of kinship in nature—witness the passage from the indigo plant and coal tar to aniline—side by side in an almost tribal way with the craft of the fathers. The history of modern chemistry is the passage from the dyer to the chemist, as well as from father to son. Ethnic and religious affinities played a part, too, dyers being often drawn from tightly knit groups such as the Jews of northwest Britain, Germany, and northeast France, as well as the Quakers of Manchester, and the Protestants of Mulhouse.[22] Behind them stand legions of dyers in India.

+ "For Germany, synthetics were the wealth of the Indies."[23] Could the great Hegel have foreseen that chemistry would displace colonies, that, being without colonies, Germany would recreate raw materials such as colors and rubber and petroleum from factories? This seems logical. Too logical. Too Hegelian. But it is true, as well. Colonization now meant the colonization of chemical bonds and molecules, which had hitherto gone their own way, free of interference.

- Chemistry here means largely *organic chemistry*, the chemistry of the carbon ring, meaning the chemistry of carbon, coal, petroleum, and the body—or, as some would have it, *organic chemistry* is the chemistry of *life itself*. There is something strange here, the world being divided between living things and not-living things, an eerie distinction, for are not inorganic things alive too? "The chemistry of life" seems synonymous with clockwork oranges, heading into Dr. Faust's sacred territories of animated beings with whom you can sit down, talk, and cut a deal.

- *Organic chemistry* is the manipulation of what had been cooked in the planet's crust after the primeval forests went under to sediment in underground marshes. Fast-growing rushes and giant tree ferns grew in swamps in hot and humid climates hundreds of millions of years ago. In that fertile soup, bacteria thrived. As the swamps sank, so the organic matter became coal or petroleum. Sometimes you can see lakes of pitch or lumps of coal on the surface of the earth.

- Organic chemistry created a conceptual leap in the relation between man and nature, thanks to the system of naming bestowed upon the oils and tars derived from coal. Names such as *benzene, nitrobenzene, naphthalene, isatin,* and *dioxindole* formed a system like a kinship table, showing the links to each other and to the mother lode. "Associative mental processes" and "thinking by analogy" became the most valuable intellectual tools.[24] Pynchon called this the work of coal-tar kabbalists.[25]

- After the *naming* came the *picturing* of the benzene carbon ring consisting of six carbon atoms, to each of which is attached a hydrogen or oxygen atom. It is said by some that that this conceptual leap was due to the German August Kekulé, who used only his last name and in 1890 told the story that sometime in the late 1850s he was dozing in front of the fire when he had a vision of atoms forming up and dancing like snakes. One of the snakes, he said, "had seized hold of its own tail, and the form whirled mockingly before my eyes."[26] This is the *ouroboros* snake, dripping in what is usually thought of as ancient mysticism, favorite of alchemists, and made much of by Jung, with his theory of archetypes.

- Mocking? Why was this snake whirling mockingly? Because the dream of the snake would lead to its self-destruction, that's why. "But the meanness, the cynicism with which this dream is to be used," says Pynchon in *Gravity's Rainbow*. "The Serpent that announces, 'The World is a closed thing, cyclical, resonant, eternally returning,' is to be delivered into a system whose only aim is to *violate* the Cycle. Taking and not giving back, demanding that 'productivity' and 'earnings' keep on increasing . . . and most of the World, animal, vegetable, and mineral, is laid waste in the process."[27]

- The "gold benzene ring with a formée cross in the center—the IG Farben Award for Meritorious Contributions to Synthetics Research."[28] This is the "great Dream that revolutionized chemistry and made the IG possible."[29]

- *The great Dream.* If you try to pin down when the snake dream emerged from the fire, you will draw a blank, as the sources, all so sure of themselves, contradict one another. Kekulé himself gave voice to the snake story some thirty years after the alleged event, and is said to have possibly been inspired by a cartoon of his model showing monkeys in a circle holding hands. This combination of shady recall and back-to-front chronologies associated with dreams and fire is why Pynchon's history, with its wisecracking wordplays and soaring fantasies, strikes me as a wonderful antidote to the role myth and dream play in the domination of nature. But Pynchon does not demystify. To the contrary. He builds on the myths already in place in science so that "the poetry of the join," as I call it, is more easily channeled away from the violation of the Cycle.

- Another story put out by Kekulé is that he came up with the idea of a three-dimensional molecular model of this ring while sitting upstairs on a London bus. The author of *The Age of Capital*, Eric Hobsbawm, sees this model as equivalent to the move from the "flat model" of accountants to the full-bodied models of architects and engineers.[30] This resonates with the story that as a young man Kekulé wanted to study architecture but attended a lecture by the great chemist, Liebig, and switched careers.

- Whether true or not, these epiphanies can be understood as testimony to the breakthrough into modernity that instead of eliminating mythology magnifies the mythic power of science (or is it the other way around—the scientific powers of myth?), from the ancient powers of fire and snakes to the upstairs of a London bus, western Europe's quintessential location for reconceptualizing time and space, as occurs in Dorothy Richardson's pre-Joycean novel, *Pilgrimage*.[31] Let us not overlook, however, the possibility that it was the representational language sought by organic chemistry in deciphering the secrets of nature that here leads the way, which literature followed.

- Once aniline had been extracted from both indigo and from coal tar, it seemed that sooner or later most everything by which we define modernity could be made in a laboratory and its associated factory, thanks to the marvelous exertions of what Walter Benjamin in 1933 called *the mimetic faculty* in an essay that begins thus: "Nature creates similarities. One need only think of mimicry. The highest capacity for producing similarities, however, is man's." [32] A pity he did not think to include chemistry.

- I say this because by imitating the carbon ring and manipulating the elements hung onto it, organic chemistry amounted to a cosmic breakthrough in the capacity to mime. *Now one could mimic nature's capacity to mimic.* This allowed for a mimesis of nature on a hitherto inconceivable scale. "Kekulé's former students and young disciples turned the ring into a tool that would contribute to the most remarkable innovative program in the nineteenth-century chemical industry."[33] The example provided here is the making of the red dye, alizarin, "the first instance of industrial replication of an organic molecule found in nature." For industrial replication, read *industrial mimesis*. Later, with plastics, as the very word has come to suggest, we now have the wrap-around, infinitely flexible substitute for most everything. With polymer chemistry developed by Farben chemists in 1939, the chemists could now decide, writes Pynchon in *Gravity's Rainbow*, "what properties they wanted a molecule to have, and then go ahead and build it . . ."[34]

- The replication of nature, meaning the replacement of "first nature" by "second," included not only *first nature* stuff such as rubber and petroleum, duplicated in chemical vats and distilleries, but the replication of *mythic nature* too, meaning making myth reality, as with poison gases and explosives. Kekulé's snakes whirling in fire with their tails in their mouths were just the beginning. What had in the nineteenth century been dependent on bird droppings hauled across treacherous seas from islands off Peru and Chile by way of Cape Horn so as to provide fertilizer for dying fields in Europe and the U.S., could now, thanks to organic chemistry and the man behind Zyklon B, Fritz Haber, be made in German factories as both explosives *and* fertilizer. Indeed, what comes across strong is the interchange between nice, innocent-sounding stuff, like fertilizer, and naked, aggressive stuff, like explosives.

• Plants set up by IG Farben to make antifreeze, hidden in German forests during World War II, could, with a flick of a switch, be converted into plants making mustard gas. I read this as fact and allegory. "Deep in the forests of eastern Bavaria," wrote Richard Sasuly at the end of World War II, "the Nazis hid their newest war plants. You can pass them on a road and see nothing. You can fly over them and again see nothing but the dense green blanket of the trees." They are perfectly camouflaged, "painted dirty greys and yellows, covered by netting where they stand in small clearings. Some of the units of a plant may be underground. Generally they are widely scattered, connected by miles of green pipes . . . they can be converted back to war production tomorrow."[35]

• As allegory, this can be read through a mythologizing lens that renders truth larger than life so that we grasp the simple core: that those miles of green pipes running concealed through the forest are with us yet, that in connecting the state to industry and both to the forest they manifest the ever more powerful domination over nature, and that this *interchange* at the flick of a switch between "nice chemistry" and "bad chemistry" is a leading characteristic of the mimetic faculty, meaning its ability to not only simulate but to dissimulate. We see it with antibiotics and vaccines, which imitate, with a difference, so as to destroy "the bad guys," and we see it in setting up plants that can convert from antifreeze to mustard gas. There is a strain in German philosophy that emphasizes this *interchangeability* as a leading historical process by which the imitative playfulness of nature—including human nature—as an end in itself is then turned against itself in a morbid enactment of mimesis. Nietzsche called it *resentiment*, meaning the transfer of life forms from play to profit. Others, with Auschwitz, Nietzsche, and what they called the drive for the domination of nature on their minds, called it *the organized control of mimesis*.[36] In Amerika it was called "scientific management," Taylorism, and Fordism. Lenin loved it. Stalin even more. Today in all walks of life it thrives stronger than ever, intertwined with everyday life and most especially with time, the way we schedule our day and our night and our bodies. Does not the very word *plant* sum this up, being both a factory and a green spurt of nature in garden and forest? Is not this ultimate deception the unforced, natural poetry, combining the manmade with the natural?

♦ *The paint factory.* The use of chemistry to destroy humans found its chemist, who, using the model of the chemical factory weekly report, chronicled Auschwitz. This was Primo Levi, in whose account humans and things operate on pretty much the same level. Here a scrap of bread speaks as much as any human and certainly more than any *mussulman*. In conversation with Primo Levi the year before Levi died (the general opinion is that he killed himself), the novelist Philip Roth makes much of the fact that Levi spent the entirety of his working life after Auschwitz as a chemist in a paint factory in his birthplace of Turin, eventually becoming a manager. Unlike Sherwood Anderson, also a paint-factory man, in Ohio, Levi seems to Roth to have thrived in this setting. Roth goes way out. "I wonder if you think of yourself," he asks, "as actually more fortunate—even better equipped to write—than those of us without a paint factory and all that's implied by that kind of connection?" (What a question!) Levi shrugs and says it's by chance things turned out like that. But early on he had told Roth that "I must admit there is no incompatibility between being a chemist and being a writer: in fact there is a mutual reinforcement."[37]

♦ *Plants that are not plants:* Primo Levi ends his book, *The Periodic Table*, talking about carbon. Each chapter of this book is dedicated to an element in the periodic table—tin, chromium, etc. But the last element he chooses is carbon, the side of life, carbon in the form of coal being what Levi got put to work on so as to make artificial rubber in the Buna plant. There is a story for each element Levi has chosen, just like people used to write a fable for each different animal. But to say this misses the point. *For the real stories are the ones told by the elements themselves* concerning their character, their relationships with other elements, and their life stories in the human world. Things, meaning the chemical elements of the periodic table, become like people, and people become like . . . ? Well, that's for you to figure out. That is what makes *The Periodic Table* a unique contribution to literature and history as much as to science, in other words to what I have called "the poetry of the join," by means of which lies the possibility not of mastery of nature but of the mastery of nonmastery.

29

COLORED BY WEATHER

I am coming to the end. All along it has been my heartfelt wish to allow color to change the way we see and hence the way we are made aware of the world at large as a body like the human body. I have done so by pointing to a peculiar aspect of color blindness that is illustrative of the blindness of habit, habit being the flywheel that allows society to function.[1] *Look! Look at color! Become aware!* is what I'm saying—Benjamin, via kids, crazy about it; Burroughs, it drips off the page; Proust, the same; Conrad's Congo, Virginia Woolf's waves, Malinowki's kula, the same—yet we so rarely see color unless it hurts and offends us. Color passes us by in the same way in which we do not notice our own breathing until it stops, by which time it's a little late. This is puzzling. It suggests that we in the West have an unconscious engagement with the color world, to which our bodies even more than our eyes are connected, and it is this force and connection, really, rather than color itself, which has gotten me going as our planet heads into the manmade onslaught of global warming and the bodily unconscious forces another type of awareness on the species.

It is not that color is banned or banned outright. To the contrary. Bright colors have wondrous powers of transgression that have been used to make contact with the gods. And even in the West, although bright color has been policed pretty severely, it is allowed now and then to play in the red-light district.

But then I want to tread carefully because color is full of kitsch traps, and just about everyone I tell I am writing on color recommends a book on color I *must* read, and I remember something in Marx to the effect that writing about money has made more men fools than has love or writing about love. Ditto for color.

Love, money, and color. Are these therefore untouchable subjects because they are foolish-making subjects about which the less said the better because there is something about them which actively resists language, not by honest confrontation but by subtle ambush and deceptions? And I'm not even thinking of boring. So many boring books on color, as if the reason color makes us foolish is that it allows us to say the first and, after that, the many things that willy-nilly enter our head and make us feel dizzy with profundity touching on the theological. Or else we drive the opposite way and perfect a system, a code, a spectrum, a pattern of contrast—you name it, no shortage of these—or a gee-whiz, wide-eyed chronology of color fashion. Color provides, it seems, a license to be stupid, willfully so. Truly a babble of tongues designed to make the mysteries of color all the more opaque. Poor color.

Or maybe not so poor, after all? Could it be that within our philosophy certain spaces have been long marked out as no-fly zones, that they remain resistant to sense-making and analysis, perhaps so other things can be made sense of and analyzed? Could it be that color, poor color, is a sterling example of such a no-fly zone and that this is because it is uncomfortably placed between meaning and force, between an idea and the body, especially the body in motion, as on those William Burroughs's inspired color walks, and this to such an extent that color itself walks? Neither fish nor fowl, color is anarchic, spreading across categories and disrupting them, which is why, I think, its most flagrant expressions are deemed vulgar and tasteless and reserved by Western culture for children, painted women, and "man in a state of nature."

One category that is in no short supply when it comes to color is "taste," as in "good taste" or "shocking taste." We could just as well say "good color." What a category! Beautifully vague, beautifully empowered—by definition indefinable and perfect for separating them from us. Could world history be built on taste, and vice versa?

Everyday yet miraculous, attracting yet repulsing, one moment in your face, next moment invisible, color in the West seems meaningful and ready for all sorts of sign-games, as with the tired orange and red alerts of the War Against Terror. Yet color is adept at sidestepping the world of signs for that of presencing, layering, graininess, washes, and other nervous impulses taking you into the image, which is how van Gogh ended up painting and which is what the Benjamin, Burroughs, Woolf, and Proust crew loved so much as—like me and my love—they thus gave color legs by means of their color walks, color being more akin to an animal than to a skin draped over a form. And they each developed a style whereby intellection and being in the world were awash in the red of Benjamin's butterfly and not only the idea of such. Such stylishness is what is called for in the no-fly zones, provided the weather is right.

With this troublemaking propensity in mind, color surely qualifies for Michel Leiris's idea of "the sacred" as that which is sought after yet feared simultaneously, ambiguous, dangerous, and loaded with prohibitions—all of which seem to play out differently between the West and most other peoples and places, which is the reason why I have made much of Goethe's occasional remarks to that effect. He noted aversion to vivid colors in his time and place, as compared with "man in a state of nature," and I have also been pleased to come across spontaneous exclamations by persons as different in character, point of view, time, and place, as Denis Diderot and John Ruskin, with regards to the sacredness of color. "Colour is the most sacred element of all visible things," wrote Ruskin. "Drawing gives shape to all creatures," says Diderot, but "color gives them life. Such is the divine breath that animates them."[2]

Why am I pleased? And why I am so aware of Goethe's crossover man who returned from fighting wars in North America with his face painted in the manner of the Indians? Because all along I have had the impression that for a long time color in the West owes a good deal of its effects to the imagination of the colonial experience, and that, furthermore, as such, this "primitivism" has long tapped into and helped shape what I call the bodily unconscious of the West, an unconscious that, following the great physiologist Walter B. Canon, I refer to as "the wisdom of the body"—a wisdom that Canon saw as highly susceptible to sorcery, at least in those places where such is the practice, and I, writing many decades later, see as both vulnerable and resistant to the most deep-seated colonization of all, that of nature now bracing itself for planetary meltdown.[3]

The domination of nature that has led to this meltdown involves at its core the rationalization of everyday life mining the bodily unconscious, most especially as regards the sun. If Isidore of Seville could point to the affinity of *calor* and *color*, meaning the heat and light of the sun in relation to color, we can equally point to the sun in yet another way, meaning the earth's movement around the sun as the constitution of time through darkness and light—Goethe's alchemical basis to color—which means the working day especially as analyzed in Marx's *Capital*. Late-nineteenth-century Taylorism, also known as "scientific management," with stopwatch in hand extended the assembly line from the factory floor to the speed up of all aspects of life such that a new word, "stress," is now in usage worldwide and there seems no stop in sight as the planet, like a tired old geezer, breathes its last.

Color resists this fate even when IG Farben and the coal-tar chemists got cranking with their synthetic world makeover. Unlike time, color could not be sped up or slowed down. Nobody knew what it was even if they knew how to fake it. Instead, color spoke to nature like the sun and it spoke of far-off people who made silk and dyed cotton in a language forever foreign, which is a good part of the reason why it so appealed and yet had to be held, as Goethe said, at arm's length. This seems to me like an ally, therefore, in disengaging the body from what Marx called "the working day," or what I will call "the schedule" that has come to budget life itself.

Of course, this may not be color itself so much as the way we put it into words, the everlastingly curious thing being that color seems to disappear once worded. You can have one or the other, at least in English, but not both. Once you speak of the tomato-red sunset, you have erased that particular tomato. This is why people get a shock when all those streams of color in Malinowski and Proust are pointed out to them, because even as careful readers they never saw or stepped into those streams before. But then there are the stories about color, and even more powerful, the stories color tells about itself, as with what I have called "Redeeming Indigo." Here color gives voice to both the thing world and to the thing world interacting with the human world.

Thus have I composed not so much a history of color as the other way around, what longingly and defiantly Nietzsche once referred to as an inquiry into the color of history, that not-yet-even-begun project. And I have found in the process of this writing that the issue is one of coming across this story or that image which might make more obvious the splice by which the senses make sense of things, things such as color, which is why I have in the final chapters, where my account gets pretty grim, drifted into what I call "poetry" as that which splices nature to second nature, as in the case of IG Farben, once the world's largest chemical company, born of color, named appropriately, and central to the power of the Third Reich. Thomas Pynchon does, I believe, much the same in his novel *Gravity's Rainbow*, as regards this strange poetry. But my account is a little shorter, although, like his, neither fish nor fowl, perfectly fitting for the mythology rampant in the join between what we call nature and the pervasive, all-inclusive mimesis of the world that chemistry provided. Once it took over from alchemy in a mighty oedipal thrust, chemistry created a new world not from alchemical lead but from coal, which did all that the alchemists had merely dreamt of in producing the rainbow plus the pot of gold at its foot. Goethe's crossover man is right there too, as the poetry of the join that he carries on his face, the face of world history. He is Madame Swann and he is mauve and he is me, too, looking at Goethe looking at that face come back from across the sea, Goethe in his black and white and various shades of gray.

The color of history connects with the history of color nowhere more meaningfully than with the way the word "plant" became used for the factory, as when aniline, the significant ingredient in indigo, cultivated by slaves and coolies, was discovered in coal tar and hence became the basis for turning the ancient forests that had become coal into "organic chemistry." Known also as the chemistry of life, this was built on the carbon ring, which in Kekulé's daydreaming was represented by the ancient symbol of a snake with its tail in its mouth, forming a perfect, living circle, only Kekulé's snake was writhing in fire, an ominous detail that was not part of the ancient symbol at all.

Struck by plants that have become plants that destroy plants, I am immeasurably taken aback by a remark of Walter Benjamin's that because death is built into novelty, "fashion prostitutes the living body to the inorganic world." Since, by my reckoning, color in the West had a great deal to do with making fashion fashionable and hence turning the wheels of capitalism, I would like to modify this remark and think of color as transmuting the human body not into the inorganic but into the organic world of plants—as we find copiously in Proust. As such, this is a body with one foot in the social world (what could be more social than fashion?) and the other in an extrasocial world of creaturely substances and things, the two together forming a perfectly fitting location for what I call the bodily unconscious. Yet as plants become plants that destroy plants, parallel to the way death is built into novelty, what is likely to happen to this perfectly fitting location?

The other location was the colony. Given color's dependence in the West on colonial fantasy and experience, I have tried to explore ethnographic field-work as that which always held the potential for a generous awareness of the investigator's body in understanding the reach of the world. Normally ignored and even repressed, this potential flares in Malinowski's diary and is subtly but infrequently carried over into his ethnographies, where we are borne away by the color wave as harbinger to profound upheavals in the bodily unconscious as it interacts with other bodies, human and inorganic, such as those waterfalls become sound passing into color on coral reefs at the base of sorcery-laden mountains. As such, his descriptions of these colorful chains of being quickly become not merely colorful but an inquisition of color itself, perturbing the practice of looking as much as what one is looking at. That is the path I am on, too; beseeching the color genie to emerge full flower so as to question our being and our notions of being's being. Why color should so easily facilitate this in Western culture I do not know, but it is there doing that, whether it be in Conrad's Congo, Primo Levi's Auschwitz as the summation of IG Farben, or Malinowski's eye for the sunset falling like a stone in the tropics over colors that flame up crazy one minute, gone the next.

Song, weather, and other *bodies* are what I would have liked to have given more space to in this regard, as so many variations of the color spirit spinning its way through the bodily unconscious—*song* because it is the handmaiden of dreams and visions in the shamanism that gave me the sense no less than the image of what I needed so as to be able to think of color as elusive and alive, like the feathers of newborn birds in the bodies of Selk'nam shamans in Tierra del Fuego, in short as *polymorphous magical substance.* Such a fairytale sub-stance, if substance it be, combines the attributes Nietzsche opposed, namely the *Apollinian* property of the image, with the *Dionysian* property of materiality, meaning, in this case of color and the feathers of newborn birds, the immer-sion, the bodily immersion, of the viewer in that image. That this opposition of image and substance was for Nietzsche likely to be a mix, not an either-or state of affairs, is radically borne out by the observation in Frazer's *Golden Bough* that magical charms frequently work this way too, combining an image of what is to be influenced with substances drawn from it as well.

To think of color as a substance with density and propensity to fluctuation and change, like the light flowing through the forest, light purple, some subtle mist of green and blue with some red and yellow in there too—was to realize more than color as in *coloring*. It was some other medium altogether, a curious light lightness, for which the term *polymorphous magical substance* seems appropriate. Such a substance helped me get out of the spot-of-color-on-the-page idea of color and pushed me into thinking of the great conjuring tricks of shamans reported the world over, tricks in which a plasma-like sense of the being of being flourishes, what Sartre called nausea, what Burroughs felt as a beautiful blue substance flowing into him, and what Eisenstein, thinking of cartooning, noted as a musicality of color and landscape. Virginia Woolf called it *waves* and had her own fantastic song of color to sing in its regard where her words melted away as the body grew from youth to old age to the imminence of death in her novel of that name, *Waves*.

As for other *bodies*, to use the phrase of the Native American anthropologist of the late nineteenth century, J. N. B. Hewitt, I take the fine-meshed connectivity between bodies to be where song and the color spirit take us to and from where they emerge. It is to what I call the *bodily unconscious* that this connectivity directs us—another sort of intelligence working, as it were, in a subterranean manner, like the signals that operate between the moon and the oceans in relation to the tides and the flow of menstruation, or the message that urges wood-boring beetles northwards along with global warming into untouched forests.

What has been called *sympathetic magic* corresponds to this sort of poetic messaging too, as with the musculature, the organs, the breathing apparatus—above all the travail of falling asleep in Proust—passing through alternating worlds such as a diver may find in descending the ocean, worlds far more revealing of reality, he thought, than the conventionalized reality perceived by waking consciousness. Indeed, so radical is the difference that to pass from one to the other is to die and then come terribly alive, which is surely what Nietzsche had in mind when he wrote that life means constantly transforming all that we are into light and flame.[4] For Proust this is a journey in the organic and now translucent depths of the mysteriously lighted viscera. Worlds of sleep—in which our inner consciousness, subordinated to the disturbances of our organs, accelerates the rhythm of the heart or the respiration, because the same dose of terror, sorrow or remorse acts with a strength magnified a hundredfold if thus injected into our veins: as soon as, to traverse the arteries of the subterranean city, we have embarked upon the dark current of our own blood as upon an inward Lethe meandering six-fold, tall, solemn forms appear to us, approach and glide away, leaving us in tears.[5]

And *weather*? Well, it was global warming and the possibility of radical changes being wrought to the bodily unconscious that took me to color in the first place, trying to use words to make manifest the heat of color and vice versa, as with the savant's savant, Isidore of Seville, who, in the seventh century AD, claimed that color and heat were the same since colors come from fire or sunlight and because the words for them were fundamentally the same, *calor* and *color*. Like the savant's savant am I, coupling words in this crazy fashion to the heat-color maelstrom that first worked its way into my consciousness in steamy heat under the harsh grey skies of the mangrove swamps of the Pacific coast of Colombia, South America, where the burning color of gold gives way to the green aura of coca and the racing white of cocaine.[6] Such is gold, such is cocaine, byproducts of the heat-color maelstrom under harsh grey skies.

And why harsh? I feel like mimicking Melville on the whiteness of the white whale, except that I speak to the greyness of the grey cloud. Why is it so appalling? Is it because of its indefiniteness, or the fact that it is the color that is the absence of all color?

I could continue, but I am cut short with the realization that you cannot separate a color from what it is a color of. Same as writing. The harshness of the grey skies has to do with the fierceness of the sun they absorb, the immense bulk of water they contain in this, the rainiest part of God's earth, and the fact that the light pierces the eye way into the back of the brain in a world where the moody grey canopy forms a parallel to the swirling estuaries and the endless drab greens of the forest. As I said, you cannot separate color from what it is a color of. Same as writing.

Eased from a visual approach to vision, color becomes the cutting edge of what Nietzsche meant here by life—not as light and flame, but our constant transformation into such. "Colored by weather" is what I have in mind, and I want to return to Benjamin's work on Marcel Proust because it strikes me as curious that Benjamin did not mention color when discussing Proust. It took Ibiza and opium via that red butterfly to bring him back to his earlier fascination with color, but it was there staring you in the face on every page of Proust, two volumes of whose famous work Benjamin had, with the help of Franz Hessel, translated into German seven years or so before Ibiza, when he was still involved with color in children's books and with the similarities between color and language.[7] Color as animal, color as the red butterfly was not seen until opium drew open the curtains looking down over the port of Ibiza. Then—with opiation of the visual field, and immersed in ideas of what he called "the mimetic faculty"—Benjamin could skip back to perceptions he held dear when writing about color in illustrations in children's books and become one of those kids himself.

As I have said, "Lost in Color" is the title for an essay I fondly fantasize that Walter Benjamin could have written if he had not taken his life in 1940 and had lived long enough to go on a color walk with William Burroughs in Paris in the vicinity of the Beat Hotel. To be lost in this way means you get absorbed into that which you absorb. Lost in color, these walks bear the imprint of the *hombre invisible* slinking lizardlike through the markets of Tangier. They also contain traces of Burroughs's esteemed companion, Brion Gysin, the painter, smuggling swirls of color out of and back into Arabic script. Calligraphy, they call it, and in the case of Sufi practice, Gysin's artwork hints at an intimate relationship between color and script in the making and unmaking of meaning.

Perhaps it goes like this, as in some Persian carpets, which, as we all know, have even been known to fly. Language with the Sufi script I have seen is animated by being embedded in frames of colors. As with medieval illuminated manuscripts in Europe, script shares the page with light and colors, which are what bring it to life. Such script has yet to become nothing more than a series of black-and-white marks, yet it seems more than likely that the long gestation of script as the play of light and color, in the West, performed yeoman's service. It is as if the black marks economically running across the whiteness of the page today are in fact the startled remnants of what before were more like actual pictures of the world and of the human imagination that went along with it—or if not pictures, then, even more interestingly, flashes of light and color. What is alarming if not miraculous, then, is what effort it took to eliminate or, should we say, de-illuminate the illumination. What have been the costs thereof? Or could it be that modern script bears, like a palimpsest, this prehistory of color and light within itself, only we don't see it any more, until some *loco hombre invisible* takes us on a color walk and cranks up the montage, the montage of words as animals yearning to be free of their cages?

Back to the red butterfly as seen under the influence of opium, same color as the poppies filling the fields, vibrating blood red in the summer haze of Ibiza. Back to Goethe, positing color as a function of the human body, itself seen as an ongoing experiment in nature's relation to culture, language being right there on the cusp where nature and culture intertwine closer than ancient ivy. This is Jean Selz with his Proust-like moment, associating the butterfly story with Benjamin breaking words up into syllables to find unexpected meanings.

"Colored by weather," wrote Proust. Once he referred to himself as an "animated barometer."[8] For a moment he could have stopped chasing girls who were really boys and thought for a moment of Friedrich Nietzsche who composed philosophy in colored weather, our Nietzsche who had, next to music, but two speeds, writing and walking, and when he went for walks, which was every day, covered himself rain or shine with a colored umbrella. To cultivate the shadow, Nietzsche loved to go on strenuous walks. "Our first question about the value of a book, a person, or a piece of music," he wrote in *The Gay Science*, "is can they walk?"[9] In Turin, where years later Primo Levi managed the paint factory, Nietzsche never went without a red umbrella to shield his pathetically weak eyes. He was getting pretty crazy then, but people remembered earlier when he was presumably sane or saner there had been a grey umbrella and a yellow one too. As for red, Lou Salome remembered him putting a red shade over the light in the Thuringen Forest resort near Jena.[10]

Rain *or* shine. And this by his own admission was the philosopher of midday, moment of the shortest shadow. There was no overarching framework of explanation, nothing to hang onto, nowhere to begin. The rug had been pulled out from under meaning itself. And this is why he chose to see reality with no division into appearance and depth, this division being the first and major mistake, or is it a snare, of "deep thinkers."

There was now no depth and therefore no appearance either. It was noontime, when the sun renders reality shadowless. Nevertheless here we have him midday, abiding by his own precept, yet at the same time cultivating the art of the shadow, albeit the shortest, so long as it was colored. From the *Prelude* to *The*

Gay Science: if you want to spare your eyes and mind, follow the sun from the shadows behind.[11]

If philosophy is the understanding—or rather the misunderstanding—of the body, Nietzsche could just as well have asked: "Is not all philosophy an understanding or rather misunderstanding of the weather?" For weather was his constant preoccupation, especially in that final year in Turin. Long before then, if I remember correctly, he wanted to emigrate to Mexico to cure his migraines by what he heard was the frequent lightning there. The effect of the weather on the colors of the lake at Sils, Switzerland, where he would go in the summers, was no less important to this man blind as a bat. But don't you know why that expression crackles? Don't bats have some sort of radarlike means of perception?

Here was the philosopher of the bleached out world of midday, moment of the shortest shadow, who then turned around and cloaked himself in shadow, colored shadow. What could be more fitting for the philosopher whom, according to Lesley Chamberlain, turned to color and music because of the absence of a suitable response to the death of god.[12]

I picture him philosophizing, striding along with those weak eyes and strong legs, holding this umbrella between himself and the light which is the sun that shines through his philosophizing. In Turin he found the color walk, just as Proust did later on the Mégélise Way, as did Mme Swann in the Bois de Boulogne, and still later as did Burroughs in Tangier and Paris, for as Nietzsche walked he was painting himself in color—sun filtered, red, grey, and yellow—the translucent colors that play like fire and water over solid colors, according to Goethe's painter friend, Philipp Otto Runge.

As he walked the color walk with those colors pouring over him like fire and water, those colors interacted as music with the rhythm of his walk. Nietzsche pointed to the magical power of rhythm in ancient times, not only in prayer as a magical snare to make the gods pliable, but in mundane activities as well, such as rowing, bailing water from a boat, and, let us add, beating indigo in a Bengali vat or just plain walking, close to blind, in Turin. Still today, he thought, even "after millennia of work at fighting such superstition," this magical power of rhythm exerts itself.[13] Throughout this book of mine I have called this "the body of the song" as much as the song of the body, which we now see as a color-walking body, following the places where music and color snare the gods, the same places where we find the color of history.

Colored by Weather

ackNowLeDCments

This color book grew out of *My Cocaine Museum,* during the writing of which I stumbled into heat, so maybe I should now call that contribution to preemptive apocalyptic anthropology *My Heat Book.* I was able to make many of the necessary—if arbitrary—connections between color and heat thanks to the generosity of Professor Karl Heinz Kohl and his colleagues in the Department of Anthropology, including Cora Bender, who invited me to give the Jensen Lectures in May 2004 at the Frobenius Institute of the University of Frankfurt, a university whose actual name is the Johann Wolfgang Goethe Universität, a nice echo to the first line in this, my color book, expressing its main argument or, if not "argument," then its connecting thread, quoting Goethe on the aversion people of refinement have towards vivid color while "man in a state of nature" loves it. That this university now inhabits what were the immaculate headquarters of IG Farben, that my pristine office was in the basement of that uniquely modernist building constructed in the late 1920s, that this building was spared saturation bombing so as to become General Eisenhower's European headquarters are facts whose historical weight bears most heavily on this, my little book on color and heat.

In the cruel winter of 1945 things were not so immaculate there. Countless refugees squatted in those pristine offices, and to warm things up burnt many of Farben's files, destroying evidence that might have ensured a devastatingly guilty verdict against the directors of this company that used slave labor at Auschwitz and elsewhere, but claimed, successfully, in all innocence of the facts, that they were victims of circumstance. In a small way, perhaps, like the images Walter Benjamin wrote about in his "Theses on the Philosophy of History," images that suddenly appear in the present as one of its concerns, this color book of mine connects with something of that history. It is a most curious feeling to be sitting as a guest in the basement of what were the headquarters first of Farben and then of the U.S. Army now liberating the Middle East—along with Farben's successors, like Halliburton, who also claim that they are mere consequence of circumstance.

Two years later I was able to sharpen the initiatory talks I had drafted in the Goethe University, thanks to an invitation from the University of Melbourne to serve as a Miegunyah Fellow. Housed in the Department of Anthropology, under the wing of Mary Patterson, I was given the chance to flaunt my wares, in the process of which I learned how wrong I was on many things, including Malinowski's shimmering whites. While there I met John Morton and some of his anthropologist colleagues at Latrobe University, it being John who introduced me via email to Michael Young, who, via that medium and his biography of Malinowski, gave generously of his time and set me straight, then straight again, on an infinitude of perspectives as well as facts, although I hasten to add that any errors and certainly attitudes are my own. Tony Birch of Melbourne University provided me with the background to his sacred-site design for Baldwin Spencer seated forlorn in the Melbourne Museum, surveying his horde of spears and boomerangs. Klaus Neumann jolted me into serious action when in all wonderment he asked why I had not mentioned IG Farben and by implication German chemistry in my talk in Melbourne redeeming indigo.

In Kolkata, Bhaskar Mukhopadhyay and my colleague Partha Chatterjee enabled me to visit nineteenth-century indigo factories, showering me with hos-

Acknowledgments

pitality, good talk, and good ideas, as did Moinak Biswas and Devleena Ghosh, it being my old friend, now *Professor of the Big Heart*, John Hutnyk of Goldsmith's college, London, who had gotten me oriented towards Bengal in the first place.

You can't write a book on color without real artists and real art historians. Laurie Monahan was in on this project from its inception, as was Anna Blume with her lessons on Vermeer and oil painting, and Nancy Goldring, whose layering of photographic slides one on top of the other has provided me with a lifeline to Goethe's interest in transparent color. And Jimmie Durham and Maria Thereza Alves were there, always, at the back of my psyche where the color sprite goes for its color walks. At our discussion group growing out of a Cooper Union aggregation, Stephan Pascher provided me with a venue and much good advice and floods of names of colorists unworthy of such an aesthetic dullard as myself. Tom Mitchell knows a thing or two about painting and photography as well, and I am much indebted to his work, his friendship over the years, his manner, really, and his colleagues at the journal *Critical Inquiry* for publishing the first section of this book as it then stood in 2006. For his dry and tender fictocritical edge, making history more real through playing chicken with its stories, I am indebted over many years to Stephen Muecke and his friends and students in Sydney.

Most of the final writing and especially the last chapters were done, as I think must be obvious from their overly morbid tone, in Berlin; to be exact in Schumannstrasse, aka by Bina Gogineni as Shamanstrasse, an act of levity that would no doubt have pleased the defunct Romantic composer and certainly helped me hold at bay the demons let loose as I turned the pages of the endless supply of books and articles on modern German history fed me by the American Academy, which sustained me for six months in 2006 with enormous affection and splendid talks, not to mention the bounty of the table. Frank Berberich, editor of the Berlin based *Lettre Internationale*, took an interest in my work on indigo and published some of that in German along with images tracked down by Esther Gallodoro. Coincidentally this article came to the attention of Mary Lance, a documentary filmmaker who is completing her film on indigo. With great kindness she has allowed me to use one of her photographs as the cover image to this book.

The University of Chicago Press has done me proud, and that owes much to

David Brent and Elizabeth Branch Dyson. Over the years, like gifted air-traffic controllers at one with technology and a love of flying they have helped me land gently.

I am grateful to Mikaela Khanya Bradbury, Madeline Hollander and Christopher Santiago for their squirreling sixth sense in the labyrinth that is the Columbia University library and for tracking down elusive images. Chris also assembled the bibliography.

Like transparent colors of fire and spirit, Bina Gogineni's light touch, and laughter hover over every page before you.

Notes

CHAPTER 1

1. The German text is a little less strident than this English translation of the verb *entefernen* as *banishment*. *To distance oneself from* seems more accurate. Goethe, *Theory of Colours*, #135, 55. Goethe's remarks on this topic are worth further quotation. See #835, 326; #836, 327; #841, 329. Take #135, for instance: "Lastly it is worthy of remark, that savage nations, uneducated people, and children have a great predilection for vivid colors; that animals are excited to rage by certain colours; that people of refinement avoid vivid colours in their dress and the objects that are about them, and seem inclined to banish them altogether from their presence." Then #835: "Men in a state of nature, uncivilized nations, children, have a great fondness for colours in their utmost brightness, and especially for yellow-red: they are also pleased with the motley. By this expression we understand the juxtaposition of vivid colours with a harmonious balance; but if this balance is observed, through instinct or accident, an agreeable effect may be produced. I

remember a Hessian officer, returned from America, who had painted his face with the positive colours, in the manner of the Indians; a kind of completeness or due balance was thus produced, the effect of which was not disagreeable."

2. Delamare and Guineau, *Colors*, 119.

3. Jünger, *Storm of Steel*, 6.

4. Proust, *In Search of Lost Time*, vol. 6, 106.

5. Letter written by Vincent van Gogh to his brother Theo, June 21, 1888, cited in Ives et al., *Vincent Van Gogh*, 77. For the characterization of the zouave as a type, see *Merriam-Webster's Collegiate Dictionary*, 10th ed., 1373.

6. Levi, *Survival in Auschwitz*, 185.

7. Ruskin, *Modern Painters*, 225.

8. Escobar, *Curse of Nemur*, 66.

9. Ibid., 65.

10. Turner, "Color Classification in Ndembu Ritual," 68.

11. Ibid., 87–88.

12. Ibid., 88–89. Turner mentions indigenous Australia, Malaysia, Africa, North America, and the ancient Hindu text *The Upanishads*, in which colors are sometimes referred to as "deities."

13. Cited in Monk, *Ludwig Wittgensetin*, 61.

CHAPTER 2

1. Goethe, *Theory of Colours*, #135, 55.

2. Woolf, "Old Bloomsbury," 200.

3. Bell, *Virginia Woolf*, 206.

4. I take this colorful term from David Batchelor's book entitled *Chromophobia*.

CHAPTER 3

1. Goethe, *Theory of Colours*, 195–97.

2. Cannon, *Wisdom of the Body*.

3. Nietzsche, *Gay Science*, #354, 211–14.

4. Warner, *A Black Civilization*, 198.

5. Doolittle (H. D.), *Tribute to Freud*.

CHAPTER 4

1. Thanks to Yehuda Saffron for this lesson.

2. Benjamin, "A Child's View of Color," 50.

3. Barthes, *Camera Lucida*, 81.

4. Albers, *Interaction of Colors*, 150.

5. Levi-Strauss, *Tristes Tropiques*, New York: Athaneum, 1974 [1955], pp.17–18

6. Levi-Strauss, *Tristes Tropiques*, 41.

7. Wolff, *This Boy's Life*, 207.

8. Pinney, *"Photos of the Gods,"* 14.

9. Malcolm, "Photography. Color," 107.

10. Ibid., 108.

11. Kramer, "Art: Focus on Photo Shows."

12. Szarkowski, *William Eggleston's Guide*, 9.

13. Bohannan, *Return to Laughter*, 90.

14. Ibid., 112.

15. Ibid., 8.

16. Archibold, "Comments about Water, and a City Doesn't Like It." *New York Times*, November 3, 2005.

17. Benjamin, "A Child's View of Color," 50.

18. Diderot, cited in Delamare and Guineau, *Colors*, 129.

19. Spiegelman, "The Comic Supplement," 11.

20. Stone, "Prince of Possibility," 74.

21. For these posters, see the art exhibition catalogue by Tomlinson and Medeiros.

22. See Garcia, "The Mario Scenario."

23. Benjamin, Convolut G, 173.

24. Colum, introduction to *Complete Grimm's Fairy Tales*, 253.

CHAPTER 5

1. Thorndike, *History of Magic and Experimental Science*, 13.

2. Burroughs, *Western Lands*, 247.

3. Burroughs, "Literary Techniques of Lady Sutton-Smith," 682.

4. Burroughs, *Western Lands*, 248.

5. Burroughs, "Literary Techniques of Lady Sutton-Smith," 682.

CHAPTER 6

1. Surya, *Georges Bataille*, 251.

2. Ibid.

3. She died young from tuberculosis in 1938, aged thirty-five. Some of her writings have been collected as *Laure: The Collected Writings*, trans. Jeanne Herman (San Francisco: City Lights, 1995).

4. Wahl, "At the College of Sociology," 101–2.

5. Letter 581 (Arles, 24 March 1889) in Auden, *Van Gogh*.

CHAPTER 7

1. Melville, *Moby Dick*, 168.

2. Burroughs, *Western Lands*, 56–57.

3. Melville, *Moby Dick*, 175.

CHAPTER 8

1. Gusinde, *Los indios de Tierra del Fuego*, vol. 1, 716–18.

2. Bridges, *Uttermost Parts of the Earth*, 716–18.

3. Albus, *Art of Arts*, 67.

4. Ibid., 93.

5. Ibid., 65.

6. Alison, "Color Me In," 15.

7. Delamare and Guineau, *Colors*, 125. (Delamare is director of research at the Écoles des Mines, Paris, studying Roman and Gallic-Roman pigments as well as modern industrial paints. A physicist and research engineer, Guineau has worked with historians on the history of pigments and has written a book on pigments and dyes from antiquity to the Middle Ages.)

8. Mumford, *Technics and Civilization*, 163.

9. Barthes, Roland Barthes by Roland Barthes, 129. Many thanks to Brigit Potter for showing me this.

10. Ibid.

11. Runge, letter to Goethe (5 July 1806), reproduced in full in Albus, Art of Arts, 80. The letter was omitted from the English translation of Goethe's color book, which was, in my opinion, a huge mistake.

12. Runge, in Albus, Art of Arts, 80.

13. Proust, In Search of Lost Time, vol. 6, 299.

14. Proust, In Search of Lost Time, vol.1, 9.

15. Ibid., 175.

CHAPTER 9

1. Benjamin, "A Glimpse into the World of Children's Books," 435.

2. Benjamin, " A Child's View of Color," 50.

3. Ibid., 51.

4. Hewitt, "Orenda and a Definition of Religion," 33–46, esp. 40.

5. Nietzsche, *Twilight of the Idols; and The Anti-Christ*, 84.

6. Hewitt, "Orenda and a Definition of Religion," 35–36.

7. Neihardt, *Black Elk Speaks*, 14.

8. Gusinde, *Yamana*, 1329.

9. Walens, *Feasting with Cannibals*, 24.

10. Boas, "Talk about the Great Shaman of the Nak!waxdax Called Fool," 41ff.

CHAPTER 10

1. Eisenstein, *Eisenstein on Disney*, 21.

2. Ibid.

3. Ibid., 98. The quotes are from another book of Eisenstein's, *Non-Indifferent Nature*, cited by the editor in the "Notes and Commentary" section of *Eisenstein on Disney*, 98.

4. Auden, *Van Gogh*, 396.

5. Neihardt, *Black Elk Speaks*, 23–24.

6. Lowie, *Indians of the Plains*, 161–62.

7. Reichard, *Navaho Religion*.

8. Ibid., 487–88.

9. Woolf, *Waves*, 286–87.

10. Maximillian, Prince of Wied, *Travels in the Interior of North America*, vol. 23, 343.

11. Ibid., 258.

12. Ibid., 260–62.

13. Maximillian, Prince of Wied, *Travels in the Interior of North America*, vol. 22, 307.

CHAPTER 11

1. Burroughs, *Naked Lunch*, 130. The ellipses are Burroughs's.

2. Ibid., 283.

3. Sartre, *Nausea*, 134.

4. Burroughs, *Naked Lunch*, 44, 45.

5. Sartre, *Nausea*, 127–29.

6. Ibid., 132.

7. Ibid., 18–19.

8. Ibid., 19.

9. Ibid.

10. Burroughs, *Naked Lunch*, 44, 45.

CHAPTER 12

1. Selz, "Benjamin in Ibiza," 353–66.

2. Benjamin, letter to Gerhard Scholem (Ibiza, 31 July 1933), in *Correspondence of Walter Benjamin*, 425.

3. Selz, *Benjamin in Ibiza*, 357.

4. Ibid.

5. Benjamin, *On Hashish*, 21–22.

6. Ibid., 20.

7. Baudelaire, "The Painter of Modern Life."

8. Benjamin, "On the Image of Proust," 242.

9. Caygill, *Walter Benjamin: The Colour of Experience.*

10. Valero, *Experiencia y pobreza*, 114–15.

11. Benjamin, letter to Scholem (Nice, 26 July 26 1932), in *Correspondence of Walter Benjamin*, 396.

12. Valero, *Experiencia y pobreza*, 117.

13. Ibid., 118.

14. Benjamin, "A Child's View of Color," 50.

15. Benjamin, "A Glimpse into the World of Children's Books," 435.

16. Burroughs, *Cities of the Red Night*, 168.

17. Burroughs, *Soft Machine*, 92–93.

18. Selz, *Benjamin in Ibiza*, 366.

CHAPTER 13

1. Young, *Malinowski*, 21.

2. Ibid., 475.

3. Malinowski, *Diary*, 298. For an account of Malinowski's early illnesses and eye issues, see Young, *Malinowski*, 37ff.

4. Ibid., 315.

5. Conrad, *Heart of Darkness*, 45.

6. Ibid., 74.

7. Malinowski, *Sexual Life of Savages in North-Western Melanesia*, 306–7.

8. Young, *Malinowski*, 475; also Stocking, *After Tylor*, 234.

9. Malinowski, *Diary*, 125.

10. Young, *Malinowski*, 400.

11. Ibid., 475.

12. Ibid., 414.

13. Ibid., 416.

14. Malinowski, *Diary*, 10.

15. Ibid., 33–34.

16. Ibid., 14.

17. Ibid., 15.

18. Ibid., 38.

19. Ibid., 40.

20. Ibid., 271.

21. Ibid., 13.

CHAPTER 14

1. Malinowski, *Diary*, 71.

2. Ibid., 11.

3. Malinowski, *Coral Gardens*, 112.

4. Ibid., 111.

5. Edmond, "Tom Harrison in the New Hebrides and Bolton," 208.

6. Malinowski, *Diary*, 62–63.

7. Young, *Malinowski*, 339.

8. Morrison, *Playing the Dark*. Thanks to Bina Gogineni for this reference.

CHAPTER 15

1. Payne, "Malinowski's Style," 438.

2. Young, *Malinowksi*, 477.

3. Malinowski, *Argonauts*, 220.

4. Ibid., 219.

5. Ibid., 318.

6. Ibid., 107.

7. Ibid., 220.

8. Ibid.

9. Michael Young has kindly pointed out to me that "harmonic synergies of music and seascape" as experienced by Malinowski are also manifest in Malinowski's diary, 230–36, and in Young's biography, 536–37.

10. Malinowksi, *Argonauts*, 108.

11. Young, Malinowski, 199.

12. Genet, *Thief's Journal*, 27.

13. Malinowski, *Argonauts*, 34.

14. Stocking, *After Tylor*, 271, 260.

15. Malinowski, *Argonauts*, 303.

16. Ibid., 131.

17. Plath, "Ocean 1212-W," 21.

18. Agee and Evans, *Let Us Now Praise Famous Men*, xlvii. Macdonald, "Death of a Poet," 232.

19. Agee and Evans, *Let Us Now Praise Famous Men*, xlviii.

20. Ibid., 11.

21. Ibid., 16.

22. Malinowski, *Argonauts*, 106.

23. Traven, *Death Ship*, 136.

24. Malinowski, *Argonauts*, 127.

25. Traven, *Death Ship*, 85–87.

26. Ibid., 287.

CHAPTER 16

1. Malinowski, *Argonauts*, 150–51.

2. Ibid., 154.

3. "Trobriand Islands—A Label," in Young, *Malinowski's Kiriwina*, 33. This piece was written by Malinowski in late 1919 to accompany a collection of Trobriand artifacts he presented to the Melbourne Museum.

4. Read, *High Valley*, 114.

5. Bohannan, *Return to Laughter*.

6. Malinowski, *Argonauts*, 336.

7. Malinowski, *Sexual Life of Savages*, 354–55; Malinowski, *Argonauts*, 335.

8. Malinowski, *Argonauts*, 339.

9. Ibid., 216.

10. Ibid., 217.

11. Ibid.

12. Young, *Malinowski*, xix–xx.

13. Ibid., 401.

14. Ibid., 416.

15. Ibid., 395.

16. Ibid., 499.

17. Ibid., 344; Young, *Malinowski's Kiriwina*, 43.

18. Malinowski, "*Baloma.*"

19. Malinowski, *Argonauts*, 4.

20. Young, *Malinowski*, 501.

21. Malinowski, *Coral Gardens*, "Documents and Appendices," 479–81n43.

22. Stocking, "Philanthropoids and Vanishing Cultures," 126. Stocking cites a 1929 article by Malinowski, "Practical Anthropology," *Africa* 2:23–39.

23. Young, *Malinowski*, 388.

24. Ibid., 163.

25. Ibid.,164.

26. Malinowski, *Coral Gardens*, 326.

27. Young, *Malinowski*, 164.

CHAPTER 17

1. Stocking, "Anthropology and the Science of the Irrational," 25.

2. Malinowski, *Coral Gardens*, plate 85.

3. Young, *Malinowski*, 498.

4. Ibid., 542.

5. Maliowski, *Diary*, 280.

6. Young, *Malinowski*, 529; Young, *Malinowski's Kiriwina*, 3–4.

7. Young, *Malinowski*, 528.

8. Young, *Malinowski's Kiriwina*, 47; Young, *Malinowski*, 496.

9. Kramer, *Red Fez*, 135–36.

10. Malinowski, *Diary*, 41.

11. Ibid., 284.

12. Ibid., 238.

13. Young, *Malinowski*, 528.

CHAPTER 18

1. Conrad, *Heart of Darkness*, 28.

2. Ibid., 36.

3. Ibid., 93, 90.

4. Ibid., 30.

5. Ibid., 32.

6. Bataille, *Accursed Share*, vol. 2, 14.

7. Conrad, *Heart of Darkness*, 46.

8. Conrad, "Outpost of Progress," 183, 184, 186.

9. Ibid., 188.

10. Conrad, *Heart of Darkness*, 52.

11. Khan, *East India Trade in the XVIIth Century*, 277–78.

12. Alpern, "What Africans Got for Their Slaves," 5.

13. Harms, *Diligent*, 80–81.

14. Hochschild, *King Leopold's Ghost*, 73, 210.

15. Harms, *Diligent*, 81.

16. Roberts, "West Africa and the Pondicherry Textile Industry," 147.

17. Harms, *Diligent*, 81.

18. Alpern, "What Africans Got for Their Slaves," 6–7.

19. Ibid., 22.

20. Schneider, "Peacocks and Penguins," 416–17.

21. Harms, *Diligent*, 372–73.

22. Ibid., 89.

23. Conrad, *Heart of Darkness*, 52.

24. Ibid., 58.

25. McKay, *Banjo*, 30. Many thanks to Bina Gogineni for bringing this book to my attention.

26. Ibid., 30.

27. Ibid., 3.

28. Ibid., 81.

29. Ibid., 62.

30. Ibid., 96.

31. Siegel, *Net of Magic*, 2.

CHAPTER 19

1. Grant, *Rural Life in Bengal*, 128.

2. Dubois, *Story of the Haitian Revolution*, 27.

3. Garrigus, "Blue and Brown."

4. Pastoureau, *Blue*.

5. Balfour-Paul, *Indigo in the Arab World*, 163–67.

6. Ibid., 21.

7. *Compact Edition of the Oxford English Dictionary* (Oxford: Clarendon Press, 1971),1:641.

8. Balfour-Paul, *Indigo in the Arab World*, 21.

9. Contreras Sánchez, *Capital commercial y colorants en la nueva España*, 27.

10. Fairlie, "Dyestuffs in the Eighteenth Century," 488.

11. Ibid., 496.

12. Ibid., 498–99.

13. Guha, "Neel-Darpan." See also Rao and Rao, *Blue Devil*, 9.

14. Guha, "Neel-Darpan," 25.

15. King, *Blue Mutiny*, 25.

16. Sealy, *Trotter-Nama*, 151. Many thanks to John Hutnyk for this book.

17. Grant, *Rural Life in Bengal*, 125.

18. Ibid., 126.

19. Hoskins, "Why Do Ladies Sing the Blues?" 151, 154.

20. Ibid., 149.

21. Goethe *Theory of Colours*, 194.

22. Hoskins, "Why Do Ladies Sing the Blues?" 144.

23. Grant, *Rural Life in Bengal*, 128.

24. Ibid., 129. The passage reads: "The operation of the beating continues for about two hours—the men amusing themselves and encouraging each other the while by sundry vehement cries and songs—generally not particularly distinguished for elegance or purity."

25. Tavernier, *Travels in India*.

26. Balfour-Paul, *Indigo in the Arab World*, 88–89; Hoskins, "Why Do Ladies Sing the Blues?"

27. Grant, *Rural Life in Bengal*, 128.

28. Benjamin, "Theses on the Philosophy of History."

29. Pastoureau, *Blue*, 167.

30. Albers, *Interaction of Colors*, 72.

31. See Bohannan, *Return to Laughter*, 75–76; and Evans-Pritchard, "Some Collective Expressions of Obscenity in Africa."

32. Evans-Pritchard, "Some Collective Expressions of Obscenity in Africa."

33. Cramer, "Songs of West Indian Negroes in the Canal Zone," 245.

CHAPTER 20

1. Percival, *Chintz Book*, 9. Many thanks to Christopher Pinney for directing me to this source. Pinney, "Creole Europe."

2. Irwin and Brett, *Origins of Chintz*, 1.

3. Thomas, "The Beginnings of Calico Printing in England," 211.

4. Douglas, "Cotton Textiles in England," 37.

5. Ibid.

6. Percival, *Chintz Book*, cited in Pinney, "Creole Europe," 136–37. Also see Mathur, *India by Design*.

7. Collins, *Moonstone*.

8. Ibid., 46.

9. Ibid., 74.

10. Benjamin, "A Glimpse into the World of Children's Books," 435.

11. Benjamin, "The Storyteller," 107.

12. Collins, *Moonstone*, 421.

CHAPTER 21

1. Schneider, "Penguins and Peacocks," 422.

2. Ibid., 427.

3. Khan, *East India Trade in the XVIIth Century*, 163, 295.

4. Ibid., 283.

5. Ibid., 163.

6. Ibid., 289–90.

7. Thomas, "Beginnings of Calico Printing in England," 213.

8. Clow and Clow, *Chemical Revolution*, 199–200.

9. Thomas, "Beginnings of Calico Printing in England," 214.

10. Ibid., 215.

11. Ibid., 209–10.

12. Tavernier, *Travels in India*, 42.

13. Michelet, *Le Peuple*, 80–81.

14. Douglas, "Cotton Textiles in England," 30, 34; Benjamin, "Paris Arcades."

15. Benjamin, *Arcades Project*, 64.

CHAPTER 22

1. Proust, *In Search of Lost Time*, vol. 2, *Within a Budding Grove*, 290.

2. Proust, *In Search of Lost Time*, vol. 1, *Swann's Way*, 13.

3. Alpers, *Art of Describing*, 33.

4. Beckett, *Proust*, 68–69.

5. Bataille, "Language of Flowers."

6. Proust, *In Search of Lost Time*, vol. 4, *Sodom and Gomorrah*, 244–45.

7. Proust, *In Search of Lost Time*, vol. 1, *Swann's Way*, 438.

8. Ibid., 439.

9. Ibid.

10. Ibid., 440

11. Ibid.

12. Ibid., 442–43.

CHAPTER 23

1. Bohanan, *Return to Laughter*, 60–61.

2. Ibid., 33–34.

3. Benjamin, "On the Mimetic Faculty," 333–36.

4. "Swimming," in the *Encyclopaedia Britannica*, by Sydney Holland , 10th ed., vol. 33 (1902), 140–41.

5. Benjamin, "Some Reflections on Kafka," 141–42.

6. Taussig, "Viscerality, Faith, and Skepticism."

7. Proust, *In Search of Lost Time*, vol. 6, *Time Regained*, 260.

8. Ibid., 260.

9. Beckett, *Proust*, 20.

10. Proust, *In Search of Lost Time*, vol. 6, *Time Regained*, 299–300.

11. Ibid., 300.

12. Neitzsche, *Gay Science*, 8.

13. Nietzsche, "Attempt at Self-Criticism."

14. Proust, *In Search of Lost Time*, vol. 3, *Guermantes Way*, 106.

15. Proust, *In Search of Lost Time*, vol. 4, *Sodom and Gomorrah*, 216.

16. Proust, *In Search of Lost Time*, vol. 3, *Guermantes Way*, 111.

17. Leiris, "Sacred in Everyday Life," 31.

18. Benjamin, "Surrealism," 179.

19. Proust, *In Search of Lost Time*, vol. 3, *Guermantes Way*, 112.

20. Proust, *In Search of Lost Time*, vol. 6, *Time Regained*, 262.

CHAPTER 24

1. Proust, *In Search of Lost Time*, vol. 1, *Swann's Way*, 45.

2. Ibid., 50.

3. Proust, *In Search of Lost Time*, vol. 6, *Time Regained*, 289.

4. Ibid., 259.

5. Proust, *In Search of Lost Time*, vol. 1, *Swann's Way*, 44.

6. Proust, *In Search of Lost Time*, vol. 6, *Time Regained*, 283–84.

7. Ibid., 284.

8. Proust, *In Search of Lost Time*, vol. 1, *Swann's Way*, 46.

9. Benjamin, "On the Image of Proust," 214.

10. Proust, *In Search of Lost Time*, vol. 1, *Swann's Way*, 148–49.

11. Proust, *In Search of Lost Time*, vol. 6, *Time Regained*, 264.

12. Benjamin, Convolut N, 470.

13. Proust, *In Search of Lost Time*, vol. 6, *Time Regained*, 289.

14. Benjamin, "Theses on the Philosophy of History," 225, 261.

15. Benjamin, *Arcades Project*, 464.

CHAPTER 25

1. Proust, *In Search of Lost Time*, vol. 1, *Swann's Way*, 3.

2. Ibid., 50–51.

3. Freud, *Beyond the Pleasure Principle*, 62.

4. Nietzsche, *Gay Science*, 110.

5. Proust, *In Search of Lost Time*, vol. 1, *Swann's Way*, 50.

6. Proust, *In Search of Lost Time*, vol. 5, *Captive*, 244.

7. Ibid., 244.

8. Ibid., 245.

9. White, *Marcel Proust*, 150.

10. Benjamin, "On the Image of Proust," 214.

11. Albaret, *Monsieur Proust*, 336–37.

12. Thanks to Roger Shattuck's *Proust's Binoculars* for this insight.

13. Barthes, *Pleasure of the Text*, 36, and "Death of the Author," 142–48.

14. Nietzsche, preface to *Genealogy of Morals*, 459.

15. Mauss, "Techniques of the Body," 70–71.

16. Benjamin, "On the Image of Proust," 211–12.

17. Proust, *In Search of Lost Time*, vol. 6, *Time Regained*, 268.

18. Proust, *In Search of Lost Time*, vol. 3, *Guermantes Way*, 5.

19. Gerard Genette, "Proust Palimpsest," 205–6.

20. Ibid., 206.

CHAPTER 26

1. Proust, *In Search of Lost Time*, vol. 1, *Swann's Way*, 158.

2. Ibid., 182.

3. Ibid., 162–68.

4. Ibid., 187.

5. White, *Marcel Proust*, 136–37.

6. Tadie, *Marcel Proust*, 670–74.

7. Kristeva, *Proust and the Sense of Time*, 11, 19.

8. Ibid., 22.

9. Goldman, *Cubeo*.

CHAPTER 27

1. Roth, interview with Primo Levi in appendix to Levi, *Survival in Auschwitz*, 185.

2. Pynchon, *Gravity's Rainbow*, 566.

3. DuBois, *Devil's Chemists*, 3.

4. Stokes, *Divide and Prosper*, 3–36.

5. Sasuly, *IG Farben*, 34.

6. DuBois, *Devil's Chemists*, 4.

7. Levi, *Auschwitz Report*.

8. Hayes, *Industry and Ideology*.

9. Ibid., 357.

10. Levi, *Survival in Auschwitz*, 72.

11. Hayes, *Industry and Ideology*, 359. The authors of *The Devil's Chemists*, published in 1952, claim some 200,000 prisoners died directly or indirectly in constructing this plant (220–21), while Simon Garfield, writing five decades later, claims some 40,000 prisoners worked there and that at least 25,000 of those died (Garfield, *Mauve*, 166–67).

12. Müller, *Eyewitness Auschwitz*. Also, Feig, *Hitler's Death Camps*, 360–61. According to Peter Hayes, profits on Zyklon B were meager. Raul Hilberg, author of *The Destruction of the European Jews*, lists extremely healthy profits for Farben's partner, Degesch, ranging from 100 to 200 percent for the years 1938 to 1943 (which is the year Auschwitz started gassing in earnest).

13. Hilberg, *Destruction of the European Jews*, vol. 3, 941.

14. Levi, *Auschwitz Report*.

15. Joffroy, *Spy of God*, 141.

16. Stern, "Fritz Haber and Albert Einstein," 119.

17. Charles, *Master Mind*, 169.

18. Charles, *Master Mind*. Stoltzenberg, *Fritz Haber*. Hayes, *From Cooperation to Complicity*, 273.

19. Charles, *Master Mind*, 26–27.

20. Joffroy, *Spy of God*.

21. Nietzsche, *Gay Science*, 70.

CHAPTER 28

1. Too late to use in my writing this book, I came across the wonderful—and wonderfully relevant—book by Esther Leslie, *Synthetic Worlds: Nature, Art, and the Chemical Industry* (London: Reaktion Books), 2005.

2. Evans-Pritchard, *Witchcraft, Oracles and Magic among the Azande*, 35–36.

3. Garfield, *Mauve*, 41.

4. Ibid., 74.

5. Marlowe, *Marlowe's Tragical History of Doctor Faustus and Goethe's Faust*.

6. Nef, *Rise of the British Coal Industry*, 201–2.

7. Kafka, "Bucket Rider," 207.

8. Clow and Clow, *Chemical Revolution*, 392.

9. Benjamin, *Arcades Project*, 565.

10. Beer, *Emergence of the German Dye Industry*, 9–10.

11. Ibid., 10.

12. Goethe, *Faust, Part One*, 53.

13. Flaherty, *Shamanism and the Eighteenth Century*, 183–207.

14. Gray, *Goethe the Alchemist*, 5.

15. Thorpe, *Coal*, 213.

16. Beer, *Emergence of the German Dye Industry*, 8.

17. Garfield, *Mauve*, 156–58.

18. Beer, *Emergence of the German Dye Industry*, 3.

19. Ibid.

20. Ibid., 148–49.

21. Garfield, *Mauve*, 98.

22. Travis, *Rainbow Makers*, 234.

23. Sasuly, *IG Farben*.

24. Travis, *Rainbow Makers*, 220–21.

25. Pynchon, *Gravity's Rainbow*, 590.

26. Garfield, *Mauve*, 92.

27. Pynchon, *Gravity's Rainbow*, 412.

28. Ibid., 243.

29. Ibid., 410.

30. Hobsbawm, *Age of Capital 1848–1875*, 284.

31. Richardson, *Pilgrimage*.

32. Benjamin, "On the Mimetic Faculty," 333.

33. Travis, *Rainbow Makers*, 163–64.

34. Pynchon, *Gravity's Rainbow*, 249–50.

35. Sasuly, *IG Farben*.

36. Horkheimer and Adorno, *Dialectic of Enlightenment*.

37. Roth, interview with Primo Levi in appendix to Levi, *Survival in Auschwitz*, 182, 186.

CHAPTER 29

1. The image of the flywheel comes from William James's book on the principles of psychology.

2. Denis Diderot, cited in Delamare and Guineau, *Colors*, 129.

3. Canon, *Wisdom of the Body*, and also his article "Voodoo Death."

4. Nietzsche, *Gay Science*, 36.

5. Proust, *In Search of Lost Time*, vol. 4, *Sodom and Gomorrah*, 216.

6. Taussig, *My Cocaine Museum*.

7. Caygill, *Walter Benjamin*.

8. Proust, *In Search of Lost Time*, vol. 5, *Captive*, 96.

9. Nietzsche, *Gay Science*, 230.

10. Chamberlain, *Nietzsche in Turin*, 130.

11. Nietzsche, *Gay Science*, 13.

12. Chamberlain, *Nietzsche in Turin*, 82.

13. Nietzsche, *Gay Science*, 83–86.

BIBLIOGRAPHY

Agee, James, and Walker Evans. *Let Us Now Praise Famous Men*. Boston: Houghton Mifflin, 1988 [1939].

Albaret, Celeste. *Monsieur Proust*. Edited by Georges Belmont. Translated by Barbara Bray. New York: McGraw Hill, 1976 [1973].

Albers, Josef. *Interaction of Colors: Text of the Original Edition with Revised Plate Section*. New Haven: Yale University Press, 1975.

Albus, Anita. *The Art of Arts*. New York: Knopf, 2000.

Alison, Jane. "Colour Me In." In *Colour After Klein*, pp. 10–35. London: Black Dog Publishing, n.d.

Alpern, Stanley B. "What Africans Got for Their Slaves: A Master List of European Trade Goods." *History in Africa* 22 (1995): 5–43.

Alpers, Svetlana. *The Art of Describing: Dutch Art in the Seventeenth Century*. Chicago: University of Chicago Press, 1983.

Archibold, Randall C. "Comments about Water, and a City Doesn't Like It." *New York Times*, November 3, 2005.

Auden, W. H., ed. *Van Gogh: A Self-Portrait. Letters Revealing His Life as a Painter, Selected by W. H. Auden.* Greenwich, Conn.: New York Graphic Society, 1961.

Balfour-Paul, Jenny. *Indigo in the Arab World.* Richmond, Surrey: Curzon, 1997.

Barthes, Roland. *Camera Lucida.* New York: Hill and Wang, 1981.

———. "Death of the Author." In *Image, Music, Text.* New York: Hill and Wang, 1977.

———. *The Pleasure of the Text.* New York: Hill and Wang, 1975.

———. *Roland Barthes by Roland Barthes.* Translated by Richard Howard. New York: Farrar Straus, Giroux, 1977 [1975].

Bataille, Georges. *The Accursed Share: An Essay on General Economy.* Translated by Robert Hurley. New York: Zone Books, 1988 [1949].

———. "The Language of Flowers." In *Visions of Excess: Selected Writings, 1927–1939,* pp. 10–14. Edited and with an introduction by Allan Stoekl. Translated by Allan Stoekl, with Carl R. Lovitt and Donald M. Leslie Jr. Minneapolis: University of Minnesota Press, 1985 [1929].

Batchelor, David. *Chromophobia.* London: Reaktion, 2000.

Baudelaire, Charles. "The Painter of Modern Life." In *Baudelaire: Selected Writings on Art and Literature.* Translated by P. E. Charvet. New York: Viking, 1972.

Beckett, Samuel. *Proust.* New York: Grove Press, 1957.

Beer, John Jospeh. *The Emergence of the German Dye Industry.* Urbana: University of Illinois Press, 1959.

Bell, Quentin. *Virginia Woolf: A Biography.* London and New York: Harcourt Brace, 1974.

Benjamin, Walter. *The Arcades Project.* Translated by Howard Eiland and Kevin McLaughlin. Cambridge, Mass.: The Belknap Press of Harvard University Press, 2002.

———. "A Child's View of Color." In *Walter Benjamin: Selected Writings, Volume 1, 1913–1926,* pp. 50–51. Edited by Marcus Bullock and Michael W. Jennings. Cambridge, Mass.: The Belknap Press of Harvard University Press, 1996.

———. Convolut G: "Exhibitions, Advertising, Grandville." In *The Arcades Project,* pp. 171–202. Edited by Roy Tiedemann. Translated by Howard Eiland and Kevin McLaughlin. Cambridge, Mass.: The Belknap Press of Harvard University Press, 2002.

———. Convolut N: "On the Theory of Knowledge, Theory of Progress." In *The Arcades Project,* 456–88. Translated by Howard Eiland and Kevin McLaughlin. Cambridge, Mass.: The Belknap Press of Harvard University Press, 2002.

———. *The Correspondence of Walter Benjamin: 1910–1940.* Edited and annotated by Gerhard Scholem and Theodor W. Adorno. Chicago: University of Chicago Press, 1994.

———. "A Glimpse into the World of Children's Books." In *Walter Benjamin: Selected*

Writings, Volume 1, 1913–1926, 435–43. Edited by Marcus Bullock and Michael W. Jennings. Cambridge, Mass.: The Belknap Press of Harvard University Press, 1996.

———. *On Hashish*. Translated by Howard Eiland. Cambridge, Mass.: Harvard University Press, 2006.

———. "On the Image of Proust." In *Walter Benjamin: Selected Writings, Volume 2, 1927–1934*, pp. 237–47. Edited by Michael W. Jennings, Howard Eiland, and Gary Smith. Translated by Harry Zorn. Cambridge, Mass.: The Belknap Press of Harvard University Press, 1999.

———. "The Paris Arcades." In *The Arcades Project*, pp. 873–84. Translated by Howard Eiland and Kevin McLaughlin. Cambridge, Mass.: The Belknap Press of Harvard University Press, 2002.

———. "Some Reflections on Kafka." In *Illuminations*, pp. 141–45. Edited by Hannah Ardent. Translated by Harry Zohn. New York: Schocken, 1969.

———. "The Storyteller: Reflections on the Work of Nikolai Leskov." In *Illuminations*, pp. 83–100. Edited by Hannah Ardent. Translated by Harry Zohn. New York: Schocken, 1969.

———. "Surrealism: The Last Snapshot of the European Intelligentsia" and "On the Mimetic Faculty." In *Reflections*, pp. 177–92 and 333–36. Edited by Peter Demetz. Translated by Edmund Jephcott. New York: Schocken, 1986.

———. "Theses on the Philosophy of History." In *Illuminations*, pp. 253–64. Edited by Hannah Ardent. Translated by Harry Zohn. New York: Schocken, 1969.

Boas, Franz. "Talk about the Great Shaman of the Nak!waxdax Called Fool." In *The Religion of the Kwakiutal Indians, Part II: Translations*, p. 41ff. New York: Columbia University Press, 1930.

Bohannan, Laura [Eleanor Smith Bowen]. *Return to Laughter: An Anthropological Novel*. New York: Anchor, 1964 [1954].

Bridges, Lucas. *Uttermost Parts of the Earth*. London: Hodder and Stoughton, 1951.

Burroughs, William S. *Cities of the Red Night*. New York: Henry Holt, 1968.

———. "The Literary Techniques of Lady Sutton-Smith." *Times Literary Supplement*, August 6, 1964.

———. *Naked Lunch*. New York: Grove Press, 2001 [1959].

———. *The Soft Machine*. In *The Soft Machine, Nova Express, The Wild Boys: Three Novels*. New York: Grove Press, 1980.

———. *The Western Lands*. New York: Viking, 1987.

Cannon, Walter B. "Voodoo Death." *American Anthropologist* 44, no. 2 (April/June 1942): 169–81.

———. *The Wisdom of the Body*. New York: Norton, 1932.

Caygill, Howard. *Walter Benjamin: The Colour of Experience*. New York: Routledge, 1998.

Chamberlain, Lesley. *Nietzsche in Turin: The End of the Future*. London: Quartet Books, 1996.

Charles, Daniel. *Master Mind: The Rise and Fall of Fritz Haber, the Nobel Laureate Who Launched the Age of Chemical Warfare*. New York: Ecco, 2005.

Clow, Archibald, and Nan L. Clow. *The Chemical Revolution: A Contribution to Social Technology*. London: Batchworth Press, 1952.

Collins, Wilkie. *The Moonstone*. London: Penguin, 1998 [1868].

Colum, Patrick. Introduction to *The Complete Grimm's Fairy Tales*. Commentary by Joseph Campbell. Illustrations by Josef Scharl. New York: Pantheon, 1944.

Conrad, Joseph. *Heart of Darkness*. Harmondsworth: Penguin, 1983 [1902].

———. "An Outpost of Progress." In *Typhoon and Other Tales*. New York: New American Library, 1962 [1898].

Contreras Sánchez, Alicia del Carmen. *Capital comercial y colorantes en la nueva España: Segunda mitad del siglo XVIII*. El Colegio de Michoacán y la Universidad Autónoma de Yucatán, 1996.

Cramer, Louise. "Songs of West Indian Negroes in the Canal Zone." *California Folklore Quarterly* 5, no. 3 (July 1946): 243–72.

Delamare, Francois, and Bernard Guineau. *Colors: The Story of Dyes and Pigments*. New York: Harry N. Abrams, 2000 [1999].

Doolittle, Hilda. *Tribute to Freud*. New York: Pantheon, 1956.

Douglas, Audrey W. "Cotton Textiles in England: The East India Company's Attempt to Exploit Developments in Fashion, 1660–1721." *Journal of British Studies* 8, no. 2 (May 1969): 28–43.

DuBois, Josiah E., Jr. *The Devil's Chemists*. In collaboration with Edward Johnson. Boston: Beacon Press, 1952.

Dubois, Laurent. *The Story of the Haitian Revolution*. Cambridge, Mass.: Harvard University Press, 2004.

Edmond, Ron. "Tom Harrison in the New Hebrides and Bolton." In *Writing, Travel , and Empire: In the Margins of Anthropology*, pp. 197–220. Edited by Peter Hulme and Russell McDougall. London: I. B. Taurus, 2007.

Eisenstein, Sergei. *Eisenstein on Disney*. Edited by Jay Leyda. Translated by Alan Upchurch. New York: Methuen, 1988 [1986].

Escobar, Ticio. *The Curse of Nemur: In Search of the Art, Myth, and Ritual of the Ishir*. Translated by Adriana Michele Campos Johnson. Pittsburgh: University of Pittsburgh Press, 2007.

Evans-Pritchard, E. E. "Some Collective Expressions of Obscenity in Africa." *Journal of the Royal Anthropological Institute of Great Britain and Ireland*, vol. 59 (1929): 311–31.

———. *Witchcraft, Oracles and Magic among the Azande*. Oxford: Clarendon Press, 1937.

Fairlie, Susan. "Dyestuffs in the Eighteenth Century." *Economic History Review*, n.s., 17, no. 3 (1965): 488–510.

Feig, Konnilyn G. *Hitler's Death Camps: The Sanity of Madness*. New York and London: Holmes and Meier, 1981.

Flaherty, Gloria. *Shamanism and the Eighteenth Century*. Princeton: Princeton University Press, 1992.

Freud, Sigmund. *Beyond the Pleasure Principle*. Vol. 18 of *The Standard Edition of the Complete Psychological Works of Sigmund Freud*. London: Hogarth Press, 1955 [1920].

Gandolfo, Daniela. "The City at Its Limits: Taboo, Transgression, and Urban Renewal in Lima." Ph.D. diss., Columbia University, 2005.

Garcia, Dr. Mario. "The Mario Scenario." Reveries.com (November 2002).

Garfield, Simon. *Mauve: How One Man Invented a Color that Changed the World*. New York: Norton, 2001.

Garrigus, John. "Blue and Brown: Contraband Indigo and the Rise of a Free Planter Class in French Saint-Domingue." *Americas* 50 (October 1993): 233–63.

Genet, Jean. *The Thief's Journal*. New York: Penguin, 1967 [1949].

Genette, Gerard. "Proust Palimpsest." In *Figures of Literary Discourse*, pp. 203–28. Translated by Alan Sheridan. New York: Columbia University Press, 1982.

Goethe, Johann Wolfgang von. *Faust, Part One*. Translated by Philip Wayne. Harmondsworth, Middlesex: Penguin, 1989 [1949].

———. *Theory of Colours*. Translated by Charles Lock Eastlake. Cambridge, Mass.: MIT Press, 1970 [1st ed. in German, 1810; in English, 1840].

Goldman, Irving. *The Cubeo: Indians of the Northwest Amazon*. Urbana: University of Illinois Press, 1963.

Grant, Colesworthy. *Rural Life in Bengal*. Calcutta: Bibhash Gupta, 1984 [1864].

Gray, Ronald D. *Goethe the Alchemist*. Cambridge: Cambridge University Press, 1952.

Guha, Ranajit. "Neel-Darpan: The Image of a Peasant Revolt in a Liberal Mirror." *Journal of Peasant Studies* 2 (1974–75): 1–45.

Gusinde, Martin. *Los indios de Tierra del Fuego*. Vol. 1, *Los Selk'nam*. Translated by Werner Hoffmann. Buenos Aires: Centro Argentino de Etnología Américana, 1982 [first published in 1931, Die Feuerland Indianer, Mödeling-Vienna].

———. *The Yamana: The Life and Thought of the Water Nomads of Cape Horn*. Translated by Frieda Schutze. 3 vols. New Haven, Conn.: Human Relations Area Files, 1961.

Harms, Robert. *The Diligent: A Voyage through the Worlds of the Slave Trade*. New York: Basic, 2002.

Hayes, Peter. *From Cooperation to Complicity: Degussa in the Third Reich*. Cambridge: Cambridge University Press, 2004.

———. *Industry and Ideology: IG Farben in the Nazi Era*. New York: Cambridge University Press, 1987.

Herle, Anna, and Sandra Rouse, eds. *Cambridge and the Torres Straits: Centenary Essays of the 1898 Anthropological Expedition.* New York: Cambridge University Press, 1998.

Hewitt, J. N. B. "Orenda and a Definition of Religion." *American Anthropologist,* n.s., 4, no.1 (January–March 1902): 33–46.

Hilberg, Raul. *The Destruction of the European Jews.* New Haven: Yale University Press, 1983 [1961].

Hobsbawm, E. J. *The Age of Capital: 1848–1875.* New York: New American Library, 1979 [1975].

Hochschild, Adam. *King Leopold's Ghost: A Story of Greed, Terror, and Heroism in Colonial Africa.* Houghton Mifflin: Boston and New York, 1999.

Holland, Sydney. "Swimming." In *Encyclopedia Britannica.* 10th ed. Vol. 33. Edited by http://www.britannica.com/memberloginSir Donald Mackenzie Wallace, http://www.britannica.com/memberloginHugh Chisholm, http://www.britannica.com/memberloginArthur T. Hadley, and http://www.britannica.com/memberlogin Franklin H. Hooper. Encyclopedia Britannica Inc., 1902.

Horkheimer, Max, and Theodor W. Adorno. *Dialectic of Enlightenment.* Translated by John Cumming. New York: Herder and Herder, 1972 [1947].

Hoskins, Janet. "Why Do Ladies Sing the Blues?" In *Cloth in Human Experience,* pp. 141–73. Edited by Annette B. Weiner and Jane Schneider. Washington: Smithsonian Institution Press, 1989.

Irwin, John, and Katherine B. Brett. *Origins of Chintz.* London: HMSO, 1970.

Ives, Colta, Susan Alyson Stein, Sjraar van Heugen, and Marije Vellekoop, eds. *Vincent Van Gogh: The Drawings.* New Haven: Yale University Press, 2005.

James, William. *Principles of Psychology.* Cambridge, Mass.: Harvard University Press, 1890.

Joffroy, Pierre. *A Spy of God: The Ordeal of Kurt Gerstein.* Translated by Norman Denny. New York: Harcourt Brace Jovanovich, 1971.

Jünger, Ernst. *The Storm of Steel: From the Diary of a German Storm-Troop Officer on the Western Front.* New York: Howard Fertig, 1996 [1929].

Junod, Henri A. *Life of a South African Tribe.* New Hyde Park, N.Y.: University Books, 1962.

Kafka, Franz. "The Bucket Rider." In *Collected Stories.* New York: Knopf, 1993.

Khan, Shafaat Ahmad. *The East India Trade in the XVIIth Century.* London: Oxford University Press, 1923.

King, Blair B. *The Blue Mutiny: The Indigo Disturbances in Bengal, 1859–1862.* Philadelphia: University of Pennsylvania Press, 1966.

Kramer, Fritz. *The Red Fez.* Translated by Malcolm R. Green. London and New York: Verso, 1993 [1987].

Kramer, Hilton. "Art: Focus on Photo Shows." *New York Times,* May 28, 1976.

Kristeva, Julia. *Proust and the Sense of Time*. New York: Columbia University Press, 1993.

Leiris, Michel. "The Sacred in Everyday Life." In *The College of Sociology, 1937–39*, pp. 24–31. Edited by Denis Hollier. Minneapolis: University of Minnesota Press, 1988.

Leslie, Esther. *Synthetic Worlds: Nature, Art, and the Chemical Industry*. London: Reaktion Books, 2005.

Levi, Primo. *Auschwitz Report*. With Leonardo de Benedetti. London and New York: Verso, 2006 [1946].

———. *Survival in Auschwitz*. Translated by Stuart Woolf. New York: Simon and Schuster, 1996 [1958].

Levi-Strauss, Claude. *Tristes Tropiques*. New York: Atheneum, 1974 [1955].

Lowie, Robert H. *Indians of the Plains*. Garden City, N.Y.: Natural History Press, 1963.

Macdonald, Dwight. "Death of a Poet." *New Yorker*, November 16, 1957.

Malcolm, Janet. "Photography. Color." *New Yorker*, October 10, 1977.

Maliowski, Bronislaw. *Argonauts of the Western Pacific*. London: G. Routledge and Sons, Ltd., 1922.

———. "Baloma: The Spirits of the Dead in the Trobriand Islands." *Journal of the Royal Anthropological Institute* 46 (July 1916): 353–430.

———. *Coral Gardens and Their Magic*. Vol 1. New York: American Book Company, 1935.

———. *A Diary in the Strict Sense of the Term*. 2nd ed. London: The Athlone Press, 1989.

———. "Practical Anthropology." *Africa* 2 (1929): 23–39.

———. *The Sexual Life of Savages in North-Western Melanesia*. New York: Harcourt, Brace and World, 1929.

Marlowe, Christopher. *Marlowe's Tragical History of Doctor Faustus and Goethe's Faust, Part I*. Translated by John Anster. Introduction by Adolphus William Ward. Oxford: Oxford University Press, 1949 [1907].

Mathur, Saloni. *India by Design: Colonial History and Cultural Display*. Berkeley: University of California Press, 2007.

Mauss, Marcel. "Techniques of the Body." In *Techniques, Technology, and Civilization*, edited and with an introduction by Nathan Schlanger. Oxford and New York: Berghahn Books, 2006.

Maximilian, Prince of Wied. *Travels in the Interior of North America*. Vols. 22 and 23, *Early Western Travels, 1784–1846*. Edited by Reuben Gold Thwaites. Cleveland: Arthur H. Clark, 1906.

McKay, Claude. *Banjo: A Story without a Plot*. New York: Harcourt Brace, 1929.

Melville, Herman. *Moby Dick*. Oxford: Oxford University Press, 1998.

Michelet, Jules. *Le Peuple*. Paris, 1846. Cited in Walter Benjamin, *The Arcades Project: The Paris Arcades*. Translated by Howard Eiland and Kevin McLaughlin. Cambridge, Mass.: The Belknap Press of Harvard University Press, 2002.

Monk, Ray. *Ludwig Wittgenstein: The Duty of Genius*. New York: The Free Press, 1990.

Morrison, Toni. *Playing the Dark: Whiteness and the Literary Imagination*. Cambridge, Mass.: Harvard University Press, 1992.

Müller, Filip. *Eyewitness Auschwitz: Three Years in the Gas Chambers*. Chicago: Ivan R Dee, 1999 [1979].

Mumford, Lewis. *Technics and Civilization*. New York: Harcourt Brace, 1963 [1934].

Nef, J. U. *The Rise of the British Coal Industry*. Vol. 1. London: Frank Cass, 1966.

Neihardt, John G. *Black Elk Speaks: Being the life of a Holy Man of the Oglala Sioux*. Lincoln: University of Nebraska Press, 1979 [1932].

Nietzsche, Friedrich. "Attempt at Self-Criticism." In *The Birth of Tragedy*. In *Basic Writings of Nietzsche*. Translated by Walter Kaufmann. New York: Modern Library, 1968.

———. *The Gay Science*. Edited by Bernard Williams. Translated by Josefine Nauckhoff. Poems translated by Adrian Del Caro. Cambridge: Cambridge University Press, 2001.

———. *Twilight of the Idols; and The Anti-Christ*. Translated by R. J. Hollingdale. London: Penguin, 1968 [1889].

Pastoureau, Michel. *Blue: The History of a Color*. Princeton: Princeton University Press, 2001 [2000].

Payne, Harry C. "Malinowski's Style." *Proceedings of the American Philosophical Society* 125, no. 6 (December 1981): 416–40.

Peignot, Laure. *Laure: The Collected Writings*. Translated by Jeanne Herman. San Francisco: City Lights, 1995. [First published in French, 1977.]

Percival, Maciver. *The Chintz Book*. London: William Heinemann, 1923.

Pinney, Christopher. "Creole Europe: The Reflection of a Reflection." Special issue ("Settlement Studies"), *Journal of New Zealand Literature*, no. 20 (2003): 125–61.

———. *"Photos of the Gods": The Printed Image and Political Struggle in India*. London: Reaktion Books, 2005.

Plath, Sylvia. "Ocean 1212-W." In *Johnny Panic and the Bible of Dreams*, pp. 20–26. New York: Harper, 1979.

Proust, Marcel. *In Search of Lost Time*. Vol. 1, *Swann's Way*. Translated by Lydia Davis. New York: Viking, 2003.

———. *In Search of Lost Time*. Vol. 2, *Within a Budding Grove*. New York: Modern Library, 1993.

———. *In Search of Lost Time*. Vol. 3, *The Guermantes Way*. Translated by C. K. Scott Moncrieff and Terence Kilmartin. Revised by D. J. Enright. New York: Modern Library, 1993.

———. *In Search of Lost Time*. Vol. 4, *Sodom and Gomorrah*. Translated by C. K. Scott Moncrieff and Terence Kilmartin. Revised by D. J. Enright. New York: Modern Library, 1993.

———. *In Search of Lost Time*. Vol. 5, *The Captive*. Translated by C. K. Scott Moncrieff and Terence Kilmartin. Revised by D. J. Enright. New York: Modern Library, 1993.

———. *In Search of Lost Time*. Vol. 6, *Time Regained*. Translated by Andreas Mayor and Terence Kilmartin. Revised by D. J. Enright. New York: Modern Library, 1993.

Pynchon, Thomas. *Gravity's Rainbow*. New York: Penguin, 1995 [1973].

Rao, Amtya, and B. G. Rao. *The Blue Devil: Indigo and Colonial Bengal*. Delhi: Oxford University Press, 1992.

Read, Kenneth. *The High Valley*. New York: Columbia University Press, 1980 [1965].

Reichard, Gladys A. *Navaho Religion: A Study of Symbolism*. Princeton: Princeton University Press, 1974 [1950].

Richardson, Dorothy. *Pilgrimage*. 4 vols. London: Virago, 1979.

Roberts, Richard. "West Africa and the Pondicherry Textile Industry." In *Cloth and Commerce: Textiles in Colonial India*, pp. 142–74. Edited by Tirthankar Roy. New Delhi and London: Sage Publications, 1996.

Roth, Phillip. Interview with Primo Levi in appendix to *Survival in Auschwitz*, by Primo Levi. New York: Simon and Schuster, 1996 [1958].

Ruskin, John. *Modern Painters*. Vol. 3. Orpington, Kent: George Allen, 1888.

Sartre, Jean-Paul. *Nausea*. New York: New Directions, 1964 [1938].

Sasuly, Richard. *IG Farben*. New York: Boni and Gaer, 1947.

Schneider, Jane. "Peacocks and Penguins: The Political Economy of European Cloth and Colors." *American Ethnologist* 5, no. 3 (August 1978): 413–47.

Sealy, I. Allen. *The Trotter-Nama*. India: Penguin, 1990.

Selz, Jean. "Benjamin in Ibiza." In *On Walter Benjamin: Critical Essays and Reflections*, pp. 353–66. Edited by Gary Smith. Cambridge, Mass.: MIT Press, 1988.

Shattuck, Roger. *Proust's Binoculars: A Study of Memory, Time, and Recognition in À la recherche du temps perdu*. New York: Random House, 1963.

Siegel, Lee. *Net of Magic: Wonders and Deception in India*. Chicago: University of Chicago Press, 1991.

Spiegelman, Art. "The Comic Supplement." In *In the Shadow of No Towers*. New York: Pantheon, 2004.

Stern, Fritz. "Fritz Haber and Albert Einstein." In *Einstein's German World*, pp. 59–164. Princeton: Princeton University Press, 1999.

Stocking, George W., Jr. *After Tylor: British Social Anthropology, 1888–1951*. Madison: Wisconsin University Press, 1995.

———. "Anthropology and the Science of the Irrational: Malinowski's Encounter with Freudian Psychoanalysis." In *Malinowski, Rivers, Benedict and Others: Essays on Culture and Personality*. Vol 4, pp. 13–49. Edited by George W. Stocking. Madison: University of Wisconsin Press: 1986.

———. "Philanthropoids and Vanishing Cultures." In *Objects and Others: Essays on Museums and Material Culture*. Vol 3, pp. 112–45. Edited by George W. Stocking. Madison: University of Wisconsin Press, 1985.

Stokes, Raymond G. *Divide and Prosper: The Heirs of I. G. Farben under Allied Authority*. Berkeley: University of California Press, 1988.

Stoltzenberg, Dietrich. *Fritz Haber: Chemist, Nobel Laureate, German, Jew: A Biography*. Philadelphia: Chemical Heritage Foundation, 2005.

Stone, Robert. "Prince of Possibility." *New Yorker*, June 14 and 21, 2004.

Surya, Michel. *Georges Bataille: An Intellectual Biography*. Translated by Krzsystof Fijalkowski and Michael Richardson. London: Verso, 2002.

Szarkowski, John. *William Eggleston's Guide*. Museum of Modern Art, 2002.

Tadie, Jean-Yves. *Marcel Proust*. Translated by Euan Cameron. New York: Viking, 2000. [French original Gallimard, 1996.]

Taussig, Michael. *My Cocaine Museum*. Chicago: University of Chicago Press, 2004.

———. "Viscerality, Faith, and Skepticism: Another Theory of Magic." In *Walter Benjamin's Grave*, pp. 121–55. Chicago: University of Chicago Press, 2006.

Tavernier, Jean-Baptiste. *Travels in India*. Vol. 1. Translated from the French edition of 1676 by V. Ball. London: Oxford University Press, 1925.

Thomas, Parakunnel J. "The Beginnings of Calico Printing in England." *English Historical Review* 39, no. 154 (April, 1924): 206–16.

Thorndike, Lynn. *A History of Magic and Experimental Science during the First Thirteen Centuries of Our Era*. Vol. 1. New York: Macmillan, 1923.

Thorpe, T. E. *Coal: Its History and Uses*. London: Macmillan, 1878.

Tomlinson, Sally, and Walter Medeiros. *High Societies*. San Diego Museum of Art: San Diego, 2001.

Traven, B. *The Death Ship: The Story of an American Sailor*. New York: Knopf, 1934.

Travis, Anthony S. *The Rainbow Makers: The Origins of the Synthetic Dyestuffs Industry in Western Europe*. Bethlehem: Lehigh University Press, 1993.

Turner, Victor. "Color Classification in Ndembu Ritual." In *The Forest of Symbols: Aspects of Ndembu Ritual*, pp. 59–92. Ithaca: Cornell University Press, 1967.

Valero, Vicente. *Experiencia y pobreza: Walter Benjamin en Ibiza, 1932–1933*. Barcelona: Ediciones Península, 2001.

Wahl, Jean. "At the College of Sociology." In *The College of Sociology, 1937–1939*, pp. 101–2. Edited by Denis Hollier. Minneapolis: Minnesota University Press, 1998.

Walens, Stanley. *Feasting with Cannibals: An Essay on Kwakiutal Cosmology*. Princeton: Princeton University Press, 1981.

Warner, Lloyd. *A Black Civilization*. Gloucester, Mass.: Peter Smith, 1969 [1937].

White, Edmund. *Marcel Proust*. New York: Viking/Penguin, 1999.

Wittgenstein, Ludwig. *Remarks on Colour*. Edited by G. E. M. Anscombe. Berkeley: University of California Press, 1978 [1977].

Wolff, Tobias. *This Boy's Life*. New York: Grove Press, 1989.

Woolf, Virginia. "Old Bloomsbury." In *Moments of Being*, pp. 181–201. New York and London: Harcourt Brace, 1985.

———. *The Waves*. New York: Harcourt, Brace, and Company, 1931.

Young, Michael. *Malinowski: Odyssey of an Anthropologist, 1884–1920*. New Haven: Yale University Press, 2004.

———. *Malinowski's Kiriwina: Fieldwork Photography 1915–1918*. Chicago: University of Chicago Press, 1998.

INDEX